Dear Timothy

Letters on Pastoral Ministry

Edited by Thomas K. Ascol

Founders Press

Published by
Founders Press
P.O. Box 150931 • Cape Coral, FL 33915
Phone (239) 772-1400 • Fax: (239) 772-1140
Electronic Mail: founders@founders.org
www.founders.org

©2004 by Founders Press
All rights reserved.
Second printing, 2006

Printed in the United States of America
ISBN 0-9713361-5-6

Dedication

To

Pastor Ernest Reisinger,

Pastor Bruce Steward,

and

The members of Grace Baptist Church,

Cape Coral, Florida

Contents

Preface 7
Contributors 13

1. Establish Priorities *Tom Ascol* 23
2. Watch Your Life *Conrad Mbewe* 37
3. Love Your Family *Tedd Tripp* 53
4. Love Your Flock *Ted Christman* 67
5. Memorize Scripture *Andy Davis* 83
6. Pray Always *Martin Holdt* 99
7. Cultivate Humility *C. J. Mahaney* 115
8. Be Courageous *Bill Ascol* 137
9. Do the Work of an Evangelist *Mark Dever* 157
10. Do Personal Work *Fred Malone* 169
11. Watch Your Doctrine *Raymond Perron* 183
12. Keep Studying *Ligon Duncan* 195
13. Learn from the Puritans I *Joel Beeke* 219
14. Learn from the Puritans II *Joel Beeke* 247
15. Preach the Word *Roger Ellsworth* 271

16. Worship in Spirit and Truth *Terry Johnson* 285
17. Train Other Men *Steve Martin* 303
18. Care for the Nations *Phil Newton* 329
19. Don't Neglect Revival *Ray Ortlund, Jr.* 347
20. Find a Place to Settle *Geoff Thomas* 359

Recommended Reading 377

Preface

I thought it was a cruel joke. It felt like I was caught up in some cosmic plot to ruin my happiness and punish my harsh attitudes toward pastors. As a child of the church I had seen my share of pastors come and go in my brief sixteen years. It had become easy for me to judge them unfairly, exaggerating their faults, ignoring their sacrifices and pretending that somehow I would always be immune to their shortcomings.

But there I was, late at night, lying on my bed with this sinking feeling that God was calling me to be a pastor. Not even out of high school and already my life was ruined! Or so I thought. Over the next five years, as God confirmed this inner call through the guidance and affirmation of the church, I found my dilemma steadily increasing. Here I was, very cynical about pastoral ministry but convinced that God was directing my life into that very vocation. I started investigating employment opportunities in social work, thinking that this line of work might satisfy that sense of inner compulsion to enter the ministry.

While considering a job to work with troubled youth, I received a call to become the pastor of Rock Prairie Baptist Church in College Station, Texas. After two weeks of emotional and spiritual turmoil, I accepted their call. The date was October 31, 1978 and it marked for me the beginning of a personal reformation of my attitudes toward pastors and pastoral ministry. It did not take long for me to realize how sinfully judgmental I had been. If that church had judged me with the same measure I had been using, I would not have lasted two months. Instead, they were patient, kind and gentle with me. They allowed me to make mistakes while I was growing into the role of pastor. By God's grace they were very longsuffering as they endured my many foibles. For that reason, I will always have a special place in my heart for that congregation.

As I look back over my early pastoral mishaps I realize that many of them could have been avoided had I received and heeded good counsel. While it is true that all the guidance a pastor needs in order to be equipped "for every good work" is sufficiently found in Scripture, there is no denying the value of godly, experienced counsel. God gives teachers to the church and even those who are called to shepherd His flock need them. As Louis McBurney so wonderfully put it in the title of his 1977 book, every pastor needs a pastor.[1]

Think of the influence of Barnabas on Paul. When everyone else was skeptical (if not scared) of the former persecutor, Barnabas took him under his wing, introduced him to church leaders and helped him get started in the work of the ministry

---

[1] *Every Pastor Needs a Pastor* (Waco: Word Books, 1977).

(Acts 9:26–30, 11:25–26). The man who was to become our Lord's foremost apostle was greatly blessed to have such an experienced minister counsel him early in his ministry.

It is a lesson Paul never forgot as he in turn invested part of his life in pastors who would serve the generations following his own. A significant portion of this investment took the form of letters. Paul's letters to Timothy and Titus serve as divinely inspired manuals of pastoral ministry. Though Paul undoubtedly gave himself in personal ministry to these men, it is the preservation of his letters to them that has served the church so well throughout history.

Letter writing is a dying art. In our age of e-mail and instant messaging fewer and fewer people seem to have the patience or disposition to compose thoughtful, significant letters. Yet, such correspondence has been a blessing to Christians of every generation. God saw fit to write a significant portion of the New Testament in the form of letters. In addition, think of how much poorer the church would be without the letters of the great Scottish Covenanter, Samuel Rutherford, which Spurgeon called, "the nearest thing to inspiration which can be found in all the writings of mere men."

The converted slave-trader, John Newton, author of such notable hymns as "Amazing Grace" and "Glorious Things of Thee Are Spoken," regarded letter writing to be a great part of his ministerial calling. "It is the Lord's will," he noted, "that I should do most by my letters." Through the republication of those letters, his work continues to this day.[2]

---

[2] See *The Works of John Newton* (reprint, Edinburgh: The Banner of Truth Trust, 1985), vol. 1.

So, while telephones and the Internet have significantly changed the way we typically communicate today, I believe that well written letters can still offer encouragement and counsel in a helpful and lasting form. The volume you now hold in your hands is an effort to prove that belief. This is a book of letters. They are written from experienced, active pastors to a young, inexperienced pastor.

"Timothy" is a composite character. He is twenty-six years old, has recently graduated from seminary and has been in his first church for six months. He and his wife, Mary, have been married for four years and they have a two-year-old son with another child on the way. Each pastor was asked to offer counsel to him on the basis of a long-term relationship and sincere interest in seeing him make a good start.

The twenty chapters that follow reflect the collective wisdom of more than 480 years of pastoral experience. Each contributor is, at the time of writing, serving a local church. Pastoral ministry is their calling. Their contributions have been made in and around the regular preaching, teaching, counseling and leadership demands that go with pastoring a local church. This fact lends credibility to what they have written.

While the letters are aimed specifically at young pastors, the counsel they contain applies to ministers of all ages and, for most of the chapters, to any serious Christian. The themes addressed are not geared to denominational distinctives and the contributors come from a variety of confessional and cultural backgrounds. My prayer is that Christian ministers will be encouraged to greater faithfulness by this volume.

Ken Puls and Barb Reisinger have been very involved in organizing and managing the details of publication. Their patience, suggestions and professionalism have made the book much better than it would have been otherwise. Amy Arens, who now is the wife of her husband and pastor, Jason, asked me to contribute to a collection of letters of encouragement that she presented to him on their wedding day five years ago when he was still a seminary student. That planted the seed in my mind for a book like this. As ever, my wonderful wife, Donna, has encouraged me in countless ways through the long process of getting the idea for this book finally into print.

For the last eighteen years it has been my joy and privilege to serve some of the most longsuffering and gracious people on earth in Grace Baptist Church. Their love for me has nurtured my own love for other pastors. I find myself today with an attitude that is exactly opposite of that which I harbored twenty-five years ago. I am amazed that God would grant me the privilege to serve a local church as a pastor. Those pastors who have served their generation and finished well are my heroes. The ones who are joyfully persevering in the work are my examples and encourage me to do the same. And those who are just starting out in the ministry stir up my hope for the future.

John Newton called the minister's work "a sorrow full of joy." So I have found it to be. Sometimes the sorrows are exacerbated by the sense of loneliness that often accompanies a pastor. Many pastors do not have a Paul or Barnabas to help them navigate those times and help them gain a fresh sight of the joys of the ministry. I hope that this book will provide many signposts that direct spiritual shepherds to paths of pastoral joy.

God placed in the congregation of Grace Baptist Church two retired pastors who have been a source of blessing to me on countless occasions. Their counsel, encouragement and support have strengthened my hand through many difficult seasons. To Ernie Reisinger and Bruce Steward, along with the members of Grace, this book is lovingly dedicated.

Tom Ascol
Grace Baptist Church
Cape Coral, Florida

Reformation Day, 2003

Contributors

BILL ASCOL

Bill Ascol has been in the pastoral ministry for twenty-five years in three different churches in Louisiana. He is the founding pastor of Heritage Baptist Church in Shreveport, Louisiana, where he has served for the past eleven years. He received a BA from Lamar University and a MDiv degree from Southwestern Baptist Theological Seminary. He serves as a member of the Executive Board of the Louisiana Baptist Convention and editor of the *Louisiana Inerrancy Fellowship LIFeLine*. He is also the coordinator of the Southern Baptist Founders Youth Conference. Bill and his wife, Karen, have been married twenty-nine years and have five children.

TOM ASCOL

Dr. Tom Ascol is the executive director of Founders Ministries (www.founders.org) and editor of the *Founders Journal*. He is the author of *From the Protestant Reformation to the Southern Baptist Convention: What Hath Geneva to do with Nashville?* He has also contributed several articles to books and journals. Tom has twenty-five years experience in the pastorate and has served as pastor of Grace Baptist Church in Cape Coral, Florida for the past eighteen years. He received a BS from Texas A&M University and MDiv and PhD degrees from Southwestern Baptist Theological Seminary. Tom and his wife, Donna, have been married twenty-four years and have six children.

JOEL BEEKE

Dr. Joel R. Beeke is president and professor of Systematic Theology and Homiletics of Puritan Reformed Theological Seminary. He is also pastor of the Heritage Netherlands Reformed Congregation in Grand Rapids, Michigan, where he has served for seventeen of his twenty-six years of pastoral ministry. He is also editor of *Banner of Sovereign Grace Truth*, radio pastor, president of Reformation Heritage Books (www.heritagebooks.org) and Inheritance Publishers and vice-president of the Dutch Reformed Translation Society. He has written or edited about fifty books and has contributed more than 1,500 articles to books, journals, periodicals and encyclopedias. His PhD is in Reformation and Post-Reformation Theology from Westminster Theological Seminary. He is frequently called upon to lecture at seminaries and to speak at conferences around the world. He and his wife, Mary, have been blessed with three children.

Ted Christman

Ted Christman is the founding pastor of Heritage Baptist Church in Owensboro, Kentucky where he has joyfully and fruitfully labored since 1973. Ted received his BA at Bob Jones University, his MDiv at Grand Rapids Theological Seminary and has pursued further postgraduate studies at Westminster Theological Seminary in Philadelphia, Pennsylvania. He is the author of *Forbid Them Not: Rethinking the Baptism and Church Membership of Young People* as well as the *Daily Bible Reading Schedule*, used by Christians throughout the United States and around the world. He and his wife, Dianne, have two children, both of whom are devoted to the Savior.

Andy Davis

Dr. Andy Davis has served as senior pastor of the First Baptist Church, Durham, North Carolina since 1988. He was born in Boston, Massachusetts and holds a PhD in Church History from The Southern Baptist Theological Seminary (1998), a MDiv from Gordon-Conwell Theological Seminary (1990) and a BSME from M.I.T. (1984). He and his wife served as church planters in Tokushima, Japan for two years (1993–1995) with the International Mission Board. Prior to that, he was pastor of a small Southern Baptist church in Topsfield, Massachusetts. Andy and his wife, Christine, have been married fifteen years and have four children.

Mark Dever

Dr. Mark Dever has been the pastor of the Capitol Hill Baptist Church in Washington, DC for nine years. He is married and has two children. He is originally from Kentucky and has attended Duke University, Gordon-Conwell Theological Seminary, The Southern Baptist Theological Seminary and the University of Cambridge. From 1995 until 2001 he served on the board of Founders Ministries. He currently serves on the board of the Southern Baptist Theological Seminary and on the council of the Alliance of Confessing Evangelicals. He has authored a number of books and articles, including *Nine Marks of a Healthy Church*. He serves as founder & senior fellow of IX Marks Ministries (9Marks.org), a ministry to encourage healthy growth in local churches.

Ligon Duncan

Dr. J. Ligon Duncan III became the senior minister of the historic First Presbyterian Church (1837), Jackson, Mississippi in August 1996. He is a native of Greenville, South Carolina and was born and reared in a Christian home. He is a graduate of Furman University, Greenville, South Carolina (BA); Covenant Theological Seminary, St. Louis, Missouri (MDiv, MA); and the University of Edinburgh, Scotland (PhD). Ligon has been in the gospel ministry for eighteen years and is but the sixth minister of First Presbyterian Church since 1896. He is also Adjunct Professor of Theology at the Reformed Theological Seminary (RTS), where he had served as Chairman of the Department of Systematic Theology, and the John R.

Richardson Professor of Theology. Dr. Duncan serves as a council member of the Alliance of Confessing Evangelicals, chairman of the Council on Biblical Manhood and Womanhood, and is the editorial director of Reformed Academic Press. He and his wife, Anne, have two children.

Roger Ellsworth

Roger Ellsworth has served in the pastoral ministry for thirty-eight years, fifteen of which have been in his current pastorate, Immanuel Baptist Church, Benton, Illinois. He is also the author of twenty books, including *The Shepherd King, A Promise is a Promise, Be Patient, God Hasn't Finished with Me Yet* and *The Guide to the Bible Book by Book*. Roger and his wife, Sylvia, have two sons.

Martin Holdt

Martin Holdt has been in the ministry thirty-seven years, seven years of which involved church planting. He is the pastor of Constantia Park Baptist Church, Pretoria, South Africa, and broadcasts the weekly radio program "Truth For Today." He is also joint editor of *Reformation Africa South*.

Terry Johnson

Terry Johnson has been in the pastoral ministry for twenty-one years. Since 1987 he has served as the senior minister of the historic Independent Presbyterian Church in Savannah,

Georgia. He is a graduate of the University of Southern California (AB in History). He received his seminary education at Trinity College in Bristol, England, where he studied under Dr. J. I. Packer, and at Gordon-Conwell Theological Seminary in South Hamilton, Massachusetts, where he served as the Byington Fellow for Dr. David Wells. He is the editor and compiler of the *Trinity Psalter* and has published *Leading in Worship*, *The Pastor's Public Ministry*, *The Family Worship Book*, *When Grace Comes Home*, *Reformed Worship: Worship that Is According to Scripture*, *When Grace Transforms: The Character of Christ's Disciples Envisioned in the Beatitudes* and *When Grace Comes Alive: The Lord's Prayer Today*. Terry and his wife, Emily, have five children.

C. J. Mahaney

C. J. Mahaney serves as senior pastor of Covenant Life Church in Gaithersburg, Maryland. He is one of the founding pastors and has served the church since its inception in 1977. He also leads Sovereign Grace Ministries, a growing family of fifty-seven local churches in six countries. In addition, he serves on the boards of the Christian Counseling and Educational Foundation (CCEF) and the Council on Biblical Manhood and Womanhood (CBMW). He is author of *The Cross-Centered Life* and has contributed to two volumes published by Crossway Books. He has also edited or co-authored four books in the *Pursuit of Godliness* book series, published by Sovereign Grace Ministries: *Why Small Groups?*, *This Great Salvation*, *How Can I Change?* and *Disciplines for Life*. C. J. and his wife, Carolyn, have four children.

Fred Malone

Dr. Fred Malone has been in the pastoral ministry almost thirty years. He has served as a field education supervisor for three seminaries and has mentored many seminary students. He holds a MDiv from Reformed Theological Seminary in Jackson, Mississippi (1974) and a PhD in New Testament from the Southwestern Baptist Theological Seminary (1989). He was a founding pastor of Heritage Baptist Church in Ft. Worth, Texas (1981–92) and has served First Baptist Church of Clinton, Louisiana, for over ten years (1993–present). He is the author of *A String of Pearls Unstrung, The Baptism of Disciples Alone* as well as many articles. He serves as a founding board member of Founders Ministries, a trustee of The Southern Baptist Theological Seminary and a trustee of Louisiana College. He also serves on the Theological Committee of the Association of Reformed Baptist Churches in America. Fred and his wife, Debbie, have been married for thirty-six years and have three children.

Steve Martin

Steve Martin has been in the pastoral ministry since 1970. He is the founding pastor of Heritage Church, Fayetteville, Georgia, where he has served for the past fifteen years. He received a BA from Wabash College in Indiana and an MA from Trinity Evangelical Divinity School. He serves as chairman of the Reformed Baptist Foreign Missions Committee of the Association of Reformed Baptist Churches of America.

Steve and his wife, Cindy, have been married thirty-one years and have two children.

Conrad Mbewe

Conrad Mbewe has served as pastor of the Kabwata Baptist Church in Lusaka, Zambia, since 1987. He received a BS in mining engineering in 1984 from the University of Zambia. He has been a columnist with the *National Mirror* (a national weekly newspaper), writing two articles per week, since 1992. He has also functioned as an associate editor for *Reformation Africa South*, a theological journal for Southern Africa. Conrad is married to Felistas and together they have two sons, a daughter and a foster daughter.

Phil Newton

Dr. Phil Newton has served as senior pastor of South Woods Baptist Church in Memphis, Tennessee since 1987, when he planted the church. He has been in pastoral ministry for twenty-six years, having served churches in Mississippi and Alabama as well. He has a BA from Mobile College (now University of Mobile), a MDiv from New Orleans Baptist Theological Seminary and a DMin from Fuller Theological Seminary. He is the author of *The Way of Faith* and has contributed to *Reforming Pastoral Ministry* (John Armstrong, ed.), *Reclaiming the Gospel and Reforming Churches* (Tom Ascol, ed.) as well as numerous periodicals. He is currently working on a book on elders and church leadership. He frequently leads international mission trips and also teaches missions at Crichton College in

Memphis. He and his wife, Karen, have been married for twenty-eight years and have five children.

Ray Ortlund, Jr.

Dr. Ray Ortlund, Jr. has been in the pastoral ministry for fifteen years. For the past five years he has served as the senior pastor of First Presbyterian Church (PCA), Augusta, Georgia. He is a graduate of Wheaton College, Dallas Theological Seminary, the University of California and Aberdeen University in Scotland. He has served three churches in pastoral ministry. He also taught at Trinity Evangelical Divinity School, Deerfield, Illinois. He is the author of numerous books including *When God Comes to Church, Let the Church Be the Church* and *A Passion for God*. Ray and his wife, Anne, have four children.

Raymond Perron

Dr. Raymond Perron has served in the pastoral ministry for twenty-six years. He was born in the Province of Quebec, Canada. He holds a MDiv from Toronto Baptist Seminary and a PhD in Theology from University Laval. Raymond is currently a national missionary with the Association of Reformed Baptist Churches of America. He started a church (Église réformée baptiste de la Capitale) in Quebec City in 1988 where he is still pastor. He is also working at another church planting project in Montreal (Église réformée baptiste de Montréal). Raymond and his wife, Diane, have been married for twenty-three years and have one son.

Geoff Thomas

Geoff Thomas has been pastor of Alfred Place Baptist Church in Aberystwyth, Wales since 1965. He received his BA from Cardiff University in Wales in 1961 and his MDiv from Westminster Seminary in 1964. He is well known as a conference speaker and is the author of *Ernest C. Reisinger, A Biography* (Banner of Truth) as well as other books. He served as an associate editor of *Evangelical Times* for ten years. He is also an associate editor of the *Banner of Truth* magazine and is responsible for the Banner of Truth website. Geoff and his wife, Iola, have three daughters.

Tedd Tripp

Dr. Tedd Tripp is the senior pastor of Grace Fellowship Church, Hazleton, Pennsylvania, where he has served as an elder since 1976 and a pastor since 1983. Tedd is a graduate of Geneva College (BA in History), Philadelphia Theological Seminary (MDiv) and Westminster Theological Seminary (DMin) with an emphasis in Pastoral Counseling. In 1979 he and his wife, Margy, founded Immanuel Christian School where Tedd served as a teacher and administrator. Both still serve on the board of ICS. Tedd is the author of the popular child-rearing book, *Shepherding a Child's Heart*. For the past eight years he has maintained an extensive ministry as a conference speaker and presenter of "Shepherding a Child's Heart" seminars. His books and video and audio materials are used throughout the world. He and his wife, Margy, have been married thirty-five years and have three children.

Chapter 1

Establish Priorities

Tom Ascol

Dear Timothy,

Donna and I are very excited for you and Mary as you settle into your new pastorate. It is an awesome responsibility and privilege to care for the souls of God's people. After twenty-five years in this ministry, I still tremble at the greatness of the task. I hope you won't think it presumptuous if I offer you a little "seasoned counsel" from one pastor to another.

One of the greatest ongoing challenges I face in my life as a pastor is maintaining a proper balance in my priorities. Every pastor has several roles that he must fulfill in order to remain faithful to his calling. You must be a student of God's Word. You must be a man of prayer. You must give leadership to the church. You must work hard to preach and teach the Word so that the people under your care are continually being formed by it into the image of Christ. You must do the work of an evangelist, and you must give yourself to personal work with individual members. All of this and more goes with the territory of serving Christ as an undershepherd of souls.

But every pastor is more than a pastor. He is first and foremost a disciple. Typically he also will be a husband and a father. In addition to this he may take on other ministry-related duties, as well. How are all of these important roles to be fulfilled without sacrificing the best on the altar of the good? It is a daunting challenge under the very best of circumstances.

A question that I often ask people I counsel is this: "What, in order of priority, has God called you to be?" It is a clarifying question because it forces an evaluation of life on the basis of what is most important. From time to time I put that question to myself and find that it helps me fight the battle for balance in my life. I would encourage you to make it a practice early in your ministry to stop and ask that question on a regular basis.

A Christian

What has God called me to be? First, He calls me to be a sincere, devoted follower of Jesus Christ. This is so basic that it is easy to take for granted and to forget about it. One great danger of the ministry is professionalism. As you will soon discover, a pastor can become very adept at doing his job. Like any other vocation, certain skills can be developed and polished in the gospel ministry. A pastor can become so proficient in his public ministry that others will regard him as very successful.

But where "professionalism" as a mentality takes over a pastor's outlook, his heart will inevitably begin to be neglected. And the heart is the primary tool of every pastor. If you are not loving God with all of your heart because you have neglected the basic responsibilities of discipleship, it does not matter how professionally "successful" you become. In reality, your apparent success will only be a sham.

Spurgeon tells of a pastor who "preached so well and lived so badly, that when he was in the pulpit everybody said that he ought never to come out again, and when he was out of it they all declared he never ought to enter it again."[1] Such compartmentalization of life may be acceptable in other professions but it is hardly agreeable with vital Christianity and much less with faithful pastoral ministry.

Many good men have been tripped up at this basic level. In fact, the gallery of fallen pastors is a sober reminder of absolute necessity to make your daily discipleship your top priority. Some of the most emotionally trying moments of my ministry have come upon receiving news that another brother has disqualified himself from the pastorate by self-inflicted moral failure. You are still young in the ministry, but make no mistake, such news will too soon make its way to your doors. Men that you know, or know of, whose gifts and graces you judge to be far superior to your own, will be discovered in scandalous sin.

How does this happen? You can be sure that it doesn't happen all at once. Disqualifying sin always has a history. And at the root of that history is the neglect of spiritual

---

[1] Charles H. Spurgeon, *Lectures to My Students* (reprint, Grand Rapids, MI: Zondervan, 1954), 17.

disciplines. As Bunyan's Christian puts it, one of the earliest steps down the path of apostasy comes when backsliders "cast off by degrees private duties, as Closet-Prayer, Curbing their Lusts, Watching, Sorrow for Sin, and the like."[2]

So, my dear young brother, guard your heart. Go to God's Word first and foremost as a believer. Remember that before you are a shepherd you are a sheep. As a pastor you need the very same things that you commend to others. Follow the wisdom of Robert Murray M'Cheyne who noted, "It is not great talents God blesses so much as great likeness to Jesus. A holy minister is an awful weapon in the hand of God."[3]

Paul said to the Ephesian elders, "take heed to yourselves." When he repeats the admonition to Timothy he adds that doing this is an essential ingredient to saving both himself and his hearers (Acts 20:28, 1 Timothy 4:16). A pastor must make it a matter of disciplined priority to read, meditate on and memorize Scripture—for his own soul's sake. We must also pray for the work of the Spirit in our lives. Anything less is spiritual malpractice.

A Husband

After being a Christian, God has called me (and you) to be is a husband. Like you, I am blessed with a faithful, godly wife. Donna and I take our covenant vows very seriously,

---

[2] John Bunyan, *The Pilgrim's Progress* (reprint, Edinburgh, Scotland: Banner of Truth Trust, 1977), 177.

[3] Andrew Bonar, *Memoir and Remains of Robert Murray M'Cheyne* (reprint, Grand Rapids, MI: Baker, 1978), 258.

which means that I am to have and to hold her above all others. Next to Jesus Christ, she is my top priority.

It is an awesome responsibility to be a husband. Jesus Christ in His relationship to the church is to be our model. Being the head of a household is a great challenge. A godly wife both needs and desires godly leadership from her husband. The call to be a godly husband includes providing such leadership. Christ calls a man to fight against the opposite and equally deadly errors of self-protecting passivity and self-serving authoritarianism in the way that he relates to his wife. A passive husband will breed frustration in a wife who desires to be led and may tempt her to become domineering. An authoritarian husband intimidates his wife and may well stifle the development of her spiritual gifts.

In Ephesians 5 Paul makes it clear that Jesus Christ is our model as a husband. His love, sacrifice and care for His bride is to be the pattern for how you relate to Mary [Gina]. She needs to be secure in your love. She needs to know that she is more important to you than your reputation or the exercise of your public gifts.

A pastor's wife may have the most difficult role in the whole church. Charles Spurgeon noted this with his characteristic wit and tenderness two years before his death. Speaking at a wedding, he said:

> If I was a young woman, and was thinking of being married, I would not marry a minister, because the position of minister's wife is a very difficult one for anyone to fill. Churches do not give a married minister two salaries, one for the husband and the other for the wife; but, in many cases, they look for the services of the wife, whether they

pay for them or not. The minister's wife is expected also to know everything about the church, and in another sense she is to know nothing of it; and she is equally blamed by some people whether she knows everything or nothing. Her duties consist in being always at home to attend to her husband and her family, and being always out, visiting other people, and doing all sorts of things for the whole church! Well, of course, that is impossible; she cannot be at everybody's beck and call, and she cannot expect to please everybody. Her husband cannot do that, and I think he is a great fool if he tries to do it; and I am certain that, as the husband cannot please everybody, neither can the wife. There will be sure to be somebody or other who will be displeased, especially if that somebody had herself half hoped to be the minister's wife. Difficulties arise continually in the best regulated churches; and, as I said before, the position of the minister's wife is always a very trying one. Still, I think that if I was a Christian young woman, I would marry a Christian minister if I could, because there is an opportunity of doing so much good in helping him in his service for Christ. It is a great help to the cause of God to keep the minister himself in good order for his work. It is his wife's duty to see that he is not uncomfortable at home; for, if everything there is happy, and free from care, he can give all his thoughts to his preparation for the pulpit; and the godly woman who thus helps her husband to preach better, is herself a preacher though she never speaks in public, and she becomes to the highest decree [sic] useful to the church of Christ committed to her husband's charge.[4]

---

[4] *Spurgeon's Sermons Preached on Unusual Occasions* (Houston, TX: Pilgrim Publications, 1978), 248.

A pastor's wife sees all of her husband's blemishes and shortcomings and yet must receive instruction in God's Word from him week by week. She lives in a fishbowl. Unrealistic expectations from the congregation can often add great stress to her life. Thoughtless comments, which may or may not be designed to hurt, can wound her deeply. If, in addition to these and other pressures, she feels that her own husband is neglecting her, the pressure can become too great to bear. As a husband, it is my responsibility and privilege to reassure my wife that she is more important to me than any other human relationship that I have. I am called to nurture and cherish her, to help her fulfill her own calling as a woman of God.

Our wives need to be reassured that they are more important to us than our ministries in the church. When this message is clearly and regularly communicated then those inevitable seasons of unusually high demands from the church are more easily weathered.

A Father

The third thing that God has made me is a father. Donna and I have six children, so I get a lot of practice at fatherhood. If pastors' wives have been singled out for special concern, pastors' kids have become proverbially notorious. Too often they are sacrificed for "the sake of the ministry." I remember sitting in my study as a young pastor listening to a retired pastor whose successful ministry was widely acclaimed. He spoke about many of the wonderful things he had experienced in the churches he had served. Then he added, "But I paid a high price for my success. My children did not get what they should have from their father, and today have turned away from the Lord and the church."

As he wept I pondered. At that time my only child was barely a toddler. The draw of never-ending needs and opportunities to minister was tempting me to neglect my family for the sake of "my ministry." But, God reminded me that, in terms of priority, He calls me to be a father before He calls me to be a pastor. My children need to know that, next to their mother, they are the most important people in my life. My congregation also needs to know this.

A pastor can easily though unintentionally neglect his children out of a misguided notion that he must always be available to minister to other people. Under the best of circumstances there will always be some disruptions in a pastor's home life. He is on call twenty-four hours a day. If a death or tragic accident involving one of the members occurs just before I head out the door to take my son fishing, our plans must necessarily change. Such demands are to be expected.

Because of this two temptations face every pastor who is a father. The first is simply to expect his child to understand his change of plans the same way that he does. As a pastor I know that it is sometimes necessary to interrupt plans in order to minister the gospel of God's grace to hurting people. But, all my young son knows is that he did not get to go fishing because somebody else needed and received his dad's time and attention. Timothy, when this kind of situation arises, be sure to talk to your child, sympathize with him and seek to make it up to him in a reasonable, intentional and timely way.

The other temptation is to become so overwhelmed with guilt because he had to change his plans that the pastor allows his child to manipulate him into actions or decisions that he would not otherwise intentionally pursue. Parenting by guilt has become all too common in our culture, and pastors are unfortunately not immune to it. But, I must confess, it is particularly unattractive when a pastor relates to his children this way. We should intentionally carve out time in our schedules for our children and then guard it scrupulously. When plans affecting your children have to be changed because of ministry emergencies, be diligent in making it up to them.

A Pastor

The fourth thing that God has made me is a pastor. This is my vocational calling. This is what occupies the bulk of my time. I am constantly amazed that God has given me the privilege to serve Him in this way. It is the highest vocational calling in the world. My responsibilities as a pastor take precedence over any recreational activities or avocations. All that is involved in shepherding the flock of God, which the Bible spells out in a fairly comprehensive way, comprises my duty. In this, my most important tasks are to labor faithfully in the ministry of the Word and in prayer. Again, these must not be carried out simply on a "professional" level. Rather, they must be taken up in the midst of my own pursuit of holiness.

There is an inevitable loneliness that goes with being a pastor. Much of the work that must be done can only be done when a man is alone with his God. Without this intimate time with God, time spent with people will not be of much value. There are a thousand "aids" available to pastors today to enable them to skirt the hard work of study and prayer. "Powerful" sermons and "guaranteed" programs are regularly marketed to pastors with shameless bravado. A man with a little ingenuity, less integrity and ample finances can keep himself well supplied with a constant stream of such resources. But he denies his calling by living off of the work of others rather than doing the work of the ministry himself.

A Helper

Beyond these four callings in my life, I also am involved in helping with other worthwhile endeavors. My work with Founders Ministries (editing the *Founders Journal*, publishing, etc.) and my involvement in my local pastors' conference and association are all important. You probably have not had much time to get very involved yet with your local pastors' fellowship. I hope that you will not neglect doing this. Not only will the fellowship be good for you (even when you are not excited about some of the programs and plans that are promoted), but also you need to recognize that God has gifted you in ways that can be a blessing to your fellow pastors.

For example, Timothy, take advantage of the fact that God has given to you both a love for and the opportunity to purchase many good books. You can be a great blessing to other pastors (and their congregations) simply by looking for and taking advantage of opportunities to recommend good books. Don't assume that everyone is as familiar with sound commentaries, inspirational biographies and good theology texts as you are. Without being officious, try to encourage the reading of good books.

No doubt other opportunities for broader ministry will come your way in time. I hope that you will be open to them and see them as ways that you can be helpful to the larger work of the kingdom. But in terms of priorities I encourage you to keep them ranked below the four things that I mentioned above. I try to keep this in mind myself, and when I do, I avoid much heartache and confusion.

Maintaining Balance

How do these priorities work? Well, those who know me best can easily testify that I do not always practice what I have written here. Though my desire and intention is never to deviate, I have repeatedly had to make mid-course corrections through the years. But that is the value of having clearly defined priorities. They provide a reliable map to make such adjustments.

Each priority builds on the ones that precede it. That is, it is only as I am faithful to the higher priorities that I can honestly engage in the other, but lower, priorities. For example, I want to be faithful in my work with Founders Ministries. But I cannot be—no matter how much good might be accomplished through my efforts—if I do that work at the expense of my pastoral responsibilities to Grace Baptist Church. If my involvement with Founders or other broader ministries prevents me from being a faithful pastor in the local church I serve, then I need to disengage from those broader works.

It is not necessary for me to be involved in other ministries in order for me to discharge my pastoral duties faithfully. But, I cannot be a faithful pastor if I neglect the higher priorities of caring for my wife and my children. In fact, according to 1 Timothy 3:4–5, a man is disqualified if such neglect characterizes his life. He must be a man who "rules his own house well, having his children in submission with all reverence (for if a man does not know how to rule his own house, how will he take care of the church of God?)."

Furthermore, I cannot be a faithful father if I fail my wife as a husband. On the contrary, one of the best things I can do for my children is to love their mother very well. No matter how well a man may think he is doing as a father, if he does not demonstrate Christ-like love to his wife, then he is doing his children a grave disservice. It seems that if the devil cannot deceive parents into neglecting their children he will tempt them to become child-centered. My children need to learn from their earliest years that their mother has a higher place in my affections than they do. That is no slight to them. Rather, it becomes a basis for security in knowing their God-ordained place in the home.

Just as I cannot be a truly helpful minister beyond my local church if I am not being a faithful pastor, and I cannot be a faithful pastor if I am not being a responsible father, and I cannot be the kind of father I ought if I do not sincerely love my wife well, so I cannot be a faithful husband if I neglect my relationship with Christ. As I have already suggested, everything else stems from this taproot.

All these priorities relate to each other as if they were levels of a pyramid. Each can be properly served with its respective importance as long as I keep them in their proper place. But when a lower priority leaps above a higher, then I am setting myself up for an unstable life. It is spiritually disastrous to put my wife above my Lord, or my children above my wife or my pastoral ministries above any of those three. It will be no slight to the church that you serve if you rank them in importance after your devotion to Christ and your family. On the contrary, the church will get more of what they need from you when you minister out of a conscious commitment to these priorities.

As I mentioned, I do not always maintain these priorities in proper balance, but I have made it a settled goal of my life to pursue them. By remembering the priorities of these callings, I am better able to establish and maintain balance in my obligations. Perhaps the most useful discipline to facilitate this balance is learning to say no. Spurgeon said that for a minister, learning to say no is of far greater value than learning Latin! He was right. No matter how much a pastor tries to do there will always be more to be done. Often I find good things screaming out for my attention should be left undone so that I can do what is better and best. When a pastor has to make those hard choices, he should do so on the basis of the priority of his callings. Then he can take heart in knowing that he has acted in faith based on the claims that God has made on his life.

Timothy, I pray that God will help you get a firm grip on your priorities while you are still young in the ministry. Give my warm greeting to Mary and your boy. Press on in your good work.

In Christ,
Tom

PS—I highly recommend the following three books:

1. *Brothers, We Are not Professionals* by John Piper (Nashville, TN: Broadman & Holman Publishers, 2002).
2. *The Christian Ministry* by Charles Bridges (reprint, Edinburgh: The Banner of Truth Trust, 1980).
3. *Lectures to My Students* by Charles H. Spurgeon (reprint, Grand Rapids, MI: Zondervan, 1954).

Chapter 2

Watch Your Life

Conrad Mbewe

Look for more stuff written by this guy.

Dear Timothy,

As your new pastorate commences, I am excited for you. I have been thinking a lot about what the Lord has in store for you. I recall several months ago when you had a number of churches beckoning you to take up their pastorates. I was anxious for you because a wrong choice could prove too costly. I am glad that you finally accepted the call to go to First Baptist Church. Humanly speaking, they have the right ambience for someone starting out his first pastorate. During these past six months as you have begun your new ministry, I have kept you in my prayers. I have prayed that the Lord will give you a long and fruitful ministry. As I have done so, a burden has grown on my heart to write to you just a few words of counsel. If it were not for the fact that I have known you for so many years, what I am about to write may be seen as presumptuous. Yet the last ten years of knowing each other has so bonded us together that I doubt you will take offense at my giving you counsel from my heart at such a time as this. In some areas I will be very personal, knowing that you will bear with my pointedness in the spirit of Scripture when it says, "Wounds from a friend can be trusted, but an enemy multiplies kisses" (Proverbs 27:6).

As I have said before, and I would not hesitate to say it again, your level of giftedness in the handling of the Word is certainly head and shoulders above an average preacher. Your mature spiritual perception, your grasp of the entire orbit of Christian doctrine, your powerful voice projection, your knowledge of the Scriptures, your flawless and seamless grasp of diction, all combine into a rich feast as your hearers sit under your ministry. Also, you have the advantage of having an enviable love for reading books and so your rich storehouse of information is ever being replenished. These facts will certainly go a long way in helping you sustain an effective pastorate to the edification of God's people at First Baptist Church and even beyond its borders.

Yet, Timothy, a full head and a full library are not enough. The future of anyone's preaching and pastoral ministry depends on how he himself develops, especially in his personal sanctification. This is why the apostle Paul advised your namesake to "watch your life and doctrine closely. Persevere in them, because if you do, you will save both yourself and your hearers" (1 Timothy 4:16). There is nothing more important in the pastoral ministry than this self-watch. Even Charles Haddon Spurgeon, whose book *Lectures to My Students* I have often urged you to read, entitled his very first chapter "The Minister's Self-Watch."[1]

---

[1] C.H. Spurgeon, *Lectures To My Students* (reprint, Grand Rapids, MI: Zondervan Publishing House, 1981).

Only in the second chapter does he proceed to handle "The Call to the Ministry." It seems to me that Spurgeon sacrifices chronological order for what he saw as the order of importance. He urges ministers to ensure that they are truly converted, that they maintain spiritual vitality and that they develop a good character.

I do not have the time now to deal with all that lies in that plea of the apostle Paul to "watch your life and doctrine closely," and so I will limit myself in this letter to the watching of your life. This must be a life-long watching. It is a watching that must ensure proper rather than warped development of your life, especially your spiritual life. Timothy, I hope you will give due weight to what I now have to say to you.

Your Self-Watch Must Be Full-Orbed

When the apostle Paul urged his young colleague to watch his life, he did not have just one area of life in mind. He wanted young Timothy to ensure a growth in life that is full-orbed, i.e. encompassing his spiritual, physical, emotional, intellectual and domestic life. I have said to you before that a preacher is not a disembodied spirit. Once he is affected, say, in the physical faculties of his being, his spiritual life will be affected as well. Therefore, it is the responsibility of every preacher to ensure that his whole redeemed humanity undergoes a positive life-long development. A well-known preacher in the United Kingdom once went to Dr. Martyn Lloyd-Jones for counsel. He felt so spiritually dry that he was seriously contemplating resigning from his pastorate. His prayer life was at its lowest ebb. He no longer sensed a love for souls. He felt a total hypocrite being in the ministry. When Dr. Martyn Lloyd-Jones heard all that this preacher had to say, he told him to take a vacation. The preacher, recalling the event, said that he was extremely disappointed that Dr. Lloyd-Jones could not give him any more counsel except telling him to take a vacation. Yet, out of respect for "the doctor" he went. His testimony was that when the time away was over, he did not need to go back to his counselor. His spiritual zest was back. He was spiritually buoyant once again. The lesson he learned was simple—all the areas of our lives are interconnected. This man had neglected physical and emotional rest, and this had a telling effect on his spiritual life.

So, seek to balance your life. The Bible says, "For physical training is of some value, but godliness has value for all things, holding promise for both the present life and the life to come" (1 Timothy 4:8). Do not neglect matters of rest and exercise while you are pursuing the arduous labors of the ministry. At your age this may sound as if it were totally unnecessary, but if you are planning for the long haul then you must run like a marathon runner and not like a hundred meters sprinter. The famous Robert Murray M'Cheyne of Scotland died on Saturday, March 25, 1843, at the early age of twenty-nine. His cry as he was dying was, "God gave me a message and a horse. I have killed the horse. Oh, what shall I do with the message?" A balanced life will avoid such a painful confession at the end of your life!

Beware of the Three "F"s

If one can consider the work of the ministry like a minefield, there are three types of landmines that have caused the greatest casualties—females, finances and fame. Beware, therefore, of the three "f"s. Many good men have started out their pastoral ministries on a very promising note but failed to get far because of being blown into the sky by one of these landmines. They have either gone off with a strange woman, or been found in serious financial scandals or allowed their growing reputation to get to their heads, and as the Bible says, "Pride goes before destruction, a haughty spirit before a fall" (Proverbs 16:18 and 18:12). Timothy, I urge you to be on your guard regarding these matters.

Why have so many good men fallen in these areas? It seems to me that it has been due to a failure to beware of sins of the heart—pride, envy, jealousy, lust, greed, anger and sloth. No wonder that history has dubbed them "the seven deadly sins"! Long before a person makes visible shipwreck of his life and ministry, his heart has been allowed to be a citadel of sin. Therefore, guard your heart, for it is the wellspring of life. Or, as someone has rightly said, the minister's heart is the heart of his ministry.

To begin with, you may keep away from physical adultery and actual theft. But if you slowly allow your ministry to be a showcase or if you allow your heart to be envious of other men's ministries, then it will not be long before you are destroyed. If you allow yourself to look at members of the opposite sex with lustful glances, again be sure that you are dangerously close to the shoal. Timothy, these are the sins that will kill the spirituality and power of your ministry long before any overt sins are visible to your people. There is no doubt that to keep your ministry alive and kicking year after year, you must train yourself to be godly.

Although Spurgeon was specifically addressing the first landmine (i.e. females), what he wrote in his first lecture in *Lectures to My Students* applies to all the others:

> The highest moral character must be sedulously maintained. Many are disqualified for office in the church who are well enough as simple members. I hold very stern opinions with regard to Christian men who have fallen into gross sin; I rejoice that they may be truly converted, and may be with mingled hope and caution received into the church; but I question, gravely question whether a man who has grossly sinned should be very readily restored to the pulpit. As John Angell James remarks, "When a preacher of righteousness has stood in the way of sinners, he should never again open his lips in the great congregation until his repentance is as notorious as his sin." Let those who have been shorn by the sons of Ammon tarry at Jericho till their beards be grown . . . Alas! the beard of reputation once shorn is hard to grow again. Open immorality, in most cases, however deep the repentance, is a fatal sign that ministerial graces were never in the man's character. Caesar's wife must be beyond suspicion, and there must be no ugly rumors as to ministerial inconsistency in the past, or the hope of usefulness will be slender. Into the church such fallen ones are to be received as penitents, and into the ministry they may be received if God puts

them there; my doubt is not about that, but as to whether God ever did place them there; and my belief is that we should be very slow to help back to the pulpit men, who having been once tried, have proved themselves to have too little grace to stand the crucial test of ministerial life.

For some work we choose none but the strong; and when God calls us to ministerial labor we should endeavor to get grace that we may be strengthened into fitness for our position, and not be mere novices carried away by the temptations of Satan, to the injury of the church and our own ruin. We are to stand equipped with the whole armor of God, ready for feats of valor not expected of others: to us self-denial, self-forgetfulness, patience, perseverance, longsuffering, must be every-day virtues, and who is sufficient for these things? We had need live very near to God, if we would approve ourselves in our vocation.[2]

THE CULTURE OF THE INNER LIFE

The last statement by Spurgeon opens the key to watching your life. It must be by keeping very near to God. It must be by the culture of the inner life. Remember that true spirituality never grows out of mere resolve. We must draw near to God.

You will soon discover, if you have not already done so, that whereas the public means of grace (such as church services) will do a lot of good to other Christians, those of us who are pastors have to rely a lot more on the private means

---

[2] Spurgeon, *Lectures*, 13–14.

of grace. This is because we are so often preoccupied with the details of our church services that we lose out on the sanctifying benefit of the injunction: "Be still and know that I am God." Therefore, for us the culture of the inner life will have to be largely the fruit of a soul that often retires for Bible reading, prayer, meditation and other private means of grace.

Sadly, you will often catch yourself rationalizing your absence from these soul-cleansing exercises by using duty as an excuse. And, granted, sometimes it will be inevitably so. But when this begins to go on week after week, then just be aware that you are on the decline and are killing the inner life of your ministry. God never intended it to be so. If your place in the closet has been empty for some time, then get back as soon as you can to your devotional exercises! It is in the place of secret prayer that the truths of the man of God become clothed in the fiber of his being. It is there that the matters of grace are kept fresh. You abandon the secret place to your own peril.

Let me be honest with you, Timothy. Although you will probably agree with everything I have said about the need to maintain the spiritual exercises necessary to cultivate your inner life, you will soon discover that it will be a real battle to do so year after year. This is because of the fallen nature, which we still carry with us despite the powerful experience we have had of God's salvation. This nature militates against everything that your renewed man longs and pants after.

The great Puritan, John Owen, whose works you must find time to read, dealt with this matter in *Indwelling Sin in*

Believers, found in volume 6 of his *Works*.[3] I have often gone back to this book when my soul has been under siege—an experience that is best described as a child of light walking in darkness. He wrote about the aversion we experience as believers for the very exercises that we know we ought to engage in for our own spiritual good. You can almost sense a groan in Owen's heart as he penned these words. He wrote:

> In these will this *aversation* and loathing oftentimes discover itself in the *affections*. A secret striving will be in them about close and cordial dealing with God, unless the hand of God in his Spirit be high and strong upon his soul. Even when convictions, sense of duty, dear and real esteem of God and communion with him, have carried the soul into its closet, yet if there be not the vigor and power of a spiritual life constantly at work, there will be a secret loathness in them unto duty; yea, sometimes there will be a violent inclination to the contrary, so that the soul had rather do any thing, embrace any diversion, though it wound itself thereby, than vigorously apply itself unto that which in the inward man it breathes after. It is weary before it begins, and says, "When will the work be over?" Here God and the soul are immediately concerned; and it is a great conquest to do what we would, though we come exceedingly short of what we should do.[4]

---

[3] *The Works of John Owen*, ed. William H. Gould, vol. 6 (1853; reprint, Edinburgh: The Banner of Truth Trust, 1981).
[4] Ibid., 183–184.

Each time I read these words my eyes are wet with tears because I know what he is talking about.

Timothy, I am concerned that you not only cultivate your inner life now, but that despite the fight with indwelling sin, you persist in these holy duties to the very end. Hence, with the apostle Paul, I must say:

> Fight the good fight of the faith. Take hold of the eternal life to which you were called when you made your good confession in the presence of many witnesses. In the sight of God, who gives life to everything, and of Christ Jesus, who while testifying before Pontius Pilate made the good confession, I charge you to keep this command without spot or blame until the appearing of our Lord Jesus Christ (1 Timothy 6:12–14).

It is not enough to throw a few good punches at the beginning of the fight, you must last the entire bout. The charge must be kept without spot or blame "until the appearing of our Lord Jesus Christ." In other words, until the final whistle! You will feel the downward pull to grow weary and tired of maintaining this single-hearted devotion and high standards of personal godliness along the way. You will be tempted to begin playing where angels fear to tread. To yield to that temptation is merely to maintain the outward form of your ministry, but inwardly you will have lost the power and passion that you once had.

BEWARE OF BAD COMPANY

Apart from the fatigue caused by the fight with the flesh (i.e. the fallen nature that still resides within us), the other source of fatigue is the bad influence of some whom you look up to in the Lord's work. Therefore, if you are to pursue a single-eyed devotion to God in ministry that will last you a lifetime, you must beware of the company you keep in your ministerial life. The apostle Paul's warning applies both to the laity as well as to those in church leadership, "Do not be misled: 'Bad company corrupts good character'" (1 Corinthians 15:33). The warning of Paul to Timothy in this regard is vital. He says to him:

> But mark this: There will be terrible times in the last days. People will be lovers of themselves, lovers of money, boastful, proud, abusive, disobedient to their parents, ungrateful, unholy, without love, unforgiving, slanderous, without self-control, brutal, not lovers of the good, treacherous, rash, conceited, lovers of pleasure rather than lovers of God—having a form of godliness but denying its power. *Have nothing to do with them* (2 Timothy 3:1–5).

There are men out there in the ministry who answer to this description. Whenever you are with them you come away feeling soiled in the soul because of their talk and attitudes. They make you feel as if you take your Christianity and ministerial functions too seriously and ought to let down your guards a little bit. From such people, Timothy, flee. Do so before their cancerous effect upon you spreads too far in your soul!

Discipline at Work

Among the "seven deadly sins" listed earlier, the last one I mentioned is slothfulness. I want to say something about this because over the years I have observed tendencies in your approach to work that need to be addressed if you are going to know a long and fruitful ministry at First Baptist Church. As you are obviously aware, Timothy, those of us who are pastors do not report for work in the same way that most in our congregations do. We do not have human supervisors to keep an eye on our time-keeping, our deadlines, our efficiency, etc. So, it is easy for us to be content with just making sure that we have prepared our Bible studies and sermons and that our evenings are sprinkled with a bit of visitation. Yet, God's people are not fools. It is only a matter of time before our people begin to ask serious questions about what on earth we do during the day. Let me, therefore, offer a few words of advice here.

Develop Office Hours

I know that you will most likely be working from your home and so it will be a real temptation for both yourself and your wife, Mary, to do as you please during the day. Resist this by developing office hours, in which you will be busy with church-related work. Your fellow elders must see that the issues related to church correspondence, ministries, meetings and members are all handled well ahead of schedule. This will not happen without developing the discipline of being in the "church office" (even if it is in your home) while your fellow elders are also in their offices. Do your personal and family business on your day off. Refuse to do so on other days, just so that you develop the habit. Help your wife, therefore, to learn to plan her shopping, visits, etc., just as the wives of your fellow church elders have to because their husbands have full-time secular jobs. Your family must not come into your office to merely chat while you work. Do not allow that.

Observe Punctuality

If there is one area that has been of major concern to me, it has been your failure at time-keeping. One can almost say that you are more often late than on time. To me, this is serious and will undermine your ministry. When members notice that you are perpetually late, they will develop a very low view of your self-discipline. It will be worse for your fellow elders who will think that you do not take your work and your appointments seriously. So, do your best to be punctual for all your church meetings and all your appointments. If you are to err, do so on the side of being too early. It is better to be too early than to be too late.

Plan Ahead and Work Hard

In calling your attention to this, I am merely laying before you what will count in the long haul at a human level. As pastors, we rarely have someone peeping over our shoulders to see whether work is getting done. We can also come up with numerous excuses for why some work has been left unattended to. Yet, at the end of the day, it is the Lord's work that suffers. And the Lord (who *does* peep over our shoulders to see whether His work is getting done) knows that the failure has been due to neglect. To avoid this situation, plan all your work in all its departments. Have your entire year before you and break it down into months and weeks. Keep a "to do" list beside you all the time. Avoid trusting your memory. Jot down everything and tick them off as they get done. Have a day each week when you revise your "to do" list, bringing it up to date and making sure that the urgent and the important are not overlooked. In due season your painstaking efforts and hard work will be evident to all by its fruit.

Without seeming to be under-valuing the place of personal prayer and Bible study, I am sure that one major reason why so many pastoral ministries are abortive is due to poor work habits. Church members begin to feel as if they are paying their pastors for only working on Sundays. If you can get the three issues I have raised into proper shape, I do not think that you will fall into that category. But, please, do so now!

Let me end with a few pungent words from Richard Baxter's *The Reformed Pastor*:

> Content not yourselves with being in a state of grace, but be also careful that your graces are kept in vigorous and lively exercise, and that you preach to yourselves the sermons which you study, before you preach them to others.... When your minds are in a holy, heavenly frame, your people are likely to partake of the fruits of

it. . . . O brethren, watch therefore over your own hearts: keep out lusts and passions, and worldly inclinations: keep up the life of faith, and love, and zeal: be much at home, and be much with God. If it be not your daily business to study your own hearts, and to subdue corruption, and to walk with God—if you make not this a work to which you constantly attend, all will go wrong, and you will starve your hearers; or, if you have an affected fervency, you cannot expect a blessing to attend it from on high. Above all, be much in secret prayer and meditation. Thence you must fetch the heavenly fire that must kindle your sacrifices . . .[5]

Amen, Baxter! Amen!

Well, Timothy, once again I rejoice with you that God has opened up a door of ministry for you. Knowing how serious you are with the things of God, I knew that it would not be long before that happened. But one thing I also know is that it will not be easy. Yet, if it is the Lord who has opened this door for you, you will find it fulfilling despite the blood, sweat and tears. I will be praying for you that His grace will prove sufficient and that, not many days hence, First Baptist Church will be a thriving center for biblical Christianity. May the Lord answer this prayer beyond what we are able to ask or even imagine. Until then, watch your life. Amen!

Yours in the bonds of the gospel,
Conrad

---

[5] Richard Baxter, *The Reformed Pastor* (reprint, Edinburgh: The Banner of Truth Trust, 1979), 61.

PS—There are a few books that I would like to highly recommend to you on the subject I have just written about. Thankfully, they are all still in print. Get them for yourself and read them again and again. They will be a real tonic to your soul.

1. *The Reformed Pastor* by Richard Baxter (reprint, Edinburgh: The Banner of Truth Trust, 1979). The first section of this powerful little book is on "the oversight of ourselves" as ministers. That section alone is worth the price of the whole book. It is a classic!
2. *The Works of John Owen*, Volumes 6 and 7 (reprint, Edinburgh: The Banner of Truth Trust, 1967, 1965). In these two volumes, I would single out Owen's work on "The Mortification of Sin," "Temptation," "Indwelling Sin in Believers" and "Spiritual Mindedness." Owen was a true physician of souls and a master in practical theology.
3. *The Christian Ministry* by Charles Bridges (reprint, Edinburgh: The Banner of Truth Trust, 1980). The second and third sections of this book deal with causes of ministerial inefficiency. It is instructive to note that almost all of them are due to a failure to watch your life.

Chapter 3

Love Your Family
Tedd Tripp

Dear Timothy,

Thanks for your call last week. I am thankful that things are going well with you in these early days of ministry. You and Mary and your young family are a great delight to Margy and me. We love you and find joy in what God is doing in your lives.

I am happy to put in writing some ideas about the pastor's family life. It is a delight to know that you are concerned with being a man of God, not only in the pulpit and pastoral ministry, but also in your home.

As you know, one of the qualifications for gospel ministry is exemplary home life. "He must manage his own household well, with all dignity keeping his children submissive, for if someone does not know how to manage his own household, how will he care for God's church?" (1 Timothy 3:4–5).

The home is a microcosm of the church. The qualities of spiritual life that give the pastor credibility at home will lend the same measure of confidence to the people he serves in the church. The spiritual vitality that enables his family to joyfully follow his leadership will give assurance to the church that they are in good hands. Home life is more than just the venue for showing pastoral skill. It is also the furnace in which those skills are forged.

The quality of your family life will either invest you with or rob you of credibility. Can you imagine a woman in the church having confidence in a pastor whose wife is unhappy? Would people ever see a man as a safe spiritual guide if his children seem wild and unruly or diffident and oppressed? Every time you preach the Word, or provide counsel or bring assurance and comfort to troubled people, the quality of your family life will give weight to your words. The goal of godliness in family life is not credibility; it is the glory of God, but the people you serve will closely observe your family life.

A busy pastor often feels torn between the needs of his family and the needs of the church. If you think about it, there is never competition between the callings of family life and the callings of gospel ministry. You are serving the church when you are serving your family. Any investment at home pays huge dividends for the church. You are modeling how the graces of the gospel effect family living for the people you serve.

As I have reflected on your questions about family living, I think of three broad headings that can organize your thinking about this part of life: Be a spiritual leader of your family. Be a husband and father to your family. Be the protector of your family.

Be a Spiritual Leader

The classic passage on this calling is Deuteronomy 6 where Moses is giving men a long-term vision. His focus is not survival or even getting through the week. The callings of spiritual leadership are so that you and your son and your son's son may know and fear the Lord (verse 2). This three-generation vision will help you resist the temptations to fall into the expediencies of the moment. As fathers, we have bigger concerns than the moment—we are concerned with where our grandchildren will be fifty years from now.

Naturally, your personal spiritual leadership is foundational for the family. Deuteronomy 6:5–7 makes this so clear, "You shall love the Lord your God with all your heart and with all your soul and with all your might. And these words of mine . . . shall be on your heart."

Your family must see the richness of your spiritual walk quite apart from your ministerial duties. Your joy in Christ, your vitality as a man of God, your kindness in the face of opposition, your clear focus on the grace of Christ (not only for forgiveness, but also for empowerment) will be the lens through which they view all your efforts to minister the grace of God to them.

Take your wife and kids into your confidence as you find comfort and strength in Christ day by day. Let them see you reading and meditating on the Word of God. Let them see you as a man of prayer and humble weakness before a God of strength. Nothing will provide your family with a sense of well being like your love and devotion to God.

Another important aspect of spiritual leadership is communicating an accurate picture of the world to your children. Deuteronomy 6 speaks to this with poignancy as well. "... these words that I command you this day are to be on your heart. You shall teach them to your children, and shall talk of them when you sit in your house, and when you walk by the way, and when you lie down, and when you rise."

Your children need to understand the nature of reality. Beyond and beneath this world of sight and sound there is an unseen world of spiritual reality that gives meaning to the world we see and touch and handle. The tree in the backyard that provides shade and nesting for birds and squirrels and a place to climb and even to build a tree fort exists at the will of the unseen God. It is His creation. It exists as a hymn of praise to His creativity, wisdom and skill. He has given it to us to enjoy that we might know about Him and worship and enjoy Him. You see, Timothy, one cannot understand the tree truly without glimpsing in the *seen* what is *unseen*.

Helping children understand the nature of reality requires imagination. Our children must see what is unseen. We Christians are people whose commitment to the unseen world of spiritual reality dictates our interpretation and response to what we do see.

The word imagination is not used in Deuteronomy 6, but the use of imagination is essential. Your son will come to you and ask, "What is the meaning of these ceremonies and rituals and rules that we follow?" (Deuteronomy 6:20). To answer this question, the father must engage the son's imagination about events in the past, about slavery in Egypt and bold and dramatic deliverance by the outstretched arm of God. Could these stories be told in ways that would impress children without engaging the imagination?

Engaging the imagination of your children will help them to see what is invisible. Eugene Peterson says it like this:

> Imagination is the capacity to make connections between the visible and the invisible, between heaven and earth, between the present and the past, between the present and the future.[1]

Think of this task of helping the children see the nature of reality as formative instruction. You are giving them ways of thinking and understanding their world that are rooted in the Bible. Our children do not live out of the events or circumstances of life, they live out of how they interpret them and how they respond to them. The key of interpretation is the being and existence of the true and living God.

Spend time in the Word with them everyday. Help them see the glories and wonders of God. Psalm 145 provides a wonderful description of this aspect of parenting, "One generation shall commend your works to another, and shall declare your mighty acts. They shall pour forth the fame of your abundant goodness and shall sing aloud of your righteousness" (Psalm 145:4, 7). Your children are made in the image of God. They are hard-wired for worship; help them be dazzled by God.

Naturally, you have to gear family worship times to the physical and conceptual limitations of the children.

---

[1] Eugene Peterson, *Subversive Spirituality* (Grand Rapids, MI: William B. Eerdmans Publishing Co., 1994), 132.

Be faithful in family worship and be sure that it connects your children to the unseen world of spiritual reality. It is what is unseen and eternal that enables us to accurately interpret what is seen.

Be a Husband and Father

I don't have to remind you, Timothy, that you must lay down your life for Mary. In Ephesians 5:25, God calls you to love Mary with the same self-sacrificing love that drove Jesus to freely give His life for the church.

Being your wife has placed many challenges in Mary's life. She lives in a fish bowl. There are many expectations of her. People look for her to intuitively understand their hopes and fears and dreams. She must be willing to give sage counsel or just a listening ear. Other women think of her as a compendium of tips for successful living. Some look for her to validate their lives. Some will envy and ignore her. She has to have the home ready for hospitality at the drop of a hat. Every parenting interchange with your son is subject to scrutiny with the analytical eye of either an imitator or a critic. She signed on to all these pressures when she became a pastor's wife.

Mary needs a husband. She needs a man who is married to her, not to the church. She is designed to flourish under the cherishing of her husband. The inspired apostle, Peter, says that you are to cherish her—to dwell with her according to knowledge. Peter says that as you cherish her as the weaker vessel your prayer life will thrive and burgeon.

Read the Bible and pray with ~~Mary~~ *Gina* every day. Take time each day to shepherd her. Give her opportunities to talk with you about her concerns, doubts and questions as well as her dreams, goals and joys. Enter into these things. Facilitate conversation letting her know that the things that move her move you as well. Help her to find refuge and hope in the grace of Christ. Remind her that grace means more than forgiveness; it also means empowerment.

Delight in her, notice her new hairstyle or new dress, take the time to look into her eyes each day, like you used to when you were first in love. Express your gratitude for the gracious way Mary entertains and makes guests feel like family. Let her know that you like her efforts at making your home look beautiful. A wife is like a lovely flower. She will blossom in beautiful color filling the room with a pleasant aroma of joy as you create an environment that encourages thriving growth. Fill her life with the sunshine of delighting in her and water her with your gracious manner and prayers. When you care for her, you are caring for the church.

When Peter speaks of the wife as the weaker vessel, he is declaring that God has ordained the husband to do the heavy lifting in family life. He is speaking not just of carrying in the groceries and awkward parcels, but that the man is to be the burden bearer. The heavy weights of family concerns, the children's education, the cares and concerns of the church, the financial struggles of living under the constraints of a pastor's wage—all these things are to be borne by the man of the house. She will, of course, shoulder them with you, but you are the one who is to do the heavy lifting. Her burden of the awareness of the weights of life will not crush her if she knows that you, as a worthy man, are shouldering the burden.

I know that you know these things and are well established in these truths, but like Peter, I am stirring you up to remember (2 Peter 1:12–13).

In loving and cherishing your wife, you create a secure and stable environment for your children. I remember my daughter, Heather, coming to me one time when she was only a little girl. She said, "Daddy, I am happy because you love me." I responded playfully, "How do you know that I love you?" "Because," she said, with far more insight than her seven years, "you love Mommy." Oh, to be able to imprint that insight in the mind of every husband and father! Loving your wife makes your children feel loved.

Actually, the opposite is true, too. Loving your children makes your wife feel loved. I remember one night when the children were little, I was crawling around on the floor playing with them. Out of the blue Margy came up behind me and threw her arms about my neck saying, "I love you so much." I responded, "Well, I love you too, but what brought that on?" She said, "I just love you." I now understand what brought that spontaneous display of affection. I was investing myself in the children and it was an investment in what meant the world to her, so it made her feel close to me.

I have always been fascinated that Ephesians 6:4 places discipline and nurture in the father's lap. Everyone knows that mothers are with the children more. Why would this be identified as a father's calling? Mothers, of course, are wired for disciplining and nurturing children. Nurturing may not come as naturally to men as to women, but God says it is your task. The fact that this calling is assigned to fathers means they must provide the leadership in childrearing.

You are God's man for leadership in the discipline, correction and motivation of the children. You have an important task as you share a vision for this task with Mary. You can be her reference for questions and her encouragement when she may be tempted to be too lenient or too harsh. You can forge partnership agreements for you and Mary about when and how to discipline. <u>It is the father's specific calling to insure that the children are brought up in the discipline and instruction of the Lord.</u>

In Genesis 18:19, God says words that are as true of us as leaders in our homes as they were of Abraham, "I have chosen him, that he may command his children and household after him to keep the way of the LORD by doing righteousness and justice, so that the Lord will bring to Abraham what he has promised to him." God will fulfill all His promises to Abraham, but He will do it in the context of Abraham's agency as one who is faithful to God.

There are many seasons to life. You are in the season of new ministry and the cares and concerns of a young family. There will be other seasons of life as you and your family mature and even grow old. It is important that you are a predictable, stable leader with integrity. Your wife and family will draw strength from seeing you live as a man who is dazzled by God and who is, therefore, full of joy and confidence in all the seasons of life.

Be a Protector

The human body is a marvel of God's wisdom and creativity. It also provides us with some handy analogies for thinking about things. The wall of a human cell, for example, is both open to what is desirable and closed to what is not. You must create walls like that for your family. Some of the protection your family needs is generic. Some of it is peculiar to a pastor's family.

Like any family you must screen out the baneful influences of the culture. One of my old seminary professors, Dr. Robert K. Rudolph, was fond of saying, "Open minds like open windows need screens to keep the bugs out." You need to provide the protection of good, well-thought through "screens" for your home. Now, while the children are young, is a good time for you and Mary to develop specific standards that you will use to filter what comes into your home. Obviously, the ordinary media offerings of a godless, anti-Christian culture cannot be brought into your home.

There will even be times when you must regulate the kind of access some people have to your children. You will need to be very discreet and wise in how you do this, but your children (and even your wife sometimes) must be protected from some of the people to whom God has called you to minister. If someone's purpose is malevolent, your family must be protected. Happily, there will not be many occasions in which that protection is needed.

You will also have to protect your family times or you will not have any. Be sure that you organize your life and ministry to allow time to spend with your family. They need time with you. Time for play and time for the quiet joys of thinking, contemplation or even reading a good <u>book together</u>. It is important that there are times in your family life, when barring a dire emergency, Daddy is just home. He is home to enjoy the family with nothing else on the agenda.

Some of this protection is simply done through managing your schedule and scheduling times when you are not available to the congregation you serve. It is a good idea for the people you serve to know that there are times when it is best for them to not call and other times when calls are welcomed. There will be emergency exceptions such as illness and death or dramatic family crisis that will override your schedule, but it is a good example to the men you serve and an encouragement to their wives to know that the pastor has family times that he protects.

It is wise for a pastor with young children to maintain his study and counseling office at the church building. If you work at home you will be distracted and unproductive. Your children will not understand why Daddy can't "come out to play." <u>If you work at the church building, then when you are home, it is to be home.</u>

A pastor's home is an open home by design. You want your family to find joy in sharing hospitality and using every gift to minister the grace of God to others (see 1 Peter 4:9–10). For that very reason it is important that you protect your family from being lost in ministry to others. There is an obvious tension here. Your home should be open so that others may be refreshed with the beauty and joys of godly living in the home. At the same time, your family needs to have the order of a normal and predictable schedule.

If you can maintain an appropriate balance here you will find that the pastor's home can be a wonderful venue for gospel ministry. In a culture in which family life has unraveled, people are hungry to see a family where there is joy and love for God and others. You can encourage in your children a hearty love for using home and family life as a setting for ministry to others. Some of our children's fondest memories are of times when guests surrounded the table and people enjoyed not only a good meal, but also, hearty spiritual conversation.

Protect your family by guarding your heart against man-pleasing. The temptation will be to place the expectations of others in the congregation on your wife and children. Richard Baxter has a wonderful section in the *Christian Directory* on the topic of the fear of man.[2] He shows how impossible a thing it is to have people pleased with you. You have a multitude to please and what pleases one will displease another. Through several helpful pages he shows the impossibility of pleasing man and the freedom of having only one to please—God.

Man-pleasing is not only impossible, Timothy, it is destructive to yourself and to your family. You and Mary must commit yourself to graciously refusing every effort made by people you serve to set the agenda for your family.

Protect your family from all the disappointments and hurts of ministry. Some of the deepest sorrows of pastoral ministry are those times when a pastor is sinned against. Perhaps his good is spoken of as evil. Or maybe he is subject to attack or charges that are unfair or untrue. You will

---

[2] Richard Baxter, *Christian Directory* (reprint, Ligioner, PA: Soli Deo Gloria, 1994), 183–195.

not serve in the same place for long without going through these times of tribulation. You do not need to defend yourself—your Defender is strong.

Your wife and children need protection during these times. They will know that you are going through stormy waters. They can pray and be sensitive to you. But they, especially your children, do not need to be dragged through your disappointments, stresses, hurts and fears. Mary's need to know is greater than the children's, but even there you can spare her some of the fine details that will only keep her up at night. The idea is not to shield Mary by struggling alone through periods of trial. You are one flesh and cannot "go it alone." Learn how to have Mary be your confidant without having her carry the burden.

God will sustain you through these trials. On the other side of this heavy weather there is always a place of abundance (see Psalm 66:10–12). When you arrive safely through the storm it will be a blessing to your wife and children not to have details to forget or struggles with bitterness to overcome.

It is a great work—gospel ministry. Sure there are trials. God never lets us go too far without helping us to see our weaknesses and profound need of His power and enablement. And as Peter says in 1 Peter 1:6–9, even in the midst of having our faith tested in all sorts of trials, we also have joy that is unspeakable and glorious. I had that experience just yesterday. As I was casting my burdens on the Lord, I was overwhelmed with a sense of His care and the goodness and rightness of knowing and serving Him. Joy unspeakable and glorious is ours even in the midst of trials. What a mighty God we serve!

We pray often for God's continued blessing on you and your family.

Running the race,
Pastor Tedd Tripp

PS—Here are a couple of titles that will encourage you in your calling as a husband and father:

1. *Your Family, God's Way* by Wayne Mack (Phillipsburg, NJ: Presbyterian & Reformed Publishing Co., 1991).
2. *The Complete Husband* by Lou Priolo (Amityville, NY: Calvary Press Publishing, 1999).
3. *Shepherding a Child's Heart* by Tedd Tripp (Wapwallopen, PA: Shepherd Press, 1995).

Chapter 4

Love Your Flock
Ted Christman

Dear Timothy,

Warmest greetings in the name of our Savior! It was wonderful to receive your last letter. Dianne and I rejoiced to hear how the Lord is establishing you, not only in the community at large, but especially among your own people. Your increased usefulness to the souls of men is a subject of frequent intercession in our family worship. Be encouraged to know that on some occasions the Lord has so enlarged our hearts concerning your needs that they could only express themselves through tears and brokenness. If only these wandering, distracted, usually too cold hearts could *always* be tender and broken!

Please express our deepest affection to Mary. She is truly a dear wife and faithful companion. We think often of our first years in the ministry and the peculiar challenges they bring to the sometimes lonely wife of a pastor. Please assure her as well of our love and frequent prayers on her behalf.

Timothy, I want to thank you for sharing the brief history of your church. I found it interesting indeed. I am especially grateful for your spiritual assessment of the congregation. I know the endeavor was time consuming, but this is an exercise you actually need to engage in continually. It will help you discern a sense of God's direction for the present and future of your ministry. For my own part, knowing something of the state of your flock helps me considerably in giving you the desired counsel.

You asked me to share some thoughts on loving your flock. I happily consent because your concern is noble and Christ-like. At the same time, I proceed with humility because I am painfully conscious of my own deficiency in loving the sheep as I ought. In fact, I thank both you and the Lord for your request. It has required me to rethink the whole matter of loving our sheep in a way that has been good for my own soul and ministry. May the Lord help me to further enlighten our minds and rekindle the flames of affection in each of our hearts.

What I am about to share with you is the result of some personal brainstorming. I simply sat down with a pad of legal paper and started recording every thought on the subject that came to my mind. Obviously, those thoughts were often random and diverse. Some of them seemed primary, while others were clearly secondary. Sooner than I expected, I had more than a full page of ideas and considerations—all related in some way to loving your flock. Immediately, the challenge became what to do with so many particulars. My approach was to organize them into logical categories and then arrange them in a reasonable order for presentation. I am probably suffering from that common ministerial disease known as "Acute Preacheritis Homileticus," but you're a pastor and likely have a touch of the same malady. I can only ask that you kindly bear with my outline. At least I haven't added a poem!

In thinking through the general subject of loving your flock, it seemed reasonable for me to raise and answer five questions. Very simply, they are: 1) Why is it necessary? 2) How does it look? 3) What must it overcome? 4) Whom should it resemble? 5) Where are its resources?

LOVE YOUR FLOCK—WHY IS IT NECESSARY?

Let me begin with the first question, "Why is it necessary?" Timothy, I am fully persuaded that you love your sheep. It is evident in what you do for them and even in how you speak of them. Nevertheless, it is good for both of us to think frequently about how we might excel still more in this love. Let me give you a few things to consider.

From the negative perspective, it must be said that if we don't love our flocks, it is proof positive that God the Father did not give us as shepherds to His flock. Neither was it the ascended Lord Jesus Christ who gave us as a gift to the Church. The Scriptures are very clear on this matter. To His people of the Old Covenant, God said, "I will give you shepherds after My *own heart* who will feed you on knowledge and understanding" (Jeremiah 3:15). I need not convince you that to have a heart after *God's* own heart is, among other things, to have a loving heart. The implications of *not* having a loving heart are more than obvious.

Since pastors are Christ's "gift" to the church (Ephesians 4:11), it is equally unthinkable that *He* would give under-shepherds who do not love His sheep. The same Savior who loved His own to the uttermost (John 13:1) implants a portion of His spiritual DNA into the heart of every true pastor.

Moreover, if we don't love our flocks, we will be utterly unable to perform any of our responsibilities with the right motive. All that we do will be perfunctory—the mechanical labors of a mere professional. I am sure you have already learned in your brief pastorate that preparing well-studied sermons, preaching with earnestness and passion, interceding fervently for each of your sheep, exercising genuine oversight to the members, giving wise and courageous leadership to the deacons and congregation, etc. is extremely hard and wearisome work! What must those same labors be for the minister who possesses no real God-given love for his people? Surely, his work is mundane to say the least and destined to become downright irksome. This is perhaps one of the primary reasons many pastors experience burnout, resign the ministry and end up selling life insurance.

Positively speaking, however, possessing just a modicum of God's heart spontaneously energizes and motivates the under-shepherd to carry out his pastoral responsibilities. Loving his sheep, he longs to help them understand the faith-increasing, sanctifying, guiding, comforting, life-transforming Word of God. Therefore, he studies *laboriously* to prepare his sermons and delivers them with a measure of earnestness and passion.

Loving his sheep and longing for their growth in grace as well as their peace and joy in the Lord, the pastor fervently carries their names into the holy place on the breastplate of his priestly intercession. There, he pours out his heart on their behalf. He can do nothing less.

The loving shepherd also makes sure that he knows the state of their souls by visiting their homes and inquiring about their spiritual health. He loves them too much to converse in vague generalities. He finds himself compelled to ask the difficult questions—the potentially embarrassing ones. He longs to know about such things as the regularity of their devotions, their progress in grace and the intimacy of their walk with God. He is deeply interested in their family worship, the state of their marriage and whether or not they are benefiting from the public means of grace. He desires to know how he may better pray for them. However, these practical concerns are not merely for the *flock* as a whole. They also pertain to *each* of the sheep individually, including the often neglected singles who grapple with their own unique challenges. Timothy, be sure of it. This kind of interest must be deeply rooted in the soil of love.

A loving pastor also understands how important it is that his sheep are *persuaded* of his love for them. This will enable them to more quickly heed his exhortations publicly and privately. J.C. Ryle said, "Once become satisfied that a man loves you, and you will listen gladly to anything he has to say."[1] Richard Baxter put it like this, "When the people see that you love them without pretense, then they will hear anything you tell them and they will bear anything you lay

---

[1] J.C. Ryle, *The Christian Leaders of England in the 18th Century*, Popular Edition (1902), 55.

upon them."² This persuasion of their pastor's love will also enable the congregation to more sweetly submit to his leadership. They know their pastor loves them. They know he only has their good in view. My dear brother, frequently affirm your love to your people publicly and privately, not only by your faithful and courageous ministries, but also by your affectionate words. Often, they should see you look into their faces and hear you say, "I truly love you in Christ. I am so thankful you're a part of this congregation."

LOVE YOUR FLOCK—HOW DOES IT LOOK?

My second inquiry is, "How does it look?" To some extent, I have already answered this question. In seeking to demonstrate how love motivates and energizes our ministerial labors, I made reference to diligent sermon preparation, passionate preaching, fervent intercession, careful oversight and courageous leadership. Where these elements are lacking, there can be no *real* love for the flock. On the other hand, it is evident that where there is such love, it will manifest itself through those very responsibilities. In other words, the portrait of a loving shepherd must always be painted with the brilliant colors of diligence, passion, fervency, carefulness and courage.

There are additional, attractive hues that must likewise contribute to the captivating portrait of a loving shepherd. They pertain not so much to his ministerial functions

---

² Richard Baxter, *The Reformed Pastor* (reprint, Grand Rapids, MI: Sovereign Grace Publishers, 1971), 32.

as to his posture and demeanor—the way he carries himself and relates to his sheep. These primary colors are *humility* and *warmth*.

To truly love our flocks in a Christ-like way, we must be men of genuine humility, "gentle and *humble* in heart" (Matthew 11:29). Among other things, the grace of humility will make us approachable. Our dear Savior was always accessible. Teachers in Israel like Nicodemus, proud Pharisees like Simon, tax gatherers and sinners, rich and poor, educated and uneducated, even little children all found the Lord to be inviting and approachable. How sad it is that so many parishioners are apprehensive to seek an audience with their minister! In some cases it is due to their own timidity and social awkwardness, but all too often the reticence is grounded in a perceived aloofness in their pastor: "He's hard to talk to. . . . It seems like he's just too busy to be spending time with me. . . . He makes me feel that he has bigger fish than me to fry. . . . I feel that his mind isn't really focused on me." These are foreboding and discouraging conclusions no member of the congregation should ever have to draw. On the subject of church members visiting with their pastor, John Stott simply says, "The more they speak to him in his study on weekdays, the better he will speak to them from the pulpit on Sundays."[3]

Referring to pastors who project a kind of sanctified superiority, Spurgeon once said to his college students, "That is the article I am deprecating, that dreadful ministerial starch.

---

[3] John R.W. Stott, *The Preacher's Portrait* (Grand Rapids, MI: William B. Eerdmans Publishing, 1961), 88.

If you have indulged in it, I would earnestly advise you to go and 'wash in Jordan seven times,' and get it out of you, every particle of it."[4] In the same lecture, the famous London pastor went on to say, "Fling away your stilts brethren, and walk on your feet; doff [cast aside] your ecclesiasticism, and array yourselves in truth."[5]

These beautiful virtues of humility, meekness and approachability ought to *especially* shine when our sheep occasionally come to advise or even correct us. Brother, a truly loving pastor is able to acknowledge before his sheep that he was wrong, perhaps that he has sinned. Even though our Chief Shepherd was never wrong or sinful, for us to be like Him in humility, we *must* be able to be constructively criticized. In the long run, we earn far more confidence from our people in being able to humble ourselves before them than in always insisting we are right. Many times we have admired the courage of Priscilla and Aquila for taking Apollos aside in order to explain to him "the way of God more accurately" (Acts 18:26). How often do we esteem the eloquent preacher for being meek enough to be sharpened by a couple of laypeople?

Another virtue essential to the Christ-like pastor is *warmth*. Loving our sheep requires us always to project and display a genuine tenderness and priestly sympathy. They must know and feel when they unburden their souls (whether it be in the confession of serious sin, the admission of spiri-

---

[4] C. H. Spurgeon, *Lectures To My Students* (reprint, Grand Rapids, MI: Assoc. Publishers and Authors, 1971), 181.
[5] Ibid.

tual coldness, the revelation of a rocky marriage or the anguishing report of the death of a loved one) that the one to whom they come for help and guidance genuinely cares. They must also feel the same interest if they come to share the happy news of an engagement or pregnancy.

Timothy, let me reiterate. Your sheep must *know* and *feel* beyond any shadow of doubt that you are gentle, tender, kind, friendly, interested, focused and warm. If they doubt the reality of these virtues, they will inevitably doubt your love. If they doubt your love, your ministerial effectiveness will be virtually paralyzed.

As I conclude the answer to my second question, listen one more time to the counsel of Charles Spurgeon. He said:

> A man must have a great heart if he would have a great congregation. When a man has a large, loving heart, men go to him as ships to a haven, and feel at peace when they have anchored under the lee of his friendship. Such a man is hearty in private as well as in public; his blood is not cold and fishy, but he is as warm as your own fireside.[6]

LOVE YOUR FLOCK—WHAT MUST IT OVERCOME?

As you have probably discovered, loving your flock is not always easy. At times it can be very difficult. This is a phenomenon we need to understand. The more aware we are of the dynamics that oppose a selfless, pastoral love, the better we will succeed in overcoming them.

---

[6] Ibid., 183, 184.

It seems to me there are enemies from within and without that rise up in opposition to the kind of pastoral love we need to possess. Those "guerilla forces" *within* are rooted in our remaining sin—partiality, selfishness, slothfulness, pride, etc. You can imagine how our sinfulness manifests itself. The scenarios are virtually limitless! A hard day's work has come to an end. You and Mary have planned an evening out, a little getaway. The babysitter for your son is all lined up. Everything looks good to go and then the phone rings. Timothy, you can finish the story. It could be a marriage problem or literally a hundred other issues. The bottom line is that in many cases the matter is sufficiently serious for you to *lovingly* set your plans aside and minister to the bleating sheep. It is Christ-like love *alone* that prevents resentment, conquers the flesh and tenderly makes the sacrifice. Time and space will not allow me to comment on the way laziness, weariness, discouragement, resentment, pride and superficiality also launch their destructive grenades. All I can say, brother, is that we must *constantly* do battle with these and other residual sins that seek to capture and imprison our love.

[Margin note: As a couple, this should be confronted beforehand]

Then there are the enemies from *without*—the potential tyranny of administrative responsibilities, the hectic pace of life, unexpected interruptions, etc. Add to these opposing forces those difficult, trying, unappreciative, criticizing, impatient, high-maintenance sheep who seem to require so much of our precious time. We try to cope with the demanding circumstances of life by prioritizing our duties and managing our time better, but these inevitable distractions still get in the way and hinder the love we long to express. The more difficult challenge is, "How do you love the *unlovely?*" God has wisely placed some of them in every congregation. Though they are wearisome and sometimes frustrating to us, they are precious to the Savior. They are the MOGs of our flock—those "means of grace" intended to make *us* more godly. Perhaps you've heard the saying, "to live above with saints we love . . . oh that will be glory! To live below with saints we know . . . now that's a different story!" Loving such sheep can only be done through the kind of love our Shepherd possesses for us. For such strength we must go to the Strong! This thought provides a natural segue to my fourth question.

Love Your Flock—Whom Should It Resemble?

When we think about the *quality* of pastoral love we desire, the natural question is raised, "Whom should it resemble?" Thankfully, we need not look long for the answer. The *ultimate* example of perfect pastoral love is clearly and indisputably the Lord Jesus Christ.

The apostle Paul spoke repeatedly of the love of Christ. In Ephesians 3:19 he described it as that which "surpasses knowledge." Perhaps the central and most awe-inspiring feature of this incomprehensible love is its *self-giving*. In that same epistle to the Ephesians, the apostle went on to say, "Christ also loved the church and *gave Himself* up for her" (Ephesians 5:25). In Galatians 2:20, Paul spoke in affectionately personal terms. He said, "The Son of God, who loved me and *delivered Himself* up for me." Referring to His own *goodness* as a shepherd, the Lord Jesus said, "The good shepherd *lays down His life* for the sheep" (John 10:11). Again, when reflecting on the quality of His love, the Savior plainly asserted, "Greater love has no one than this, that one *lay down his life* for his friends" (John 15:13).

Dear brother, if the most Christ-like thing a husband can do for his wife is to give himself up for her, then surely the most Christ-like thing we can do for our sheep is to give ourselves up for them. The love we need to emulate is essentially about sacrifice. The consummate "lover" is our precious Savior. As we pursue our ministries and strive for increased conformity to Him, "beholding as in a mirror" the glory of our Lord, we *will* be "transformed into the same image" (2 Corinthians 3:18). We will look more like *Him* and our love will look more like *His*. If through God's kindness our ministries are lengthy, we will find a thousand ways to lay our lives down for the flock, often to the point of exhaustion, until the very day of our death.

Another critical virtue exemplified in our Lord's character is *patience*. Every time I read through the Gospels, I am overwhelmed with how graciously He endured the unbelief, ignorance, dullness, ingratitude and pride of His disciples. On one occasion He had to say to the twelve, "Have I been *so long* with you, and yet you have not come to know Me?" (John 14:9). On another occasion He said, "O foolish men and *slow of heart to believe*" (Luke 24:25). Frequently, we hear Him tenderly lament, "O you of little faith" (Matthew 14:31). On the very eve of His crucifixion, when His heart was heavy with the prospect of divine abandonment, His weak, unbelieving, dull-of-heart disciples actually entered into an argument "as to which one of them was regarded to be greatest" (Luke 22:24). How did the One whom we should resemble respond? *Always, always, always* with the gentleness and self-composure of patience. Timothy, our disciples are no different than the Lord's. They, like their pastors, also struggle with unbelief, ignorance, dullness, ingratitude and pride. Our duty is to help them out of these sins with a patient and longsuffering love that resembles the Savior.

Love Your Flock—Where Are Its Resources?

Dear brother, I come now to my last question, "Where are its resources?" When you consider the necessity of loving your flock, how it looks, what it must overcome and whom it should resemble, surely you join me in feeling overwhelmed. Upon contemplating such matters, we find ourselves spontaneously crying out with the apostle Paul, "Who is adequate for these things?" (2 Corinthians 2:16). Of course, the answer is "No one!" However, the same apostle, only a few verses later, points us to our true hope. He says, "Our adequacy is from God" (2 Corinthians 3:5). The responsibility to love our sheep in a way that is truly pleasing to the Lord is momentous. Sometimes it even seems impossible. The encouraging fact remains that *all* of the resources for such a difficult assignment are readily available. They are to be found in the triune God of Scripture. We simply must flee to His Word and throne.

With regard to His Word, we should continually search its sacred pages for direction and guidance as to *how* we should love the flock. Therein we find for our instruction an abundance of precepts, principles and examples, especially in the words and works of the Savior. The life and ministry of the apostle Paul is also pregnant with helpful counsel. The book of Acts and the Epistles reveal much about the heart of a loving shepherd. Concerning God's moral precepts it has been said, "Law is love's eyes, without it, love is blind." The same is true for pastoral love. Without the eyes of Scripture, its love is blind. You and I have no right to love Christ's sheep the way *we* think they should be loved. We are responsible to love them the way the Chief Shepherd requires.

In addition to bowing before His Word, we must also continually bow in prayer before His throne. There we may take up the prosperous occupation of begging. As you well know, in the kingdom of God, beggars become rich.

Timothy, I previously spoke of the triune God. Here is what I had in mind. God the *Father* gives shepherds after His own heart (Jeremiah 3:15). The exalted *Son* of God gives pastors to the church (Ephesians 4:11). God the *Holy Spirit* makes "overseers" (Acts 20:28). We simply need to fall before the gracious throne of this God and plead with the respective Persons of the Trinity to mold us into all that we need to be. He who gives and makes true pastors is able to make them *better* pastors—i.e. more loving. Before His throne of grace we ought often to present holy arguments. We should plead, "Oh God, I want a heart more like Yours so that I may better love *Your* sheep. I'm asking You to make me like Yourself! How can You decline my request?" Surely the Lord would be pleased with such prayers! Surely He will answer such prayers! John Piper graphically describes prayer as "the coupling of primary and secondary causes."

He goes on to characterize it as "the splicing of our limp wire to the lightning bolt of heaven."[7] With a resource of such infinite power, may we find ourselves fervently and frequently begging for such grace.

Brother, I thank you for your patience in reading this longer than normal letter. I readily acknowledge that I have only scratched the surface. I am also painfully aware of my own failure to love my sheep as I ought. This sin of omission is a matter of frequent confession on my part. As I conclude, Timothy, please remember to whom our sheep belong. I say "our sheep," but in reality they are *not* ours. They belong to the One whom we are privileged to serve—the Chief Shepherd. This is just one more sobering reason why we must *never, ever* approach "lording it over" them (1 Peter 5:3). Rather, with all of the God-like love we can acquire, we must imitate the Lord of whom it is said, "Like a shepherd He will tend His flock. In His arm He will gather the lambs and carry them in His bosom. He will gently lead the nursing ewes" (Isaiah 40:11).

May the Lord graciously and abundantly pour into our unworthy souls ever-increasing measures of His own love for the sheep. Please covenant with me to petition God for more of this wonderful gift. Timothy, if you are able to receive one brief and final exhortation from a spiritual father, humbly receive this one. *Love your flock!* Baxter says, "See that you feel a tender love in your breasts, and let the people feel it in your speeches and see it in your

---

[7] John Piper, *Brothers, We Are Not Professionals* (Nashville, TN: Broadman and Holman Publishers, 2002), 58.

dealings. Let them see that you are willing to spend and be spent for their sakes."[8]

Give our warmest regards to Mary and assure her of our prayers for a good pregnancy and the safe delivery of another healthy child. As you give us occasional updates, we will continue to intercede for the Lord's blessing on your church. I humbly ask that you remember the ministry of Heritage in the same way. Until we correspond again, "The Lord bless you and keep you. The Lord make His face shine on you and be gracious to you. The Lord lift up His countenance on you and give you peace" (Numbers 6:24–26).

Sincerely your fellow servant in the gospel,
Pastor Ted

PS—You asked about books that might be helpful on the subject of loving your flock. I highly recommend these titles:

1. *Lectures to My Students* by Charles H. Spurgeon (reprint, Grand Rapids, MI: Zondervan, 1954).
2. *The Reformed Pastor* by Richard Baxter (reprint, Edinburgh: The Banner of Truth Trust, 1979).
3. *The Preacher's Portrait* by John R. W. Stott (Grand Rapids, MI:. Eerdmans, 1961).

---

[8] Baxter, *Reformed Pastor*, 32.

Chapter 5

Memorize Scripture

Andy Davis

Dear Timothy,

    I can't tell you how glad I am to hear of your new ministry as a senior pastor! I still cherish those times that we shared in prayer as you wondered from the depths of your heart whether or not God was calling you into ministry. To see you grow from the unbeliever you were when we first met to this point now is one of the greatest joys I have ever experienced in ministry. Of course you must remember how apprehensive you were to open up to me on our first conversation, little realizing that I would someday be one of your best friends. As I talked to you about life after death and Christ's atoning sacrifice for sins, I felt as though the Holy Spirit was personally selecting each Scripture verse just for you, like a skilled surgeon selecting each surgical tool, "as though God were making His appeal" through me (2 Corinthians 5:20). What was all the more amazing was that I had left my Bible at home and had to rely on my Scripture memorization to share the gospel verses with you. It is of that precise topic I want to speak now—the value of Scripture memorization to every aspect of your life as a pastor.

Timothy, I yearn for your life and ministry to count fully for the glory of God and the growth of His kingdom. But my greatest prayer for you is that you not forget how central the Word of God is both to you personally and to the church over which you are now an under-shepherd. In order to stay spiritually healthy and protect yourself from the temptations and attacks of the devil, you must continually saturate your mind in the Word of God so that you can avoid all the snares he will lay for your feet. One of the hardest parts of pastoral ministry is to realize how vital to the church is your personal walk with Christ. Thus, you are a strategic and attractive target for the Evil One. If he can drag you down, many others will go down with you. This is parallel to the situation of King David and the people of Israel and Jerusalem. When David sinned by taking a census of the fighting men in Israel, it was the people who paid the price in a plague at the Lord's hand (1 Chronicles 21:14). So also when David sinned by committing adultery with Bathsheba and when he confessed his sin in Psalm 51, he was very concerned about the prosperity of Jerusalem: "In your good pleasure, make Zion prosper, build up the walls of Jerusalem" (Psalm 51:18). Sin is a "luxury" a pastor cannot afford—the cost to his people is staggeringly high. Therefore, when the devil prowls around your way, seeking to destroy your family, all that you have planted in ministry, and your very life as well, remember that our Lord Jesus Christ answered the devil with one memorized Scripture after another: "Away from me Satan, for it is written..." (Matthew 4:10).

This brings me to another aspect of your personal walk with God that will be foundational to the fruitfulness of your pastoral ministry: following God's leadership and guidance through absolute moment-by-moment obedience. Pastors are constantly feeling the need for guidance in their ministries—"What should I do now, Lord?" Christ's answer points the way. While in the desert, the devil tempted Christ, "If you are the Son of God, tell these stones to become bread." Jesus answered, "It is written: 'Man does not live on bread alone, but on every word that comes from the mouth of God'" (Matthew 4:3–4). Timothy, for the longest time I felt this verse was simply instructing me that I needed to have a daily quiet time. I have recently dug into the Old Testament context and come to realize that that application does not go deep enough. Jesus was quoting from Deuteronomy 8:3, and the context of that verse is vital:

> Be careful to follow every command I am giving you today, so that you may live and increase and may enter and possess the land that the Lord promised on oath to your forefathers. Remember how the Lord your God led you all the way in the desert these forty years, to humble you and to test you in order to know what was in your heart, whether or not you would keep His commands. He humbled you, causing you to hunger and then feeding you with manna, which neither you nor your fathers had known, to teach you that man does not live on bread alone but on every word that comes from the mouth of the Lord (Deuteronomy 8:1–3).

God led Israel step by step through the wilderness, humbling the people and causing them to look to God for their every need and their every direction, whether left or right. In effect, God trained Israel to stare at His mouth and to live and move only at the words of God's mouth. This was equally underscored in their movements from place to place as they followed God's leadership by the pillar of cloud and fire:

> Whenever the cloud lifted from above the Tent, the Israelites set out; wherever the cloud settled, the Israelites encamped. At the Lord's command the Israelites set out, and at His command they encamped. As long as the cloud stayed over the tabernacle, they remained in camp. When the cloud remained over the tabernacle a long time, the Israelites obeyed the Lord's order and did not set out. Sometimes the cloud was over the tabernacle only a few days; at the Lord's command they would encamp, and then at His command they would set out. Sometimes the cloud stayed only from evening till morning, and when it lifted in the morning, they set out. Whether by day or by night, whenever the cloud lifted, they set out (Numbers 9:17–21).

So, in effect, the Lord Jesus Christ was saying, "Satan, I will not eat except at the Lord's command. I do not live by bread alone but by every word that comes from the mouth of God. When God gives the word, I shall eat again!" Now of course, we expect God to "give the word" for the direction of our lives expressly through the written Word of God. But this understanding of the Old Testament context of Christ's quote has made clinging to "every word that comes from the mouth of God" so much more vivid in terms of personal daily obedience. This is where the guidance you will seek for every aspect of your ministry will come from.

Scripture memorization is thus beneficial to your private life before God. It is also beneficial to the health of your family. I am so delighted that God is blessing you and Mary with another child! Parenting is such a great joy and a challenge too. But realize this, to paraphrase Jesus, "What would it profit a pastor to gain a 'successful church' and lose his family?" Or, to put it more biblically, "If anyone does not know how to manage his own family, how can he take care of God's church?" (1 Timothy 3:5). Your wife needs your constant love and affection, Timothy. Memorizing Ephesians 5 has blessed my marriage constantly. As I drive home from a hard day at the church and my eyes are selfishly on myself, the Holy Spirit presses the words of Scripture again with a clarion call: "Husbands, love your wives as Christ loved the church and gave Himself up for her . . ." and "He who loves his wife, loves himself" (Ephesians 5:25, 28). In effect, the Spirit says "Get your eyes off yourself, Timothy, and love your wife." Often times, God has used whatever passage I have been memorizing to bless my prayer times with my wife or as a means of God's leadership of me as I act as spiritual head in our marriage. This discipline will also help protect your marriage from the incredible stresses associated with pastoral ministry.

In the same way, saturating your mind with Scripture will enable you to teach it to your children and disciple them properly. Your children are your primary disciples—don't lose them while seeking to gain the world for Christ.

Again, the wisdom of Deuteronomy guides your parenting as the priest of your family:

> Hear, O Israel: The Lord our God, the Lord is one. Love the Lord your God with all your heart and with all your soul and with all your strength. These commandments that I give you today are to be upon your hearts. Impress them on your children. Talk about them when you sit at home and when you walk along the road, when you lie down and when you get up (Deuteronomy 6:4–7).

Timothy, I don't really know how you can obey this in any practical way if you don't give yourself to memorization. To "talk about them when you sit at home and when you walk along the road," you must have them committed to memory, or else bring a Bible along. Even more telling is the word "impress" (in the NIV; "teach them diligently" in many other versions). This exact same word is used for the whetting of God's glistening sword in Deuteronomy 32:41 and means "to sharpen." Do you remember that discipleship camping trip we took with the other guys in our Bible study? Do you remember how Kevin took out the whetstone and began sharpening his axe before getting firewood ready for us? He rubbed the whetstone against the blade again and again and again, over and over, until the blade was sharp. This is exactly what happens to your mind when you are memorizing verses, repeating them again and again. And there's no short-cut to getting the verses down perfectly—it's as simple and as hard as repetition over time, day after day, month after month. That is precisely what

Accept it and do it.

God wants you to do to the minds of your children—sharpen the Word of God into them through repetition. ASAP!

That reminds me of another illustration from that camping trip. Do you remember when I had you guys each get a small stone from the river and one from the forest? I had you put the forest stone in your left hand and the river stone in your right and hold them out so we all could see. Do you remember the immediate difference between the forest stone and the river stone? Steve said, "Yeah, the forest one's all dirty!" So I had you all wash your forest stones in the river—now they were completely clean and free from dirt and leaves. But were they identical? No! Timothy, you were the first to see the difference. The forest stone was sharp with jagged edges but the river stone was perfectly smooth. Then I had you put your forest rocks in the river while we ate dinner—franks and beans as I recall. After dinner, you fished the same stones back out of the river and they still looked jagged and rough. You could see the point I was making—a forest rock only becomes perfectly smooth through years and years of being totally immersed in the mountain stream. So it is with your mind and the Word of God. Sanctification occurs when you have totally immersed your mind day after day, month after month, years after year in the constantly flowing truth of Scripture: "Do not conform any longer to the pattern of this world, but *be transformed by the renewing of your mind*. Then you will be able to test and approve what God's will is—His good, pleasing and perfect will" (Romans 12:2). Scripture memorization is one of the most powerful tools God has used in my life to purify me from evil desires and to sanctify me for His glory.

Now Timothy, I want to speak to you also about your outward ministry as pastor. I know you well enough to understand how much you desire to have a fruitful ministry in your new church. Realize that this desire is a godly one and openly spoken of by Christ, as I will mention in a minute. However, even a godly desire for fruit can be twisted into a selfish desire for an "empire." Avoid playing a numbers game, in which you measure "success" by how big your worship services have grown since you got there. Remember, we are seeking to "make disciples of all nations," not draw an ever-larger crowd. Yet, desiring salvation for the lost and growing maturity for the saved is evidence of God's work in your heart. Yearn for fruit—not just a little, but a lot of it!

How does Scripture memorization relate to this? Well, I may be going out on a limb, but I think that Jesus may have had it in mind (at least in some ways) when He said to His apostles the night before He died, "If you remain in me *and my words remain in you*, ask whatever you wish, and it will be given you. This is to my Father's glory, *that you bear much fruit*, showing yourselves to be my disciples" (John 15:7–8). Of course, you remember the powerful illustration of the vine and the branches that preceded this teaching. (By the way, Timothy, I still have that dead branch taken from a grapevine on my desk as a motivator to me that, only by abiding in Christ will I bear fruit. You should get one for your office.) Abiding in Christ means constantly reckoning or considering ourselves spiritually grafted into Him, with His life-giving sap flowing through us by the Holy Spirit. Only this way will you be able to bear fruit that will last. Yet I believe that God has shown me the incredibly powerful way that Scripture memorization plays in that "abiding." Jesus said, "If you abide in me [i.e. through personal faith in me, made alive by my Spirit], *and my words abide in you,*" only then will you bear eternal fruit through prayer in His name. I could easily address the importance of prayer at this point, but I am focusing on the concept of Christ's words abiding in you. I looked it up in the Greek a moment ago, just to be sure, and it is plural—if Christ's *words* abide in you. That means His nouns, verbs, adjectives, subordinate clauses, etc. These have to abide in you moment by moment. How can this be done better than by committing them to memory? Scripture memorization is a God-blessed path to spiritual fruitfulness in your ministry.

This is amazingly practical. Let's say it is Tuesday and you have to visit Mrs. Beecham after her gall bladder operation. As you are walking down the sidewalk that leads to the hospital, you are reviewing whatever chapter you are memorizing at that time—perhaps Philippians 2 on the humility of Christ or 2 Corinthians 1 on how God brings us through terrible trials so that we may comfort others with the comfort He used with us. As you sit by Mrs. Beecham's bedside to talk with her, out of the overflow of your heart your mouth speaks Scripture. Someone once said, "When all you have is a hammer, the whole world begins to look like a nail." In like manner, you begin to find a practical use for encouragement and exhortation to almost any passage of Scripture you're memorizing. Your counsel becomes saturated with the "very words of God" (1 Peter 4:11). I have heard it said that John Wesley rode more miles on horseback than any man that ever lived and all the while, he was reading the Bible. Like it was said of Bunyan, his mind was so saturated with Scripture, his blood was "bibline." So let it be with you.

Timothy, I want to be very clear about what I'm advocating. I am urging you to memorize whole books of the Bible, rather than just individual verses. Many people print memory systems with "key verses" they choose. Memorizing individual verses is better than memorizing no verses, but memorizing whole chapters and books is better than doing individual verses. Why? Several reasons:

1) It honors the testimony that Scripture gives about itself: "All Scripture is God-breathed and is useful for teaching, rebuking, correcting and training in righteousness" (2 Timothy 3:16), and "Man does not live on bread alone but on every word that comes from the mouth of God" (Matthew 4:4). God does not waste His breath, so there are no superfluous words in Scripture. And you will find that some of your most powerful moments of conviction, insight and encouragement will come from unexpected places in the Bible.

2) Since so much of Scripture is written as a flow of thought, with the author making some overall point through logical argumentation, memorizing the whole passage enables you more readily to grasp the central thought. You won't loose the forest for the trees. Nor will you lose the trees for the forest. The whole book of Hebrews will come together as a sym-

phony of united truth, and each individual verse in the train of thought will sing its own tones with a new clarity. This "forest and the trees" benefit will also help you build a sound biblical and systematic theology overall, while at the same time understanding and preaching/teaching individual verses properly as well.

3) You will be less likely to take verses out of context as a result of memorizing the whole book. One of the most common ways that people who oppose you will seek to blunt the force of your case in a doctrinal dispute is, "You're taking that out of context!" Careful work on the whole book will help you avoid that error.

4) Your joy will keep increasing, as will your awe at the miraculous infinity of truth in the Scripture, as you continue to discover new truths day after day, month after month. The discipline of memorizing whole books will take you into uncharted territory, and since "All Scripture is God-breathed and useful . . ." (2 Timothy 3:16) you will derive benefit from the journey of discovery. Suppose a rich uncle died and gave you an old abandoned silver mine near Tucson, Arizona. After you scrape together enough money for a plane flight there, you stop at a hardware store and buy a lantern and a shovel. The shopkeeper asks what you are doing and you tell him. He laughs, saying, "There's been no silver out of that hole in the ground in decades, if there ever was any!" Thus, you enter your inheritance with skepticism,

pushing aside cobwebs and old boards. Suppose on the one hand, you spend six hours poking around the tunnels and find nothing but rocks and dirt. Do you think you would ever enter that mine again? But suppose instead you find some tunnel that it seems no one had ever explored. You begin digging and after an hour of hard labor, your efforts are rewarded with an unmistakable sparkle—a new vein of silver! How likely would you be to return with renewed efforts to explore that tunnel? Would you even wait another day? So it is with memorizing passages of Scripture that you wouldn't ordinarily choose—you discover things you didn't expect and your love and joy for the Bible ascends to the skies. You will never get stagnant but will be a constantly renewing fountain for your people.

5) Finally, memorization of extended portions of Scripture most readily lends itself to the best style of preaching for you—expository. Timothy, I realize you have a disposition toward expository preaching and see the danger of following a merely topical approach. You already believe that preaching week by week through books of the Bible is the best way to avoid your own blind spots and to protect you from avoiding "hot potatoes"—controversial topics no one wants to cover. As you remember, we have spoken about Paul's example, that he did not hesitate to proclaim to his people the whole will of God (Acts 20:27). In this way alone can we see the Word of God fully sanctify your people as God intends.

Can you see how memorizing whole books will give a richness and depth to your preaching that would be impossible without it? You will be expounding verse after verse that you have already meditated deeply upon through endless repetition. As you are preaching, your people will feast on your deep meditation as you are show them things from Scripture they've never seen before, though they've been over those passages since childhood. They're not getting shallow baby-talk and they will thrive. While you are preaching, the Holy Spirit will be able to take up other verses that you have stored up and will enable you to cite them powerfully and accurately, because you understand them thoroughly. When you are writing your sermons, you will have a built-in concordance of cross-references that will give you all the support and depth you could ever desire. Scripture memorization is a rich and powerful ally to expository preaching. For these reasons and others, I advocate memorizing extended portions of Scripture over individual verses.

Now, if you feel that your memory is not good enough, you will be surprised to find how God will improve your memory as you work on this discipline. My missions professor at Gordon-Conwell Theological Seminary, Dr. J. Christy Wilson (who has since gone to be with the Lord), related a story about a plumber he knew who made a simple goal of memorizing John 3:16. He had such incredible difficulty that, after working on it daily for three months, he still couldn't recite it without error! What's even more amazing, however, is that this persistent saint never gave up, as most of us would have. Once he succeeded in achieving his humble goal, God blessed him by enabling him to memorize over 2000 verses of Scripture over the next five years! God was merely testing him to see if he would be faithful. And the Lord has power over your brain, Timothy. "Then He [Christ] *opened their minds so they could understand the Scriptures*" (Luke 24:45). This means Christ did something within their brains to enable them to understand. He can do the same work in you to enable you to memorize. Only be faithful to work hard and He will bless your humble efforts.

Timothy, I have already reminded you of the value of Scripture memorization in *evangelism* from your own conversion when I first spoke to you. Witnessing with extended portions of Scripture memorized gives you a freedom and versatility to bring the whole counsel of God's Word to bear on the suffering soul of a lost person. The exact same thing is true in the pastoral counseling you will do. Many pastors abandon the doctrine of the sufficiency of Scripture when it comes to the *counseling* of troubled souls. Scripture memorization will help you to see that we already have "everything we need for life and godliness" (2 Peter 1:3) through the knowledge Scripture has given us of God Himself. Worldly psychology will reveal itself to be the man-made fraud it is compared with sound biblical counsel. Scripture memorization has deeply enriched my *prayer life*, enabling me easily to pray back to God His own words. And in the area of *stewardship of time*, memorizing Scripture is the best way to "make the most of every opportunity, because the days are evil" (Ephesians 5:16). Timothy, the days fly by quickly. Soon, you and Mary will be old and gray. Soon your children will be grown. Soon, you will stand before Christ to give Him an account of each second you spent on earth. Think of all the hours you spend driving, walking, sitting, showering, mowing the lawn, shaving, waiting for a plane, etc. Fill those moments with prayer and with Scripture memorization, and you will not regret even one tick of the clock spent on memorization when Christ calls you to account for your stewardship.

I close with an incredible promise of blessing on every area of your life because of your commitment to this discipline:

> Blessed is the man who does not walk in the counsel of the wicked or stand in the way of sinners or sit in the seat of mockers. But his delight is in the law of the Lord, and *on His law he meditates day and night.* He is like a tree planted by streams of water, which yields its fruit in season and whose leaf does not wither. *Whatever he does prospers* (Psalm 1:1–3).

Timothy, I love you in the Lord. My prayers are with you, and may God richly bless each day of your ministry. I will always be your friend, eternally your brother.

For the glory of our King,
Andy

PS—I know of no books dedicated to the extended memorization of Scripture other than my own pamphlet, *An Approach to the Extended Memorization of Scripture*. It is available at our website (www.fbcdurham.org) under the "Writings" section. Others have written ably on the spiritual discipline of memorization itself. Two I would recommend are:

1. *Spiritual Disciplines for the Christian Life* by Donald Whitney (Colorado Springs, CO: NavPress, 1991).
2. *The Spirit of the Disciplines* by Dallas Willard (San Francisco, CA: Harper & Row, 1988).

Many people put out topical memory systems and that is of some excellent benefit. But again, Timothy, I am advocating memorizing whole books as God leads.

Chapter 6

Pray Always
Martin Holdt

Dear Timothy,

Like you, my ministry commenced when I was in my mid-twenties, and to say that there was a degree of fear and trepidation about the awesome prospect of being a pastor and a preacher is an understatement. Looking back, I thank God for the advice given me by older men in the ministry. Through them, I learned and *continue* to discover insights about an effective ministry. What was passed on to me by faithful men who have left a legacy of ministerial fruitfulness has been to my eternal benefit, and I pray that as you stand on the threshold of your pastorate God might use me to profit you in the same way.

When I was a third year theological student, I was anxious to know if, when one day I graduated, I would find myself in God's work and service, enjoying, in the biblical sense of the word, success. I noted that a certain pastor in our country was exercising a ministry that was being owned of God. I wrote to him and asked pointed questions about his success and his ministry. His reply consisted of two-and-a-half pages of sound pastoral advice. His answer to my question about prayer was modest and humble, but it did indicate one thing: prayer was a major factor in his life. My years of training were invaluable, but I have often wondered why there was never as much as a mention of the theology of prayer. In the history of Presbyterianism, the whole matter of the pastor and his commitment to intercessory prayer was an integral part of the ordination service, particularly when it came to addressing the man and his duties and responsibility to his congregation. Tragically, prayer is an under-emphasized part of the pastor's calling today.

Cast your mind across the stretches of biblical history. There is one continuous account of men inspired by God the Holy Spirit, calling upon the living God and imploring His mercy in times of need. With Abraham, for example, the biblical record is clear. He understood the part prayer played in his powerful pilgrimage. God disclosed to him the secret of His purposes, and when He did that, Abraham rushed to the throne of grace to implore the mercy of God upon the righteous in Sodom. Would God, for the sake of fifty, forty, thirty and fewer righteous, spare those who were worthy? God heard his cry and remembering Abraham, delivered Lot.

The life of Jacob teaches us that when the covenant is in force, where sin abounds, grace does much more abound. Can you find a more moving prayer than Jacob crying, "I will not let you go except you bless me?" Is the Author of Scripture not telling us that we have in Jacob a man who at least understood one thing, that in the providence of God, it is impossible to consider a pilgrimage of faith if intercessory prayer does not feature prominently?

What shall we say of Moses? God once declared that the people were worthy of immediate judgment. Moses then came to the fore and made his plea. There is holy argument and content in his prayer. Hear him plead: "God, what about Your reputation? What will the heathen say? How can this be?" What holy respect, what an anxious plea, what concern for the honor of the living God! If he did it once, he did it again and again, as he stood between an ungrateful, rebellious people and a sin-avenging God. Here was a man of God, arguing the case on the grounds of God's holy and gracious Name, and God remembered and spared the nation.

Every chapter in redemptive history features men at prayer. Take Nehemiah and the broken-down walls of Jerusalem. He appears as a man given to intercessory supplication. Ezra was exactly the same. David stressed the necessity of prayer. All the prophets were characterized as intercessors of the first rank.

Consider the example of Jesus. We excuse ourselves from prayer because of our busy schedules. Was there ever a man as busy as Jesus? Have you ever noticed, Timothy, the setting of Mark 1:35? It reads: "Now in the morning, having risen a long while before daylight, He went out and departed to a solitary place and there He prayed." The Holy Son of God was spending the early hours of the morning, before the rising of the sun, approaching His heavenly Father, renewing His spiritual strength and vigor as He prepared Himself for the coming day.

Jesus' whole life is interspersed with prayer. As He approaches the cross, He takes His disciples with Him. He again teaches the necessity of praying. It was an inseparable part of His preparation for that baptism of suffering. Have you ever read anything more soul-moving than His high priestly prayer? In Gethsemane and in the agony of the cross, the Son of God was preoccupied with communion with the Father even as His holy wrath was being poured upon His darling Son in order to pay for the sins of His elect people. Even then, He had the mind to pray! Timothy, it would be absurd not to see the importance of walking in His steps.

Acts 6 is a fascinating passage. It begins with these words: "Now in those days when the number of disciples was increasing, the Grecian Jews among them complained against those of the Aramaic-speaking community because their widows were being overlooked in the daily distribution of food. So the twelve gathered all the disciples together and said, 'It would not be right for us to neglect the ministry of the Word of God in order to wait on tables. Brothers, choose seven men from among you who are known to be full of the Spirit and wisdom. We will turn this responsibility over to them and will give our attention to *prayer* and the ministry of the Word'" (emphasis mine).

Notice, first of all, unprecedented church growth bringing with it the unusual demands for pastoral attention. The church was multiplying because of a sovereign act of God. With it came an unexpected pastoral problem, which threatened to get out of hand. Some of us would have panicked. The apostles, however, refused to allow the issue to entangle them and consume their time. They delegated the responsibility.

Can you imagine a leadership today with a hands-off attitude to a matter as serious as that? Starvation was the issue! The first ministerial function, as far as these men were concerned, was prayer. They had learned well. The two functions of the ministry, prayer and preaching, cannot be separated. Ministers must of necessity pray as all people do. They must of necessity do what all Christians do: begin the day with prayer, pre-empt the day with prayer, point the day with prayer and end the day with prayer. But they must go beyond that.

The people of the early church, according to Acts 2:42, gave themselves to prayer. But the pastors went further. They refused to undertake a noble responsibility in the local church in order to pursue to a far greater degree the essential ministry of prayer. Calvin said that pastors have a greater reason to pray than anyone else, for their big concern is the common salvation of the church. At this point the example of Moses becomes instructive to all pastors.

While prayerlessness abounds, unbelief and secularism is making inroads into the evangelical church. Our only hope today is an abandonment to prayer. Prayer is our common duty, but it is particularly the duty of those of us who are called to the ministry. In the Old Testament, people expected prayer of their leaders. Samuel considered it a sin not to pray for the people. David prayed and the plague was stopped. Hezekiah prayed in a national crisis, and God heard.

And yet, Timothy, for all of their diligence and faithfulness, these Old Testament saints could not pray as we may with our faith in the knowledge of Jesus Christ. They could not pray as we do in the full consciousness of the glorious privileges set out for us in Hebrews 10:19–22:

Therefore, brothers, since we have confidence to enter the Most Holy Place by the blood of Jesus, by a new and living way opened for us through the curtain, that is His Body, and since we have a great Priest over the house of God, let us draw near to God with a sincere heart in full assurance of faith, having our hearts sprinkled to cleanse us from a guilty conscience and having our bodies washed with pure water.

Study Paul's prayers. Study the details. Study the passion, the precision, the emphasis, the pastoral heart. As he carries upon his heart the burdens of the churches, he knows that by God's divine appointment, his highest calling, as an under-shepherd of the flock, is to invoke the Great Shepherd on behalf of the flock.

There is no special efficacy in ministers' prayers. Only Christ has efficacy. The basis of our praying is always, and shall always be, the mediatorial work of Christ. Our work as pastors is not to present a sacrifice for men, but to persuade them to believe a Sacrifice already offered. However, it is precisely on that basis that we plead with God on behalf of men.

In that sense, prayer is our highest work. It is hard work. It is a fight against the adversary. It is a battle against the flesh. It is essential work. The minister who does not pray for his flock is no minister at all. He is proud because he does his work as if he can succeed without God's power. He shows no pity because he does not realize that his people's greatest need is the Lord's divine favors upon them. Be assured of this, if he does not pray, he will pay a high price.

Consider the sobering remarks of John Smith:

Prayer is the life and soul of the sacred function; without it, we can expect no success in our ministry; without it our best instructions are barren and our most painful labors idle. Before we can strike terror into those who break the law, we must first, like Moses, spend much time with God in retirement; prayer often gains a success to little talents, while the greatest without it are useless or pernicious. A minister who is not a man of piety and prayer, whatever his other talents may be, cannot be called a servant of God, but rather a servant of Satan, chosen by him for the same reason that he chose the serpent of old because he was more subtle than any beast of the field which the Lord God had made. What a monster, oh God, must that minister of religion be, that dispenser of the ordinances of the gospel, that intercessor between God and His people, that reconciler of man to his Maker, if he sees himself not as a man of prayer.

God often gives those blessings meant for the people in answer to the pastor's prayer. We are to bring their needs before Him, we are to lament their sin, we are to pray for the sinner's conversion and for the saint's edification, and woe to us if we do not! While ministers need to be in the forefront of the ministry of prayer, all who believe need to have the same concern. If ever the church is, by God's design, to blossom, Christians must learn to pray.

Ministers do not follow a career. A minister is captive to divine service and he cannot serve God without prayer. When Paul writes to the Romans, he wants them to know this (Romans 1:8). Following his introduction, and before he moves into the rest of his letter to the church in Rome, he employs the oath saying, "God is my witness, whom I serve with my spirit in the gospel of His Son, that without ceasing I make mention of you always in my prayers" (1:9). He employs the oath to assure believers of his work in this regard. It is the first duty he mentions.

I might mention here that on a number of occasions in my life I have heard preachers inveighing against what they call "shopping-list praying." If by that they mean that we are not to pray by demanding of God things on a list, then I identify with their aversion to this kind of praying. However, I believe, in recalling two Old Testament examples, that it is the duty of the pastor to pray for his entire congregation by name. The Scriptures say of Aaron that he bore a breastplate with the names of the children of Israel on his breast. Take note also of Samuel's example when he said, "As for me, far be it from me that I should sin against the Lord by failing to pray for you" (1 Samuel 12:23a). It has been a great help to me to have my personal prayer book! There is nothing Anglican about it! It is a notebook with a pocket on the inside cover for a small white card with short-term items for prayer, items such as speaking engagements, needs that will pass away and other such temporal matters. For the rest of the book, the pages consist of verses of Scripture, which I repeat in prayer as they focus my attention on God and His ways. Then I have on the list the names of the members of the church I pastor and their children as well as other pastors and institutions for which I feel the need to pray. Included in those pages are items such as the church's finances, the singing and the worship in the church and the various departments of activity such as the youth. If that is "shopping-list praying" then I would argue that someone who goes to shop with a shopping list at least knows what he wants to buy and does not return home disappointed that he has forgotten something!

There are far too many things that are expected of the pastor. If we did all that was expected of us, we would never pray. If you go back to Acts 6, you will notice that when that priority was established, the results were phenomenal. Our ministry is not results-orientated, but when by God's design, these men did what it was their duty to do, "the Word of God spread and the number of the disciples multiplied greatly in Jerusalem, and a great many of the priests were obedient to the faith." It may not always be the same with us, but our work will never be unblessed. There will never be evangelistic potency without intercessory prayer.

Timothy, the following ten important features of biblical praying should be remembered:

1. *Necessity.* God has no dumb children, much less dumb servants. When that Pharisee of Pharisees, Saul of Tarsus, was converted, he immediately commenced praying. When the angel announced this conversion to Ananias, the chief description that was given of Saul was, "Behold, he is praying." It was as if the angel were saying, "He's never done it before." Previously he went through the motions. Now that he's experienced the Spirit of adoption and is an heir of God and a joint-heir with Christ, he is praying and his voice is heard. It has now become a necessity for him. Without prayer a man cannot be a Christian.
2. *Urgency.* It follows that the moment a newborn soul begins to appreciate the glories of his translation from the kingdom of darkness to the kingdom of

Light, he also begins to see the world as a place in which God's name has been dishonored. He then urgently implores in terms of, "Will You not revive us again that Your people may rejoice in You?" (Psalm 85:6) and, "It is time for You to act, O Lord; for Your law is being broken" (Psalm 119:126). The denial of God's authority and sovereignty is a call for divine action. Do you know something of that urgency?

3. *Value its critical importance.* We are helpless without it. We get nowhere without it. Our Lord came back from the Mount of Transfiguration to a sad scene: a group of helpless disciples in the face of incredible human need. They say to Him, "What is wrong?" He tells them that, in essence, they have yet to learn to pray. How are we going to break through gates of brass? We, too, sometimes seem to stand so helpless before human need. Have we forsaken the secret place of the Most High to our own sad loss and the powerlessness of the pulpit? May God awaken us!

4. *Helplessness.* In Psalm 50:7–12, God declares His self-sufficiency. In that context He teaches us our dispensability and helplessness. God does not need our prayers. We need Him. He does not need us! Prayerfulness is Calvinism at its best. It is a simple, open, honest declaration in the presence of God, of total helplessness. If salvation is of the Lord, and if people are to be converted, it shall be by God's grace and by God's power and through the gospel. It is never because of who I am, but in spite of it all. The propensity to pride is there, and it will destroy us if

we are not on our guard. If we do not pray, God is not at a loss as to what to do about a situation.

When Mordecai tried to impress upon Esther the importance of her intervention in the national crisis that was threatening the future existence of the Jews, and when she was more concerned about her own self-protection than anything else, his message amounted to this: "Have you ever considered, Esther, that you are not indispensable? If you do nothing about it, deliverance will arise from another quarter. God is not dependent on you. But, who knows? Perhaps you have come to the kingdom for such a time as this? Why not rise to the occasion rather than lose out?"

Timothy, if you and I cease to pray, God's plans will continue. He will still build His church, the gates of hell will not prevail against her, and every man, woman and child destined to be brought into the kingdom of God will be brought. But *I will suffer for my prayerlessness.*

5. *Constancy.* Paul exhorts us in 1 Thessalonians 5:17 to "pray without ceasing." David prayed seven times a day; Daniel, three times a day. Luther, meeting a friend in the street, would say, "Brother, do I find you praying?"

6. *Content.* Why were prayers ever recorded in Scripture? Why did the Holy Spirit deem it important that we should have columns and columns of Holy Writ given to the prayers that were offered by Daniel, Nehemiah, Paul and Jesus Christ? He did it so that you and I could be taught how to pray. Oh, that

prayers would assume a more biblical character! Oh, that prayers would be an expression of the will of God as it is set down in Scripture!

7. *Importunity*. That is, understanding God's will and bringing it before Him for His attention, continuously and persistently. It is giving God no rest until He gives peace to Jerusalem. After all, it is the will of God that His Jerusalem, the body of Christ, should be resplendent with His glory, and a praise to God in the earth. If the church is not what it was called to be, should we not implore the mercy of God to make the body of Christ an honor to His name in this poor miserable world? Did Jesus not give us the parable of the importunate widow in the words of Luke 18:1, "That men ought always to pray and not lose heart?" How serious are you about your concern for the church of God?

8. *Certainty*. This means faith. That has nothing to do with God giving us a type of blank check for us to fill in the details. Faith is founded in God's will. Faith discovers the heart of God in the pages of Scripture. Faith acquaints itself with the vision of God. Faith reads moving prayers, such as John 17. "Father," prays Jesus, "I desire that they also, whom You gave me, may be with me where I am, that they may see the glory which You have given me, for You loved me before the foundation of the world, and I want them with me, all of them." Faith takes cognizance of this expression of the Savior's will and carries it to God all over again. It lays it at His feet. Faith pleads: "Father, Your people, for whom Christ

prayed, need to be carried on eagles' wings. Take them safely through the passage of this wicked and hostile world. Take them through the gates of death into their eternal home in glory." Martin Luther might have sounded impudent in the manner in which he prayed when he was overheard to say, "Father, I will have my will because I know that my will is Your will." However, he had understood the Father's will and had given expression to it in prayer.

9. *Extent.* When the believer has a mind that reaches far beyond the limits of men's little minds and looks beyond the horizons to see and understand the glorious purposes of God in redemption, he prays in keeping with God's goal in redemption. "Ask of Me, and I will give You the heathen for an inheritance (Psalm 2:8)," says the Father to the Son. The believer takes it up in prayer. His highest joy and his greatest delight is to know that rebels bend the knee to the Son of God, that they touch the scepter stretched out to them, and that they are then saved by grace. The believer, on bended knee, covets one thing more than anything—that Christ should have a following, a following that adores Him. He longs for a following that admires Him. Every intercessor can identify with Spurgeon, of whom Archibald Brown once said, "He loved Him, he adored Him, he was our Lord's delighted captive." When Paul prayed, he thought big. See his prayer in Ephesians 3:14–21. Think big when you pray!

10. *The goal.* The goal is the glory of God. "Hallowed be Your name." "Let the name of George Whitefield

perish," said that man, "But let the name of Christ live on and on forever!" When Jesus Himself lifted up His eyes to Heaven, He said, "Father, the hour has come, glorify Your Son that your Son also may glorify You. And now, O Father, glorify me together with Yourself, with the glory which I had with You before the world was" (John 17:1,5). The believer responds immediately with a hearty, "So be it."

In conclusion, let me make one or two practical suggestions. I was converted under the ministry of the most godly man I have ever known. His name was Victor Thomas. He was spirituality on two feet, the epitome of humility and a mighty expositor. He is in heaven now. One day when he and I were alone, he said, "Martin, whenever you can, pray aloud." This practical advice has helped me over the years. The Psalmist himself said, "With my voice I cry aloud to the Lord." Admittedly, there is such a thing as prayer that is not audible. Hannah is said to have mumbled a heart-felt prayer that was inaudible. Then there was Nehemiah who had no option but to send up a silent prayer to the God of heaven when the king asked him a question and he wanted to give a wise answer. There will, of course, be times when you too will follow these examples, but you will need to discover what I have, since given that first bit of advice about praying, that verbalizing and voicing your requests to God is a simple but meaningful biblical injunction.

In Zechariah 8:20, we read, "Thus says the Lord of hosts: Peoples shall yet come, even the inhabitants of many cities; the inhabitants of one city shall go to another saying, 'Let us go at once to entreat the favor of the Lord, and to seek the Lord of hosts; I am going.' Many peoples and strong nations shall come to seek the Lord of hosts in Jerusalem, and to entreat the favor of the Lord." Here you have a sudden awareness of the incredible importance of intercessory prayer. With a fresh sense of urgency, the people began to invoke the mercy of God, and then Zechariah continues: "Thus says the Lord of hosts: In those days ten men from every language of the nation shall grasp the sleeve of the Jewish man saying, 'Let us go with you, for we have heard that God is with you.'" Oh, that God would repeat those mercies again! Can you imagine, Timothy, ten of your neighbors begging you to take them with you to church? Oh, that God would awaken us! We have the truth. We do not say that arrogantly. Jesus' words to Peter apply to us: "Blessed are you, Simon bar Jonah, for flesh and blood has not revealed this to you, but my Father who is in heaven." If the Word of God is ever to make a powerful inroad into the strongholds of evil and sin, all of us shall have to take seriously the matter of intercessory prayer.

I close with a quotation from a great American minister of an earlier generation. Gardiner Spring said:

> The time was when the pastors of the American churches valued the privilege of prayer; they were not only men of prayer, but they prayed often for and with one another. Their reciprocal and fraternal visits were consecrated and sweetened by prayer, nor was it any unusual thing for them to employ days of fasting and prayer together for the effusions of God's Spirit upon themselves and their churches, and they were days of power, days

when God's arm was made bare and His right hand plucked out of His bosom, nor was it difficult to see then wherein the great strength of the pulpit lies. He that is feeble among them shall be as David, and the House of David shall be as God.

God be with us and God awaken us, and God make us intercessors for His glory, for His honor, for the well-being of His church and for the rescuing of the nations.

Soli Deo Gloria,
Pastor Martin Holdt

PS—I commend to you most heartily the chapter in C. H. Spurgeon's *Lectures to my Students* on the Preacher's Private Prayer. A little volume by Derek Thomas called *Praying the Savior's Way* (Fearn, Ross-shire: Christian Focus Publications, 2001) is all about letting Jesus' prayer reshape your prayer life. This book is worth more than I can tell. I urge you to read as many books on the subject of prayer, but especially the Scripture's teaching on what is surely together with the study of the Word of God *the* most important part of a pastor's work.

Chapter 7

Cultivate Humility

C. J. Mahaney

Dear Timothy,

    I trust that you are being overwhelmed by God's grace as you survey the wondrous cross. Thanks for your recent letter. It's always such a joy to recognize your writing on the envelope and then to read of God's faithfulness at work in your life, even through the challenges. Thank you for sharing your struggles with me. I count it an honor to pray for you and to offer whatever counsel I can.

    Even before your letter, Timothy, I found myself thinking about you. I suppose this is due to all the activities associated with the twenty-fifth anniversary of Covenant Life Church. In recent weeks I've been shown several photos of myself from a quarter-century ago, when we were a few dozen people meeting in a basement and I actually had hair! I was just about your age then, and I still remember so well what it's like to be a pastor in his twenties with a young family and a small congregation.

But it's not the similarities between us that strike me most. It's the differences. You have so many advantages that I did not. Unlike me twenty-five years ago, you have fathers in the faith. You have a history of membership in strong, mature churches that have modeled much of what it means to be a local representation of the body of Christ. Most important, you have a solid grasp of essential biblical doctrines, chief among them the glorious gospel of our Savior. These are things I so yearned for when I was your age. What a challenge it was, especially for a young pastor, to pursue his calling without an older man in the faith to come alongside him and be his Paul! Having faced that, I made a commitment early in my ministry, as you know, to do what I could to help prepare the next generation of leaders, and God in His mercy has granted me those opportunities. When I now observe young men like you, who are actively cultivating and benefiting from such relationships, it brings me great joy.

There was one recent event during our anniversary celebration where you came to mind quite clearly. A man named Jim, fairly new to the church, told us how he had recently heard Gary, one of our pastors, enumerating some evidences of God's grace that have been present at Covenant Life Church from the beginning. A few years ago, Jim had been in a church that, tragically, suffered a serious split. So as Gary read through these evidences of grace, Jim paid close attention, trying to learn what had been different about the two churches—why they had such different experiences.

Gary noted how at the inception of our church we had a love for God's Word. And Jim said to himself, "Yup, we had that." Gary told how we were in love with Jesus Christ and grateful for His substitutionary sacrifice on the cross. And Jim thought, "Yeah, we had that, too." We loved grace and worship. "Sure, we had that." We believed in the importance of relationships, and once again Jim thought, "Yes, we certainly had that." Finally, Gary noted how there was an emphasis on humility, especially among the leaders. And Jim thought, "Oh . . . no. That we did not have."

In my Bible reading this morning I came upon Isaiah 66:1–2. That's when I knew I had to take some time this afternoon to write you. Timothy, this is a passage that, by grace, the leaders of Covenant Life Church have sought to apply from our earliest days. I believe it will help you with the challenges you are currently facing. You are no doubt familiar with the passage, but please read it carefully:

> Thus says the LORD: "Heaven is my throne, and the earth is my footstool; what is the house that you would build for me, and what is the place of my rest? All these things my hand has made, and so all these things came to be, declares the LORD. But this is the one to whom I will look: he who is humble and contrite in spirit and trembles at my word."

Like you, my friend, the Israelites had a lot going for them. They had a unique identity. They had the Torah. They had the law of God, the covenant and the temple. But they lacked humility—they had allowed pride to flourish unchecked. So God draws their attention away from the temple and toward their hearts. He tells them that their preoccupation ought not to be with the grandeur of externals, but with the internal. "This is the one to whom I will look: he who is humble and contrite in spirit and trembles at my word."

Timothy, I'm not saying that I consider you an unusually prideful man. But I do think that pride is at the root of several of the challenges you've described to me. Surely, due to remaining sin, all of us are prone to pride. And as a minister of the gospel, pride has the potential in your life to leverage itself through your ministry, doing damage that extends far beyond your own family.

Perhaps you have read what John Stott wrote about pride: "At every stage of our Christian development and in every sphere of our Christian discipleship, pride is our greatest enemy and humility our greatest friend."[1] As best I can tell, pride was the first sin—among angels and among men. And it would appear that pride is the essence of all sin, as well as the sin God finds most offensive. The proud man heads up the list of God's seven hated abominations in Proverbs 6. When referring to pride, the Bible uses words like *hate*, *abomination*, and *detestable*. Stronger language, Timothy, is simply not available.

Besides the things I "hate" in the humorous sense—things like cottage cheese and professional sports teams from New York—I do in all seriousness genuinely hate abortion; I genuinely hate racism; I genuinely hate child abuse. But set these side by side with the supremely pure, holy and unalterable hatred that God has for the sin of pride, and they will appear as nothing but casual disinclinations. We

---

[1] J. I. Packer & Loren Wilkinson, eds., *Alive to God* (Downers Grove, IL: InterVarsity Press, 1992), 119.

simply cannot overstate how deeply God detests and abhors pride.

Why does God so hate pride? Charles Bridges summed it up well, "Pride lifts up the heart against God. It contends for the supremacy with him."[2] Pride is an attitude of self-sufficiency and independence toward God and of self-righteousness and superiority toward others. It robs God of the honor and glory due Him. It takes many forms but has only one goal: self-glorification. No wonder then that God opposes the proud (1 Peter 5:5).

Oh the perils of pride! I've seen it ruin pastors, marriages, families, relationships, churches—all this among sincere believers. But for all the very real perils of pride, there is also the rich promise of humility. For our God is not only passionately opposed to pride, He is decisively drawn to humility. The omniscient One is aware of all things—nothing escapes His notice—yet He actively searches for one thing. His attention is uniquely drawn to humility: "*This* is the one to whom I will look." The humble man will receive grace, and not opposition, because his motive is to glorify God, not himself. God will always support and extend favor to a humble man who pursues God's will.

Timothy, during the past decade I've seen your knowledge and love of Scripture grow strong and deep. I know you can, yourself, give accurate and effective sermons on pride and humility. But if you'll allow me a digression, I have a point to make before moving on.

---

[2] Charles Bridges, *The Commentary on Proverbs* (reprint, Carlisle, PA: The Banner of Truth Trust, 1968), 228.

Imagine a number of churches, each one led by called, gifted and committed men. Each one holding a high view of Scripture and of sound doctrine and devoted to the centrality of the gospel. Each one filled with committed, servant-hearted believers who love the Lord Jesus in sincerity. Over time, some of these churches thrive, but some do not. Why is that? At the risk of oversimplifying, I think I know the answer.

Many people, of course, believe the Bible. Many pastors know it extremely well. Many recognize that it is our only truly reliable guide for life and faith. But strong churches—that is, churches in which the members are growing in sanctification and increasingly glorifying God in their public and private lives—are churches in which the leaders do not merely teach sound doctrine. They also lead in and model the consistent application of biblical truth to all of life.

So this I can say with full confidence. A decade from now, your ministry will have been fruitful only to the extent that you have both taught Scripture accurately *and* applied it consistently—to yourself, your family, your fellow elders and your church. It is not biblical truth alone that builds effective churches. It is, by God's grace, the *application* of biblical truth.

When Gary said, "there was an emphasis on humility, especially among the leaders," he was talking about application. The proper application of Scripture will always emphasize the weakening of pride (your greatest enemy) and the cultivation of humility (your greatest friend). I'm convinced this has made a huge difference here. It will make a difference in your church, too.

I've covered all this, Timothy, so that I can share with you some specific ways in which I have sought to tremble at God's Word. Surely this phrase speaks of something far beyond mere mental assent. The proud man may respect God's Word, he may believe it, he may teach it, but to tremble before it is the exclusive preserve of the humble. So, what practical steps can a pastor take to cultivate humility and thus tremble at God's Word?

For years I have had a list of practices. They derive from the three decades I have spent thus far seeking to grow in grace. Some are items of specific daily application—these I really do seek to observe every day. The other items are not so much items of daily application as they are areas of emphasis and of regular, consistent application throughout the year. For lack of a better term, I call them my annual list. These are things with which I seek to concern myself as a matter of close attention, that my character may continue to be informed by their pride-subduing, humility-inducing effects.

I know of no better way to grow in humility than to observe some set of concrete, tangible practices. Here are the ones that, by God's grace, have proven effective for me. I'm not encouraging any strict emulation of these. I offer them for your consideration and, I hope, for your provocation. Custom-design your own list. But for the sake of your family and your church, you must have a list.

The first item on my annual list is to study the attributes of God. Focus especially on God's incommunicable attributes, those having no reflection or illustration in man or indeed anywhere in creation. (Note how, in the Isaiah

66 passage I quoted, God draws our attention to His unique and unparalleled greatness.)

Consider, for example, that God is infinite. He has no boundaries, no edges. He is also omnipresent. He has no center, no one point of concentration, no single place where His essence is located, for He is fully and equally present everywhere—within creation and beyond it. The *New Bible Dictionary* says, "When we say that God is infinite spirit, we pass completely out of the reach of our experience."[3]

Truly, my friend, this is the deep end of the theological pool. This infinite One is self-existent and self-sufficient. Everything in creation, from you and me, to the heavenly beings, to the atoms of gas in deepest space, is in complete dependence on God's sustaining attention for mere moment-by-moment existence. But before time, through all of time, and outside of time, God depends ever and only upon Himself. We are like the grass that withers and fades, but He alone possesses the power of sheer *being*. As Matthew Henry wrote, "The greatest and best men in the world must say 'By the grace of God I am what I am.' But God says absolutely—and it is more than any creature, man or angel, can say—'I am that I am.'"[4]

Such contemplation will inevitably weaken your pride. The greater your awareness of the difference between yourself and God, the more you will experience and express humility. How good of God to offer us in His Word a glimpse

---

[3] J. D. Douglas, et al., (eds.), *New Bible Dictionary* (Wheaton, IL: Tyndale House Publishers, Inc., 1962), 427.

[4] Matthew Henry, *Commentary on the Whole Bible,* vol. 1 (Old Tappan, NJ: Fleming H. Revell Company, n.d.), 284 [Exodus 3:14].

of His unfathomable other-ness, that we might have it as an unerring aid to humility!

For many of the items on these lists, I'm going to recommend some reading. I want to identify several of the books that have had a profound and lasting influence on my ministry and on this church. So, for God's incommunicable attributes, you must at some point read Chapter 11 of Wayne Grudem's *Systematic Theology*, titled "The Character of God: Incommunicable Attributes—How is God Different From Us?" Or you could read the equivalent chapter in *Bible Doctrine*, which is the abridged version of that volume.

Second, never stray from the cross. Live as one who continually surveys—and from close range—the wondrous cross on which the Prince of Glory died. As I've told you before, I can do no more, and I can surely do no better, than to draw your attention to the centrality of our Savior's sacrifice.

A friend told me of an opportunity he once had to interview Carl Henry, a truly humble man who, as you know, is perhaps the foremost evangelical scholar of the latter half of the twentieth century. He asked Dr. Henry, then in his late seventies, how he had remained so humble for so many decades. Dr. Henry replied, "How can anyone be arrogant when he stands beside the cross?" I am under no delusions that my character approaches that of Dr. Henry, but two books that have been invaluable in helping me to stand beside the cross are *The Atonement* (Leon Morris) and *The Cross of Christ* (John Stott). One quote from the Stott book: "The cross does not flatter us, the cross undermines our self-righteousness. We can stand before it only with a bowed head and a broken spirit."[5]

Third, study the doctrines of grace. As you immerse yourself in the study of election, calling, justification and perseverance, you will be reminded that all we have and all we are as Christians begins with God, ends with God and depends on God. These rich doctrines leave no room for self-congratulation. Mark Webb writes, "God intentionally designed salvation so that no man can boast of it. He didn't merely arrange it so that boasting would be discouraged or kept to a minimum. He planned it so that boasting would be absolutely excluded. Election does precisely that."[6]

Personal arrogance and a true appreciation of reformation theology cannot long co-exist; truth will drive out the lie of pride. For me, one very helpful book in this area has been Anthony Hoekema's *Saved by Grace*.

Fourth, study the doctrine of sin. I read about a sign on a store's dressing-room mirror that stated, "Objects in mirror may appear bigger than they actually are." Timothy, when you allow the doctrine of sin to inform your self-perception, this will not be your experience. Grasping the depth and depravity of one's sin forbids any inflated view of self.

The best way to prepare for your study of sin is first to study God's holiness, for there and there alone do we encounter the complete absence of sin. Search the Scriptures

---

[5] John Stott, *The Cross of Christ* (Downers Grove, IL: InterVarsity Press, 1986), 12.
[6] Mark Webb, "What Difference Does It Make?" *Reformation & Revival Journal* 3, no. 1 (Winter 1994).

thoroughly on the topic, and by all means read R.C. Sproul's *The Holiness of God*. Then, when you begin to study the doctrine of sin itself, you will bring to the task a proper perspective. For your reading here, none can improve upon John Owen, especially *Temptation and Sin* in Volume Six of his collected works. An abridged version is available as a book titled *Sin and Temptation*. Also, Kris Lundgaard's *The Enemy Within* is essentially a simplified and modernized interpretation of Owen's work that is nevertheless quite effective.

Fifth, apply the doctrine of sin. Noting that all men are sinners, Mike Renihan further observes, "Sinners fall into two more distinct classes: those who admit their sin and those who don't. Those who admit themselves to be sinners fall into two more classes: those who do something about it and those who do not."[7] Timothy, the humble pastor is the man who does something about it, especially through confession and the pursuit of correction.

It's not difficult to acknowledge one's pervasive depravity. What's difficult is specifically to confess an area of personal depravity. Obviously, one must first confess sins to God. But we are also called to confess, as appropriate, to individuals. You know how strongly I feel that every pastor, even in the smallest church, must have a team of men to whom he is accountable. God will surely send you such men. Your job is to find them, enlist them to help you and be transparent before them, confessing freely and regularly.

Let these confessions be full and specific, not selective and partial. Confess overt acts of sin as well as present

---

[7] Mike Renihan, "A Pastor's Pride and Joy" *TableTalk* 53 (July 1999).

temptations, and let grace and forgiveness be yours in abundance. It's a sad truth that whenever a pastor disqualifies himself from ministry through a failure of personal character, a long-standing lack of confession has invariably been present.

Another vital means of applying the doctrine of sin to your own life is to invite and pursue correction in areas of character. In this regard, a pastor must be gently persistent, in public and in private. Eventually, the majority of the members in your church should feel truly welcome to point out to you any instance in which it appears you have behaved sinfully—or indeed, any area in which you could simply be doing a better job. Would your wife, your friends and those who serve with you in your church say you are easy to entreat? Alfred Poirier had an excellent article on this topic titled, "The Cross and Criticism."[8]

The items I've just covered will help any Christian grow in humility, but the ones that follow apply specifically to pastors.

- Study diligently, but recognize your theological limitations. As your children grow up, Timothy, you will at various times be peppered with theological questions you simply can't answer. Our son Chad, who recently turned nine, asks lots of these, and often I just have to say, "I don't know, son." (I say

---

[8] Alfred Poirier, "The Cross and Criticism" *The Journal of Biblical Counseling* 17, no. 6. This article is included in the booklet, *Words that Cut* (Billings, MT: Peacemaker Ministries, 2003).

it so often that by now he may be thinking you don't have to know very much to be a pastor.) Members of your congregation will ask hard questions, too. Let us be appropriately affected by Calvin's estimate that even the best theologians are probably right only 80 percent of the time. So, on my best day, what's my percentage? Half of that? Moreover, as far as I know I've never had an original thought. When I teach or counsel, I'm benefiting from the labors of better and wiser men who have come before me. If I can see anything, it's only because I stand on their shoulders—and I don't ever want to leave anyone with a different impression. When instructing or counseling, an awareness of your limitations will have a softening and humbling effect on your attitude, your tone of voice and your conversation.

- Just before you preach, read Spurgeon. Whenever possible, I attempt on Saturday night to find and read a sermon by Charles Spurgeon on the topic or text I will be addressing the next morning. Spurgeon shows you how it's supposed to be done, which reminds you that you can't do it that way. Reading the Prince of Preachers invariably lowers my opinion of my own material and increases my dependence on God.
- Use unflattering illustrations of yourself in your sermons and counseling. My sermon preparation isn't complete until I have attempted to insert an appropriate personal confession or illustration that will humble me. Based on comments I've received over

the years, these are often the most memorable things I say (which is itself pretty humbling). This practice also presents to all gathered a provocative example of humility.

- Recognize your relative unimportance. A pastor is a vital means of grace to his church and to those he serves. Yet at the same time, no one is indispensable. Charles DeGaulle pointed out that, "Graveyards are filled with indispensable men."

Were I to die before completing this letter, what would happen? There would be some mourning among those who love me. Within a few months, it would mostly subside. In six months, for nearly everyone, I'd be nothing but a warm memory, a vaguely familiar voice on some old, neglected tapes. God, in His mercy and love for the church, will have richly anointed my replacement until his effectiveness clearly surpasses mine. As for me, I won't care. I'll be in heaven!

- Prepare to be replaced. I'm just here keeping this seat warm for somebody else. The timing may be uncertain, but one day I will be replaced. So will you. Our repositioning is inevitable. You would do well to begin preparing your heart for that change even now, so that when it happens you will be able to respond in a way that will bring glory to God and honor to His church.

- Play golf as often as possible, and make sure you play with guys who won't hesitate to draw attention to the awful shots you will inevitably make from time to time. I know of no sport so effective as golf at promoting humility.

I've got to move quickly now through the daily list. (I'm taking Carolyn on our weekly date tonight, and I'm eager to complete a few small preparations.) In the morning, this list helps me set the tone for the day. It helps me throughout the day to take advantage of those innumerable mundane moments that can be transformed into means of experiencing God's grace. And it helps me close out the day fully aware that His grace makes all good things possible.

First, begin the day acknowledging your dependence upon God, your need for God, and your confidence in God. Timothy, I'm talking the *first thoughts* of the day. When that alarm goes off, I'm immediately seeking to direct my heart to God that I might express my dependence on Him. I continue purposefully to cultivate this attitude as I prepare for the day. If not, my thoughts will—without fail—drift toward self-reliance.

Second, as you turn your thoughts to God, set the tone for the day by expressing gratefulness to Him. "Thankfulness is a soil in which pride does not easily grow,"[9] and thankfulness begins with the gospel. The best way I have found to battle the forgetfulness and distraction that so easily hinder our gratitude is—as Jerry Bridges says—to preach the gospel to yourself every day. So begin each day doing just that, and then direct your gratitude to God because of the gospel.

---

[9] Michael Ramsey, *The Christian Priest Today* (London: SPCK, 1972), 79.

As the day progresses, purpose to recognize and express gratitude for the innumerable "Post-It notes" that God places around us to remind us of His grace. It is said of Matthew Henry that to encounter him was to become aware of an alert and thankful observer of answered prayer. I want to be like that. Ingratitude is the mark of a proud man, but to consistently express thankfulness is to deal blow after mortifying blow to my self-glorifying arrogance.

Third, practice the spiritual disciplines every day. I'm convinced this is best done in the morning, in part because it further sets the day's tone of dependence upon God. The spiritual disciplines are a daily declaration and demonstration of my need for God and my dependence on Him. I find Charles Hummel's words striking: "When we fail to wait prayerfully for God's guidance and strength, we are saying, with our actions if not our lips, that we do not need him."[10] I believe that our inconsistency in practicing the spiritual disciplines is not due primarily to an absence of self-discipline, but to the presence of self-sufficiency. Practicing the spiritual disciplines is a daily means of weakening prideful self-sufficiency and cultivating humility.

Fourth, seize your commute to and from the church office to memorize and mediate on Scripture. When William Wilberforce was serving in the House of Commons, he used his daily one-mile walk from his home to Parliament to recite from memory the whole of Psalm 119. Now that is time well spent.

---

[10] Charles E. Hummel, *Tyranny of the Urgent* (Downers Grove, IL: InterVarsity Press, 1967).

Fifth, all day long, at the moment you become aware of burdensome cares, cast them upon the Lord, who cares for you. Where there is worry and anxiety, there is the pride of self-reliance. The humble man, though he may be responsible for many things, is free of care—he is care-free. His life is characterized by joy and peace, for it is impossible to be worried while trusting in the Sovereign One.

Timothy, we are not like cordless drills that can go all day on a single charge. I do not expect my morning devotions to sustain me at 2:30 in the afternoon or even at 11:00 in the morning. All day, every day, I need to keep directing my thoughts to God, keep standing close to the cross, keep offering thanks for innumerable evidences of grace and keep casting my cares on the One who cares for me with such perfect love and faithfulness.

Sixth, when the work day concludes, instead of simply leaving for home, I seize the opportunity to cultivate humility. No matter how "successful" or "unsuccessful" my day has been (in my limited estimation), I acknowledge that God is the only One who ever perfectly completes His daily to-do list, and I commit all that remains undone to His safe keeping. Tomorrow, I'll come back and, by His grace, try again.

Then, at the end of the day, I seek to transfer all glory to God. Puritan Thomas Watson wrote, "When we have done anything praiseworthy we must hide ourselves under the veil of humility and transfer the glory of all we have done to God."[11] Thankful for such precious advice, I take a few

---

[11] Thomas Watson, *A Body of Divinity* (Carlisle, PA: The Banner of Truth Trust, 1992), 17.

moments in the evening just to mentally review the day. For every evidence of fruitfulness or progress I've witnessed or experienced that day, I try to specifically acknowledge to God the undeniable fact that He alone is responsible.

As a pastor, I may be a means of grace in the lives of others, but I can't save anyone! I can't convict anyone of sin or bring a soul to repentance. I have no power in me to effect sanctification in anyone's life. Our churches are testimonies to the greatness and graciousness of God—not monuments to our leadership and preaching.

On one occasion when Charles Spurgeon was addressing his Pastors College students, he told them, "Your ministry is poor enough. Everybody knows it, and you ought to know it most of all."[12] Now, was he pointing out that this class of students was particularly incompetent? Not at all. He went on to inform them that preaching is ever and only effective because God keeps His promise that His Word shall not return void. Isaiah acknowledged to God, "You have done all our works for us" (26:12), and this, as the *Expositor's Bible Commentary* notes, is "a profound truth, blessedly destructive of spiritual pride."[13] God is the prime mover behind every means of grace. *Soli Deo Gloria!*

Finally, before going to sleep at night, I acknowledge that sleep is a gift from the Creator to the creature. I don't just passively fall asleep. I seize that daily opportunity to weaken pride and cultivate humility by acknowledging Him

---

[12] Charles Spurgeon, *Lectures to My Students* (reprint, Grand Rapids, MI: Zondervan Publishing House, 1981), 194.
[13] *The Expositor's Bible Commentary*, ed. Frank E. Gaebelein, vol. 6 (Grand Rapids, MI: Zondervan Publishing House, 1986), 165.

who neither slumbers nor sleeps. Sleep, for me, is a daily reminder that I am far from self-sufficient. Let me put it this way: I have a desperate, irreversible, physiological need to spend a substantial portion of every twenty-four hours in a state of mental and physical incapacity, utterly helpless and completely useless. Is this not comical? God then uses this time to strengthen and restore me for another day—a day in which I will invariably fail to obey Him fully, yet by grace He will somehow redeem my actions to produce a measure of fruitfulness. How can this not be humbling?

Well there you go, my friend—my annual list, my daily list and some suggestions for application. None of these ideas originate with me. Whatever wisdom you may find here has its source in Scripture and in the insights of teachers far more gifted and mature than I. All I do is collect the wisdom of others and pass it along. I pray that these thoughts will inspire you to establish patterns of your own that will serve you for the rest of your life, as these have served me.

So let us devote ourselves daily to the purposeful application of Scripture, that we might avoid the perils of pride and experience the promise of humility. And let us do so motivated by grace. For however intentional our efforts, and however much we might see God's grace at work in sanctification, we do not rest in our accomplishments or good intentions, as if they could ever earn us anything before a Holy God. We claim no merit in what we do. Rather, we rest in the finished work of the Savior. We are God's, and enjoy His favor, only because Another has perfectly fulfilled all the righteous requirements of the law. Jesus Christ is the only One who has ever been perfectly humble, completely contrite in spirit and fully observant of what it means to tremble at God's Word. We rest ultimately in Him—in His perfect life and substitutionary sacrifice for our sins.

Write again soon, Timothy. I'll be eager to hear what God in His marvelous grace has been doing in you and through you.

With love to you and Mary through our glorious Savior,
C. J.

PS—You asked for a recommended reading list. Here are the cites for the materials I've mentioned. Enjoy!

1. *The Discipline of Grace* by Jerry Bridges (Colorado Springs, CO: NavPress, 1994).
2. *Systematic Theology* by Wayne Grudem (Grand Rapids, MI: Zondervan, 1995).
3. *Bible Doctrine* by Wayne Grudem (Grand Rapids, MI: Zondervan, 1999).
4. *Saved By Grace* by Anthony A. Hoekema (Grand Rapids, MI: William B. Eerdmans Publishing Company, 1989).
5. *The Enemy Within* by Kris Lundgaard (Phillipsburg, NJ: P&R Publishing, 1998).
6. *The Atonement: It's Meaning and Significance* by Leon Morris (Downer's Grove, IL: Inter-Varsity Press, 1983).

7. *The Complete Works of John Owen* edited by William Gould (reprint, Edinburgh, Scotland: The Banner of Truth, 1980).
8. *Sin and Temptation* by John Owen (reprint, Bloomington, MN: Bethany House, 1996).
9. "The Cross and Criticism" by Alfred Poirier in *The Journal of Biblical Counseling* 17, no. 3, (1999).
10. *The Cross of Christ* by John Stott (Downer's Grove, IL: Inter-Varsity Press, 1986).
11. *The Holiness of God* by R. C. Sproul (Carol Stream, IL: Tyndale, 1998).

Chapter 8

Be Courageous
Bill Ascol

Dear Timothy,

I am excited to hear that you have recently been called to your first pastorate. After twenty-five years in the pastoral ministry I can tell you that there is nothing quite as exhilarating and challenging as shepherding the flock of God over which the Holy Spirit has made you an overseer. Leading, feeding and protecting the people of God, as we make the dangerous journey from this world to the world that is to come, will require much "evangelical courage" on your part. By evangelical courage I mean that unconditional commitment to minister the gospel with compassion, regardless of the consequences and no matter the cost. I like to use the word *evangelical* to modify courage because some forms of courage may have more to do with bravado than with bravery, more with braggadocio than with boldness. Such courage (if it can rightly be called that) can be hurtful rather than helpful if manifested in the life of a gospel minister. Courage that is not evangelical—that is, not driven by gospel motives and desires—might lead a man to approach the pastoral ministry very much like he would the role of a corporate CEO, military commander or even a cattle driver. These models are not based on God's Word, and they run counter to the spirit and conduct expressed by the apostle Peter when, writing in the role of an elder, he appealed to his fellow elders to be faithful pastors over the people of God as they lived and labored in the midst of them (1 Peter 5:1–2).

A double-sided dilemma that will ultimately face a gospel minister is the temptation either to "go soft" or to "be harsh" as he labors among God's people. The temptation to "go soft" often comes when the minister has various perks dangled before him with the unspoken qualification that, "All these can be yours as long as we see eye to eye on things." Access for the minister and his family to private swimming pools, tennis courts, camp houses, vehicles and various other activities and opportunities can blur a minister's judgment. When it becomes necessary for him to take a stand for righteousness, he may be faced with the unhappy providence of becoming unpopular with the one providing the perks. Failure on the part of the minister to exercise evangelical courage in the face of this temptation may well have the effect of relegating him to the latest "preacher boy" to come along and to be controlled by "the powers that be." This often emboldens some in their sinful ways, while at the same time discourages the spiritually-minded who had hoped that at long last a man of God had come among them to proclaim God's Word in a principled way. This is exactly why the apostle Paul cautions a minister to keep himself disentangled from the world (2 Timothy 2:3–4). One of the lessons you would be wise to learn right now, Timothy, is that the hardest ground you will ever have to gain in ministry is ground that you once held and voluntarily surrendered.

Equally dangerous is the temptation to be harsh with the people of God. Again, it is popular in some evangelical circles today to view the pastorate very much the way one would view the positions of a CEO, military commander or cattle driver. All three of these roles have their rightful place in the world, but they are disastrous when imported into pastoral ministry. The pastor who comes under the influence of any one of these attitudes toward the ministry runs the risk of developing a view of the people of God as pawns to be used or manipulated for often less than noble ends. The "CEO" may use the people under his care to build something that looks like his kingdom here on earth, not unlike the Pharaohs in the days of the pyramids. He may be harsh toward the people, viewing them as expendable for the sake of "the cause." The "military commander" is only different from the CEO by degrees. He is still an autocrat, however, and justifies sacrificing the people of God in the name of "victory." Authoritarianism, in its harshest expression, can turn a congregation's journey together into a spiritual Bataan death march, where the wounded are "executed" on the side of the road along the way. People under the lasso of the "cattle driver" fare little better, being driven along toward a tragic end. Too often these ill-fated models of pastoral ministry are proposed and embraced all in the name of the pastor "playing the man." The problem with these three approaches is that they have more to do with managing, maneuvering and moving than with ministering as under-shepherds. Shepherds lead, feed and protect—tasks that are often missing in the ministries of the CEO, military commander or cattle driver. Timothy, do not let any well-intended ministerial expert bully you into adopting any of these contemporary styles of ministry.

The challenge, it seems to me, is to negotiate a biblically-based, God-centered, Christ-exalting, Holy Spirit-empowered middle path between these two ditches of "going soft" or "being harsh." By going soft you run the risk of becoming little more than the congregation's puppet. By being harsh you may well take on the appearance of the church's pope. You must resist the efforts of anyone who would push you into the former ditch, while at the same time resist your own temptation to jump into the latter ditch. Both of these extremes must be avoided in the spirit of Jesus Christ.

Some congregations, particularly those who have experienced a high turnover of short-term pastorates, tend to view their pastor from the standpoint of someone whom they have "hired." He is their employee, on their payroll, and therefore subject to a set of rules and expectations (almost always unwritten and unspoken) that are very different from the rules and expectations under which the rest of the congregation lives. For example, he is always expected to be present at Sunday services (both morning and evening), mid-week prayer meeting, outreach visitation, church-wide work day, etc. For everyone else in the congregation these gatherings are opportunities that are optional. Why is it this way? "Because," they say, "that's what we pay him to do." The same congregation that would never agree to exercise corrective church discipline in the case of an erring member will very often not blink an eye when it is suggested that the pastor should be forced to leave the church. Why is this? "Because," they argue, "we hired him and we can fire him." In such a setting the pastor tends to be treated somewhat like an indentured servant. He often lives in the church's parsonage and therefore may feel the pressure to keep the "church's house" and the "church's yard" in a condition that meets the approval of even the sharpest critic.

He may be made to feel like a man who lives and enjoys the livelihood he does only because he is allowed to do so by the chief decision-makers in the church. Perhaps the pastor is put in the embarrassing situation of having to go to the church treasurer, inquiring when he might expect to receive his paycheck. He may have to get approval from the deacons for time off to preach a Bible conference elsewhere, attend a conference for his own soul's nourishment or simply take his family for a brief vacation. In fact, a vote of the whole church may be required before any of these undertakings can be scheduled. Whenever he is introduced to anyone in the community by one of the long-time church members, he is likely to be identified as "our little preacher," particularly if he is young or just beginning his journey in pastoral ministry. This may sound like a caricature, but sadly it is not. While it is true that not every church is like this, there are enough to cause concern and alarm. I pray that the congregation to whom you are ministering is not anything like what I have described above.

When any or all of these characteristics begin to manifest themselves in the face of a man's pastoral ministry, he may succumb to the temptation to knuckle under and live a ministerial life of frustration, feeling very much like a hireling who is stuck between the proverbial rock and hard place. Many men of God, however, are not willing simply to succumb to such treatment. Instead they will resist this demeaning of the office of pastor. In so doing there is the danger of reacting in a way that is unhealthy. Too often, in the name of "courage," a minister will take on an air of haughtiness, carrying on as one whose office entitles him to live above the congregation's wrong-headedness concerning his office. He may even resent the negative attitudes toward him. In an effort to provoke the respect that the Scripture says is due to a gospel minister, he may begin demanding this respect in a way that resembles a popish tyrant. Timothy, it must be remembered that we are all frail creatures of dust and men of like passions, vulnerable to the possibility of knee-jerk reactions when things do not go our way or when we are not recognized as those called of God to preach the gospel. But high-handed demagoguery on the pastor's part is not the answer to low-handed demeaning on the part of church members toward the God-ordained office of pastor in a local church. It may fairly be said that much more harm and mischief has come to the true sheep of Jesus Christ—as well as to the reputation of Jesus Christ Himself—as a result of a pompous power-play on the part of a pastor or group of elders than has ever come as a result of pastors being belittled, ill-treated and lightly esteemed. In fact, Timothy, I would be so bold as to suggest to you that it takes more evangelical courage to endure such reproach from those who claim to be the people of God than it does to rise up and strike down the rebellious and stiff-necked in the name of defending the gospel. The fact still remains, however, that every church in which the Lord places us to serve as pastor will be a church in need of "reforming and becoming reformed." There will be various aspects of the ministry that are in need of being re-formed and restored to a shape and pattern that more exactly reflects the standard set forth for churches in the New Testament.

What is a gospel minister to do, then, when he finds himself newly called to a church that is in need of being brought into conformity with various biblical precepts? Timothy, believe me when I tell you that your personal relationship with the Lord Jesus Christ, your stable relationship with your wife and family, your knowledge of sound doctrine and theology, your exegetical and pastoral skills as well as your people skills and capacity to communicate effectively, must all be buttressed by a deeply-rooted evangelical courage—the unconditional commitment to minister the gospel with compassion, regardless of the consequences and no matter the cost. As you labor in your first pastoral charge, I want to encourage you to have the evangelical courage to cultivate those you have been called to serve, to confront those whose sins are destructive to themselves or to others and to confess your faults to those against whom you sin.

Evangelical Courage to Cultivate Those You Have Been Called to Serve

First, you must always remember that God has called you to be a pastor to His sheep—those who are safely folded in the congregation and those whom He will call in the course of your ministry. Furthermore, the sheep under your care are comprised of little lambs, wounded sheep, maturing sheep and erring sheep, all with different appetites concerning the gospel meals you desire to feed them. The wise pastor will patiently cultivate the sheep, feeding them the biblical truth according to their capacity to receive it. It takes evangelical courage to cultivate the sheep in their various situations, since you will face several temptations in your attempts to pastor such a variety of sheep.

The little lambs will need to be fed the sincere milk of the Word (1 Peter 2:2). They will need digestible portions of the precious truths of God's love for sinners shown in Jesus' sufficient sacrificial death and victorious resurrection. They will need to be taught the simplicity of walking by faith in the blood and righteousness of Jesus Christ, a blood and righteousness that constantly avails for them. They must learn that walking by faith means trusting in the promises of the gospel as if spoken personally to them. It will be important for them to know that this faith in Jesus Christ is most powerfully and joyfully expressed when it bears fruit in a willingness to repent of and confess their sins to others when others have sinned against them, as well as in a willingness to forgive others when others sin against them. There are so many "first lessons" that little lambs need to take in, but they cannot take them in all at once. Nor will they necessarily master them the first time they are taught to them. Cultivating a healthy "feeding regimen" that will provoke a steady appetite in a young Christian will take patience and forbearance. The courageous minister will fight against the temptation to become impatient with, or discouraged concerning, the progress of growth in grace of the little lamb. It will take evangelical courage to continue ministering the gospel with compassion fueled by an unconditional commitment, regardless of the consequences and no matter what the costs.

In any congregation there are wounded sheep—those who have been deeply hurt by others in the congregation or worse yet, hurt by previous encounters with those serving in the role of God's under-shepherd. You should not be surprised that these wounded sheep have learned not to trust the one who would offer his hand to feed them with words of life and healing. They will most likely be inclined to stay away from the ministry altogether or at least take a "wait and see" posture concerning the value and sincerity of your ministry. Again, great patience will be needed to bear with them, while at the same time you fight the temptation to take their reticence to benefit from your ministry as a personal rejection of you—or worse yet, of the gospel. Time has a way of leveling everything, and if approached in a redemptive way by the gospel minister, can be his friend in ministry.

In time everyone faces great need—even wounded sheep. It is often in the time of great need that the faithful pastor is allowed by God to exercise critical pastoral care in the life of the wounded sheep. A greater, more pressing pain experienced in the present may cause the deeply hurt church member to place on the back burner a deep pain from the past. It is at this point that the gospel minister must summon up a large measure of evangelical courage and be willing to wade into the middle of the hurt, even at the risk of facing initial continual rejection by the wounded sheep. I say initial because the heart of every one of Jesus' sheep beats with His love and mercy—no matter how damaged it has become—and this mercy will ultimately express itself to those who are merciful. When you prove the sincerity of your love to the wounded, you earn the right to speak to them of things eternal. When you accumulate this kind of pastoral collateral, you will gain their ears as well as their hearts.

Some of the most delightful pastoral experiences occur between the pastor and the maturing sheep—those who demonstrate a healthy appetite for the Word of God and who manifest a genuine appreciation for sound doctrine. Ideally, these should be the leaders in the congregation. These are the ones who ask the right questions, draw the right conclusions and exhibit a growing appetite for the meat of the Word. They do not tire of hearing (or of telling) the "old, old story of Jesus and His love." They also very often express a "Berean spirit" in their willingness to search the Scriptures to see if the things learned under your ministry are taught there (Acts 17:10–11). They are not afraid of Bible doctrines that they have not previously been taught. They just want to know, "What does the Scripture say?" The maturing sheep will be most inclined to be jealous for the glory of God in their lives and in the life of the congregation, even if they do not know how to express this with theological precision. They will have a desire to see Jesus Christ exalted, convinced that He must increase and they must decrease. The maturing members of the church are most likely to be those who are faithful to pray together for the progress of the gospel through the ministry and who will give thanks to God for sending them a faithful gospel minister. It might be asked, "Why would evangelical courage be needed to minister to such as these?" The answer lies in the temptation to spend most of your time with them, running the risk of overlooking the needs of the less mature. Make no mistake about it, pastors are to equip the saints to do the work of the ministry (Ephesians 4:12), and we are to teach the things that we have seen and heard to faithful men who will be able to teach others also (2 Timothy 2:2). Gospel labor among the maturing sheep is enjoyable, even if the minister finds himself tired in a satisfying way. Another temptation, however, is that the pastor is susceptible to taking the praise directed toward him by the mature believers and turning it into an occasion for pride, boasting and thinking more highly of himself than he ought. It is also among this group that the minister is most likely to "drop his guard" in a bad way. It may well be that some of those who are most excited about your ministry now will one day turn against you and reject the truth that you expound.

Rejoice, Timothy, if the Lord has been pleased to surround you with a core group of maturing disciples who are hungry for the Word and who seem to hang upon every word you utter. But guard your heart, lest you become like King David who began to "believe his own press clippings" (2 Samuel 8:13; 11:1–2).

Perhaps the most difficult group to which a pastor tries to minister are those who are erring sheep. At one time they gave every appearance of having a vital interest in biblical Christianity and seemed sincerely to want to grow in grace as disciples of the Lord Jesus Christ. But now they have turned away. Perhaps their sinfulness expresses itself in habitual neglect of Bible study, worship or other crucial meetings of the church. As professing Christians they bear the name of Jesus Christ. Perhaps they have brought shame to Christ's name by undertaking a destructive lifestyle that is both dangerous to their souls and scandalous. Perhaps they have become troublemakers and are stirring up strife in the congregation. Whatever the nature of the sinful pattern, the erring sheep can take a spiritual and emotional toll on the pastor who takes seriously his responsibility to attempt to recover them.

The diligent pastor may discover in his attempts to recover those who have been overtaken in a fault (Galatians 6:1) that he is not dealing with one who is truly a sheep. It may be that the individual "professed" faith in Jesus Christ but has never really "possessed" true saving faith in Jesus Christ (Acts 8:13–23). Because this cannot necessarily be known immediately, the pastor must wade into the matter as one who is trying to recover someone who has the indwelling presence of the Holy Spirit in his life. When it is discovered, however, that the "erring sheep" is in actuality a "goat" or even a "wolf in sheep's clothing," then the mission changes from the redemptive corrective discipline of a wayward disciple to the redemptive corrective discipline of, as well as the evangelistic witness to, an unconverted church member. Much evangelical courage is needed for this task because it can be tasteless at times and may well result in the maligning of the character of the pastor who dared to undertake the rescue according to biblical teaching. The erring member is often all too willing to "bite the hand that feeds him," and he will not hesitate to sully the reputation of those who venture to tell him that all is not well with his soul.

You will need large doses of evangelical courage to engage in the ministry of recovering the erring sheep. The temptations are two-fold. First there is the temptation to be a coward and not attempt to recover the erring sheep. The rationalizations for this are many. Perhaps this person is very influential in the church (or the relative or close friend of a very influential person in the church) and you do not want to upset him. Perhaps you don't want to run the risk of offending the godly people who may not yet have the biblical acumen to understand. Perhaps you fear you will lose your influence or even your ministry! This is where it is important to remember that evangelical courage is the unconditional commitment to minister the gospel with compassion, regardless of the consequences and no matter the cost. The other temptation is just as dangerous, however. It is the temptation to deal harshly with the erring sheep (or goat or wolf in sheep's clothing), acting as if the goal of corrective discipline is to cut them off, washing your hands of them and having nothing else to do with them. This approach, however, turns redemptive corrective church discipline on its head and becomes an offense not only in the congregation but in heaven as well.

Because the erring one may well turn out to be unconverted, he is likely to make threats against the pastor. The danger the pastor faces in such a situation is to go into self-defense mode. However, the pastor is placed over the flock by God to protect the sheep from those who would scatter and tear them—not necessarily to protect himself. (This is why a plurality of elders can be a blessed arrangement in a church—but that is a discussion for another letter!) The shepherd is to lay down his life for the sheep. Timothy, if you find yourself facing the challenge of rescuing an erring sheep, summon up the evangelical courage to undertake the effort in such a way that you guard your heart against cowardice, harshness and the subtle danger of becoming self-defensive.

Evangelical Courage to Confront Those Whose Sins are Destructive to Themselves or Others

Every pastor who is worthy of the name desires to have a ministry whose tone is irenic—primarily peaceful and edifying. However, the reality of remaining sin, the inevitability of sinful outcroppings in the life of the congregation and the importance of challenging the lost with the gospel claims of Jesus Christ, mean that there will be times when the tone of the ministry will be one of evangelical confrontation. The gospel minister must be willing to confront his hearers in preaching and in counseling if they are to take the Word personally unto themselves.

Confrontational preaching is not scolding or browbeating the people of God, nor is it turning the sacred desk into a bully pulpit in which a preacher grinds his latest axe or tongue-lashes his most recent foe. Rather, confrontational preaching is applicatory preaching—pressing the claims of the Scripture to the hearts and minds of the hearers. Many preachers are very skilled at giving their congregations the meaning of the text. Faithful exegesis must be intertwined with flaming exhortation. When Peter preached at Pentecost he not only told the crowd that the crucifixion of Jesus Christ was God's previously planned way to save sinners, but he also pointedly told his hearers that their own wicked hands had put Jesus to death. This confrontational, applicatory proclamation was used by the Holy Spirit to prick the hearts of many who initially inquired how they might be delivered from their sin. They ultimately came to faith in Jesus Christ (Acts 2:22–41). It will take evangelical courage to preach to your hearers in such a way as to afflict the comfortable and comfort the afflicted in one and the same message. You must enter the pulpit with the burning reality that the first person in the audience who must be taken note of is God Himself. He must be pleased with your labors, whether anyone else is or not. The temptations to avoid in such a privileged endeavor are two-fold. There is the temptation to hold back on application and let the hearers figure the implications out for themselves. In doing this, the pastor may be feeding the flock but he is not leading nor is he necessarily protecting them. The other temptation is to blister the hearers from the pulpit in something akin to an angry tirade. While it is true that Jesus Christ Himself became angry, His was a righteous anger (Matthew 21:12–13). Our anger is seldom of such a noble character. Remember that the wrath of man does not produce the righteousness of God (James 1:20).

Most of the occasions that will require confrontation in the ministry have to do with those who, as I have previously observed in this letter, have fallen into gross negligence or destructive sin that, if left unchecked, will destroy themselves or others in the congregation. No pastor enjoys going to a member in the congregation and telling him his fault. In fact, I am leery of the pastor who finds enjoyment in such a task, just as I would be leery of a parent who looks forward to and derives some pleasure from spanking his disobedient child. The Lord Jesus Christ has called us, however, to go to such a one and tell him his fault (Matthew 18:15). We are to do this in a spirit of gentleness and meekness, determining not to be quarrelsome, in the hope that God will grant the erring one repentance leading to the further knowledge of the truth. The Scripture likens this to the rescue of a POW (2 Timothy 2:24–26) who may or may not want to be rescued.

There must be loving confrontation in which a redemptive rebuke is given as a means, hopefully blessed by God, to help the wayward one to see his sins, confess and repent of them and return and be restored unto fellowship. It has been said that growth in any relationship will necessitate caring enough to confront another when he is in sin. Again, this will take evangelical courage if this labor of close pastoral ministry is to be engaged in with any God-honoring effect. Because it is so easy not to go to an individual and confront him in his sin, you must fight against the temptation to do nothing. All of the excuses in the world you might be able to muster against going will melt in the face of the words of Jesus, who said, "If you love me, keep my commandments" (John 14:15). There is also the temptation to confuse loving confrontation with legal condemnation. You are not the judge and jury called by God to execute an arbitrary sentence on those whose lives have proven to be a dismal disappointment in the journey. You are a pastor going after a wayward sheep with the hope of recovering him back to the fold. If in the process of this he proves not to be a sheep at all, then he must be lovingly removed from the fellowship for the glory of God, the name of Christ upon the congregation, the good of the genuine sheep within the church and the good of his own soul because he is deceived about his own spiritual condition. All of this, however, is to be done in the hope that the gospel witness to such a wayward person will ultimately bear fruit in the saving of his soul. You must have the courage to risk the relationship and rest in the providence of God, whether or not the erring one ever returns.

Evangelical Courage to Confess Your Faults To Those against Whom You Sin

It is important that a faithful pastor have the evangelical courage to make an honest assessment of himself and of his faults. If you are to be a pastor who earns the right to speak to the people under your care, feeding them the Word of God for the nourishment of their own souls, leading them by precept and example into the paths of righteousness and holiness and protecting them from the world, the flesh, and the devil, then you must have an honest assessment of yourself. It is true that some will take advantage of your willingness to acknowledge that you, too, are a sinner, saved only by the mighty grace of God. Some may even see this as a weakness and seek to exploit it. Most, however, will appreciate being led by one who acknowledges that he also battles with remaining sin (Romans 7 does not make us think any less of the apostle Paul, but rather helps us to identify with him). They can identify with such and will believe that you are able both to sympathize and empathize with them in their struggles. Transparency and vulnerability are precious marks of a servant of Jesus Christ.

The wise pastor, when his sin is brought to his attention, will always be willing to confess it, repent of it and demonstrate the power of the gospel to make men holy by bringing forth the fruit of repentance in his life. He will at the same time always be willing to forgive those who sin against him. He does this in a two-fold way. First, pastors (as well as all Christians) must nurture a continual forgiving attitude in their hearts, ready to express this to those who have sinned or will sin against them. The Lord Jesus Christ demonstrated this on the cross when He said, "Father, forgive them, for they do not know what they are doing" (Luke 23:34). He was not formally forgiving all of those who had participated in His crucifixion. Rather, He was demonstrating a forgiving heart toward those who had wronged Him. (It was actually at Pentecost that many received forgiveness for their sins—after they had confessed them and repented of them.) The martyr Stephen showed at his death that He had learned this lesson from his Lord when he made virtually the same statement to God as his accusers were stoning him to death (Acts 7:60). This forgiving attitude was mightily used by God to touch the heart of Saul of Tarsus, who was greatly moved by what he saw and heard.

In addition to a forgiving spirit, the pastor must also be willing to express formal forgiveness when one who has sinned against him comes and confesses the sin with a repenting heart. Speaking words of forgiveness that are followed by tangible evidence of forgiveness can be a tremendous object lesson of the reconciling power of the gospel and the reality of unconditional gospel love. Never miss an opportunity to attempt to effect reconciliation. Your congregation will be blessed to have modeled before them the essence of what it means to be saved by grace.

Timothy, I have probably told you much more than you wanted to know about life in the ministry, so I will close my letter with this exhortation from the Scripture spoken by God to His servant, Joshua:

> Only be strong and very courageous, that you may observe to do according to all the law which Moses My servant commanded you; do not turn from it to the right hand or to the left, that you may prosper wherever you go. This Book of the Law shall not depart from your mouth, but you shall meditate in it day and night, that you may observe to do according to all that is written in it. For then you will make your way prosperous, and then you will have good success. Have I not commanded you? Be strong and of good courage; do not be afraid, nor be dismayed, for the Lord your God is with you wherever you go (Joshua 1:7–9).

Timothy, May the Lord bless you and keep you, and make His face shine upon you, and be gracious unto you. May the Lord lift up His countenance upon you and give you peace (Numbers 6:24–26).

Your fellow servant in the gospel,
Bill Ascol, Pastor

PS—I want to encourage you to read a few books that I hope will strengthen you in your ministry, such as:

1. *Too Great a Temptation*, by Joel Gregory (Irving, TX: Summit Publishing Group, 1994).
2. *Jonathan Edwards: A New Biography* by Iain Murray (Edinburgh: The Banner of Truth, 1987).
3. *Biography of D. Martyn Lloyd-Jones* (2 volumes) by Iain Murray (Edinburgh: The Banner of Truth, 1983, 1990).
4. *Healing Spiritual Abuse* by Ken Blue (Downers Grove, IL: Intervarsity Press, 1993).
5. *Shepherding God's Flock* edited by Roger Beardmore (Harrisonburg, VA: Sprinkle Publications, 1988).
6. *The Reformed Pastor* by Richard Baxter (reprint, Edinburgh: The Banner of Truth Trust, 1979).

Chapter 9

Do the Work of an Evangelist
Mark Dever

Dear Timothy,

Good to hear from you again. I'm sure that, by God's grace, you'll weather the storms that you're facing. The difficulties that you're finding about scheduling family time, committee meetings, preparation time for preaching and so many other things are completely normal. One concern that you didn't mention (which, I have to be honest, concerned me a little bit) was evangelism.

Real evangelism is one of the first things to vanish when you begin working in the ministry. Before then, you've likely had a secular job or you've been in school and you've been used to being around non-Christians without ever "having your cover blown." You've naturally had time with non-believers and you've not been someone who would put them off. In fact, one of the things that made me encourage you to consider the ministry was the evident concern you've always had for evangelism. Remember that a concern for the salvation of friends is one of the things you even first found attractive in your wife!

When you go into the ministry, all of a sudden, you're a marked man by everything from your business card to your work mates to your time. You have a conversation with someone at the store or on the plane and they find out you're a minister (and especially, I've found, when you're a "Baptist preacher") and the conversation just closes down. I don't want to be too bleak here. Maybe one time in five or ten it is actually an advantage, but usually it's anything but. Too often, people load on you every bad experience that they've had with a pastor or a church or even some Christian relative. On top of all this, if you find your church growing, then you'll find that your time is even more pressed. Church members can see all too easily when you're not doing something inside the church; they usually don't think too much about whether or not you've got any natural outlets for meeting non-Christians.

I've just re-read what I've written to you, Timothy, and I feel that I need to back up a little bit. I generally know when someone goes into the ministry because they like to work only with Christians and doing church things, that this person probably isn't called. The person who is usually best is the person who is quite good in a non-Christian work environment but who is willing, for the sake of the kingdom, to be called back "behind the lines" as it were, to spend his life supplying those who are on the front lines of ministry. As a pastor, I am in a position that is both frustrating and privileged. It is frustrating in that I really enjoy opportunities to spend time with non-Christian friends, relatives and neighbors. Because I am a pastor, I have to work intentionally to create such opportunities. But my position is also a privileged one, in that I get to meet at least weekly (and I think you said that you have two weekly meetings) with a few hundred people and work to equip them to share the gospel with their friends and family during the week ahead. Being a minister of the Word is a calling that has its price in personal evangelistic opportunities but that also affords great opportunities to encourage others.

Now, all of this is simply about your *personal* evangelism. At the heart of your full-time calling is the command to spread the evangel to others. And much of your activity doing that will be public. Timothy, you've got an incredible opportunity at the church where God has placed you to declare the gospel. Not only your church community and neighborhood, but the whole city needs to hear the gospel. There are thousands and thousands of people within an hour's drive of where you are who have never carefully considered the gospel. You are one of a relatively small number of men called to proclaim the gospel there and you've even got a whole community of people (your church) who are setting aside a portion of their income to help you to do that full time. Do you see the privilege you have?

I've always found it amazing to reflect on the fact that God uses us in His purposes. He has determined that He will save His own; we know this from Romans 9. But when we keep reading in Romans 10, we see that this same God has determined that He will not do it without the gospel being preached and that requires churches sending preachers and preachers preaching. And that's where you and I come in. God has decided to include us in making sure that Beth and Michael and Rachel and Andrea and Marilyn and Bob and Kurt and Ryan and Jason and so many others come to know Him. I remember you're excitement when David became a Christian your junior year in college. That was in part because of your faithful evangelism, but it was also because he had been convicted by hearing the minister at your church there. Timothy, you are now that minister for many people.

Every time you step into the pulpit and preach a sermon, one of your aims should be to have sinners converted. Spurgeon has a marvelous lecture on this in his *Lectures to My Students*.[1] It is called, "On Conversion as Our Aim." In it, he maintains, "as a rule, God has sent us to preach in order that through the gospel of Jesus Christ the sons of men may be reconciled to him."[2] He acknowledges that the glory of God is our chief aim and that sometimes a ministry is not blessed with conversions, but normally, he said, the preaching of the gospel is intended to result in the reconciliation of sinners with God.

Some will tell you that you can only be evangelistic in your preaching if you conclude your sermons with a call to come down to the front. Surely you understand both the ridiculousness of thinking that's necessary, and yet the pastoral prudence involved in when and how you help your congregation to separate an "altar call" from conversion. The best way that you can do that is simply by making clear in the normal course of your expositional preaching the nature of true conversion. Also speak and teach clearly

---

[1] C. H. Spurgeon, *Lectures to My Students* (reprint, Grand Rapids, MI: Zondervan, 1954), 336–348.
[2] Ibid., 336.

about how baptism is to function in a New Testament church. And don't be too hasty to change long-standing practices, unless you absolutely have to. Teach them into asking for change themselves, before you try to lead the uncomprehending into change.

And always, *always* be giving invitationals, in the sense of inviting sinners to repent and believe the good news, in every sermon. If your church members hear that heart in your message and see it lived out in your life, they will be more open to listen to your teaching on how to evangelize. They just need to know that there is no excuse to not evangelize. Here at our church, we're seeing more people converted and joining the church now that there's no altar call than they ever did when they used one.

But do remember always to preach the gospel when you preach. You can preach more than that, but never less. I remember preaching a sermon on Ecclesiastes a few years ago and having a good friend come up to me and say what a marvelous sermon it really was, except that the gospel wasn't in it. I felt cut to the quick. Since then, I've always tried to be better about keeping the conversion of sinners as not my only object, but one of my main objects in every sermon.

Now, honestly, Timothy, just between us, has the conversion of sinners been in your mind as you've ascended the steps to the pulpit these last few Sundays? Has your mind been all on Deuteronomy (I believe you said you were preaching through the Ten Commandments on Sunday morning, is that right?), or have you had in mind how the text of Scripture you are preaching from is to be preached with a view of seeing men and women come to Christ. Timothy, I'm particularly concerned about this now, because you are young in your ministry. You've hardly been there six months, but you are establishing the pattern that your people will come to know and expect from you for years. Are your sermons going to be sermons that they would want to invite their non-Christian husband, or their neighbors or their friends at work to come hear?

Let that last question hang in your mind. I want you to think about that because too many ministers feel that their ministry of feeding the sheep has nothing to do with their ministry of proclaiming the gospel. But it does! And I hope that you can grasp this early on in your ministry. Lloyd-Jones in *Preaching and Preachers*[3] implores preachers always to establish separate evangelistic services with special preaching in the weekly meeting of the church. I'm not sure that I agree with that, but I do think that the point he makes about the need for teaching to be part of our evangelism and for evangelistic preaching to be part of our teaching is true.

We just can't get away from the gospel! Timothy, the passion that I've heard from you in the past about evangelism and that I hear from you now about faithfulness and your church being successful, I also long to hear from you about the privilege and necessity of evangelism as a priority in your ministry. Brother, if it's not a priority in your ministry, it will not be in your church, either.

---

[3] Martyn Lloyd-Jones, *Preaching and Preachers* (Grand Rapids, MI: Zondervan, 1971).

Last summer on vacation, I read the letters of A. W. Pink.[4] He's an interesting fellow, sad in some ways, but helpfully plain. He was reflecting on the state of gospel preaching in Australia in the 1920s when he wrote:

> General religious conditions here are very similar to those which obtain in the USA. The vast majority of the churches are in a sorry state. Those that are out-and-out worldly are at their wits' end to invent new devices for drawing a crowd. Others which still preserve an outward form of godliness provide nothing substantial for the soul; there is little ministering of Christ to the heart and little preaching of "sound doctrine," without which souls cannot be built up and established in the faith. The great majority of the "pastors" summon to their aid some professional "evangelist," who, for two to four weeks, puts on a high-pressure campaign and secures sufficient new "converts" to take the place of those who have "lapsed" since he was last with them. What a farce it all is! What an acknowledgement of their own failure! Imagine C. H. Spurgeon needing some evangelist to preach the Gospel for him for a month each year! Why do not these well-paid "pastors" heed 2 Timothy 4:5 and *themselves* "do the work of an evangelist," and thus "make full proof of their ministry"?
>
> The great need of Australia today is for God-sent and God-anointed men, who will not shun to declare all the counsel of God; men in whom the Word of Christ dwells

---

[4] A. W. Pink, *Letters of A. W. Pink* (Edinburgh: Banner of Truth Trust, 1978).

richly, so that they can say with the apostle, "Woe is me if I preach not the Gospel"; men on whom rests the fear of God, so that they are delivered from the fear of man. Will Christian readers in distant lands join us daily in prayer that the Lord of the harvest will raise up and thrust forth more of his laborers into this portion of his Vineyard?[5]

Timothy, that's not just the need for Sydney, Australia, it's the need of your city, too. Something each of these men I've mentioned—Spurgeon, Pink, Lloyd-Jones—had in each of their different ways was passion—a passion for God that translated into a passion for people to come to know Him.

One of the most fruitful things you can do is to meditate on what it means to be separated from God by your sins. Remember what it was like before you were a Christian? Meditate on the fearfulness of the state of those who are separated from God and realize that it is your tremendous privilege to tell people the good news that there is a way that their sins can be forgiven and that they can be given a fresh start, a new birth! Sometimes these phrases become old-hat to us, but I remember someone who became a Christian here a few years ago telling us that, before she was a Christian, she thought that we must have some very good writers at this church because our material contained the imagery of "a new birth" and "a new creation." Timothy, sometimes we forget how claustrophobic and soul-destroying this world is to someone who doesn't know God and is at enmity with Him. Make friends with non-Christians and pray that God grow a love in your heart for Him.

---

[5] Iain Murray, *Arthur W. Pink* (Edinburgh: Banner of Truth Trust, 1981), 42.

Timothy, the God we serve is the God who left the ninety and nine to go seeking for the lost one. Pour over Luke 15 in prayer and ask God to give you a heart for the lost, like that woman had for her coin, like that shepherd had for his sheep, like that father had for his son. Pray that lost people become precious to you. If they do, it will affect the way you prepare and the way you preach. It will affect the way you plan your own schedule and the way you lead your church. There's nothing wrong with being reformed in your theology *and* planning for evangelism. A certainty of God's blessing should only encourage us to be bold in the use of means, not to become lazy in them.

Evangelism is sharing the gospel. To tell it, you have to know it, and not everyone knows it, Timothy. That puts a special responsibility on the shoulders of those who do, and especially on those, like you and me, who have been called to this ministry. I hope you haven't gotten the idea that evangelists are only people like Finney or Moody, Graham or Palau, people who work full-time at this. At the center of our ministry should be sharing the gospel. All pastors are called to be evangelists. Indeed, evangelism is to be a central part of our work, and sometimes that may mean teaching our people that. But, Timothy, what a worthy work it is! Scholars leave a volume of pages called their *magnum opus*—their great work. The pastor's great work, our *magnum opus*, should be the great body of people evangelized by our faithful ministry. Oh, brother, early on in your ministry there *do* make evangelism a priority in your prayers and practice, in your preaching and your living.

I've been here at my present church for eight years now, and I wouldn't want you to think that I've got this all sorted out. Just a couple of months ago I was sharing with the congregation that I felt the one place we were particularly not doing all we should is in the area of evangelism. So I certainly don't mean to present myself in this letter to you as one who has all the answers. Having said that, I am at least certain that this is to be a central concern for both you and me, because we're both called to be ministers of God's Word.

As for me coming there to preach for you sometime, I think that if I did that, I would love to do so in some evangelistic capacity. You did so well in Greek, and you're such a good, budding theologian, that I can't imagine I would add much to what you can already offer them. Perhaps I could meet with you and your church leaders to talk about baptism, congregationalism, discipline and elders—those things people are always asking me to come talk about. But I wonder if what would be best would be for us to come up with a topic for me to address in an open venue, in which I would present the gospel. Your congregation could be informed, be praying, invite friends. I know it's not much, but it may be a start in helping you to become more intentional in your evangelistic planning and practice, and you've got to start somewhere. When you write me again, I want you to tell me about some non-Christians you've recently spoken to about the gospel and about some who've talked to you about the gospel after hearing you preach. Does that sound fair?

I'd better go now. Do let me hear from you again soon, especially if you're going to tell me how you're planning to do the work of an evangelist.

With fraternal affection as a
co-laborer in the gospel,
Mark

PS—Here are some of my suggested resources:

1. For more specific ideas on evangelism, you could see my chapter on "Pastoral Success in Evangelism" in *Reforming Pastoral Ministry*, ed. John Armstrong (Wheaton, IL: Crossway Books, 2001).
2. Probably the best book on thinking through evangelism theologically is *Evangelism and the Sovereignty of God* by J. I. Packer (Downers Grove, IL: InterVarsity Press, 1961).
3. And well worth a read for how to share the gospel in a God-centered way is Will Metzger's great book *Tell the Truth* (Downers Grove, IL: InterVarsity Press, 1981).
4. Reformed-friendly evangelistic literature can be found from St. Matthias Press (www.matthiasmedia.com). Check out more about their "Two Ways to Live" gospel presentation.
5. There are also some good comparisons of various evangelistic Bible studies out there at the website for IX Marks Ministries (www.9marks.org).

Chapter 10

Do Personal Work
Fred Malone

Dear Timothy,

Greetings in the name of our dear Lord Jesus Christ. As you enter into your first pastorate, I feel the necessity of writing to you about the need, responsibility and usefulness of doing personal work in the ministry.

Sometimes, other voices mean well in their advice to young pastors yet neglect some simple biblical principles. For instance, the apostles gave themselves to the Word of God and prayer (Acts 6:4). Certainly this is the priority in the pastoral ministry. All of our knowledge and strength comes from a study of God's Word and prayer. Our public ministry of the Word is the foundation of all we do. However, neither our Lord nor His apostles neglected personal work with individuals in carrying out this priority. We cannot allow well-meaning advisors of young pastors to call them to ignore personal work with the priority of the study and preaching of God's Word. We must do both, as I will prove to you.

Another voice young pastors hear often is that of large church pastors who say, "I do not do counseling. I do not visit the hospitals. I do not have time to visit in the homes of my people. I let the staff be the first line of doing personal work." This is a CEO mentality but certainly not the mentality of the Lord, His apostles or of the great pastors in Christian history. We have Bunyan, Spurgeon, Lloyd-Jones, Baxter, M'Cheyne, Manley, Judson, Wayland, Chantry and many others whose ministries were marked by the highest level of ministering the Word publicly, while at the same time giving their time and lives to do personal work. Do not allow corporate models of ministry negate the clear teachings of Scripture to pastors nor the wonderful examples of godly men who literally died ministering to individuals.

I would like to outline for you the necessity of personal work, the foundation of personal work and clear examples of personal work from the Scriptures. I will also list a few suggestions that, I believe, will enhance your opportunity to apply the Word of God to the individual cases of men.

Personal Work Is Commanded By God

Paul's Pastoral Epistles are full of commands to young Timothy and Titus to do personal work. He commanded them to: "instruct certain men" (1 Timothy 1:3); "rebuke an older man . . . younger men . . . older women . . . younger women" (5:1–2); "instruct the rich" (6:17); "entrust to faithful men" (2 Timothy 2:2); "correct those in opposition" (2:25); "silence empty talkers" (Titus 1:11); "reject a factious man" (3:20). And if these commands are not clear enough, remember that Paul devoted a whole letter to write one individual on behalf of another (Philemon). Paul demonstrated as well as taught the need for pastors and elders to do personal work. He emphasized this need even amidst the commands to study to show yourself approved unto God as a workman not ashamed. He never intended that the priority of study and public ministry be used as an excuse to ignore personal work with individuals.

Charles Bridges said in *The Christian Ministry*, perhaps the best book ever written on the subject:

> Preaching—the grand lever of the Ministry—derives much of its power from connexion with the Pastoral Work; and its too frequent disjunction from it is a main cause of our inefficiency . . . The Pastoral work is the personal application of the pulpit Ministry to the proper individualities of our people . . . For this purpose, we must acquaint ourselves with their situation, habits, character, state of heart, peculiar wants [lacks], and difficulties . . . The indolent are slumbering—the self-dependent are falling back—the zealous are under the influence of spiritual pride—the earnest are becoming self-righteous—the regular, formal. Then there is the enquirer, asking for direction—the tempted and perplexed, looking for support—the afflicted, longing for the cheering consolation of the gospel—the convinced sinner, from the slight healing of his wound, settling in a delusive peace—the professor, "having a name that he lives; but he is dead." These cases cannot, in all their minute and diversified forms, be fully treated from the pulpit. It is

therefore in his Pastoral character that the Minister "watches for souls as one that must give account."[1]

Such quotations could be multiplied from Matthew Henry, John Owen and other Puritans. However, it is sufficient to recognize that personal work is a command of God in the Scriptures. After all, the pastor is included in Jesus' standard of judgment:

> I was hungry and you gave Me something to eat; I was thirsty and you gave Me drink; I was a stranger, and you invited Me in; naked, and you clothed Me; I was sick, and you visited Me; I was in prison, and you came to Me . . . Truly, I say to you, to the extent that you did this to one of these brothers of mine, even the least of them, you did it unto Me (Matthew 25:35–37, 40).

Timothy, we are commanded to do personal work. Do not be misled that the pastor is exempted from such commands because he is a busy pastor (Hebrews 13:17).

---

[1] Charles Bridges, *The Christian Ministry* (reprint, Edinburgh: The Banner of Truth Trust, 1980), 343–344. Bridges references Hebrews 13:17 as a sobering text for all pastors of any size church. His section on pastoral work includes illustrations on how to minister to each of these kinds of men. They are a worthy study to increase the pulpit's application of God's Word to various kinds of hearers—a neglected area of homiletics today.

Personal Work Requires a Theological Foundation

Paul commanded Timothy, "Pay close attention to yourself and to your teaching; persevere in these things; for as you do this, you will insure salvation both for yourself and for those who hear you" (1 Timothy 4:16). Although we are charged with paying close attention to sound teaching, could it be made more clear that Paul also requires that you first apply sound teaching to your own soul? In other words, make sure that your own relationship to God and to His Christ is real, genuine and theologically sound. This theological necessity is the foundation for your entire work.

For example, if you intend to preach justification by faith alone in Christ alone, do you understand and live in that justification yourself? Do you daily remember the mountain of sin and sins that deserve God's wrath? Do you daily flee to Christ risen and ascended to depend upon His once-for-all shed blood and His imputed righteousness to assure you of your standing with God? Do you believe that your "Christian sins" are as covered by the blood and righteousness of Christ as well as your "pre-Christian sins"? Do you believe that on your best day of ministering to others that your best works still are mixed with sin and ignorance, needing atonement and the imputed righteousness of Christ to be made an acceptable sacrifice to God? Do you daily depend upon sovereign grace and justification by faith alone yourself?

You see, Timothy, to do personal work you must believe that God does personal theological work with you.

You must believe that you are accepted and loved by sovereign grace through justification by faith alone. You must believe that God's love in Christ is unchangeable, constant and benevolent, even when you fall into a sin. How else will you give the sinful sheep of Christ the impression that you accept them, love them and grieve for them when they fall into sin? How else will you communicate grace when you must speak to them, confront them and seek to bring loving correction? If you preach justification by faith alone, you must live in it first. Then you will be able to have a loving, forgiving, patient and persevering spirit toward individuals in your ministry.

Along with justification, you must also pay close attention to yourself in sanctification by faith exercised in Christ as you seek to love Him and keep His commandments. If your pursuit of holiness degenerates into a law-based, works-performance relationship with God, then your pastoral ministry will reflect a condemning, angry, works-performance relationship to Christ's sheep. Yes, sanctification gives due attention to the law of God (the Ten Words and more). However, sanctification works by faith in the justifying grace of the Lord Jesus Christ. Only justified men pursue sanctification under the grace of God. If a husband does not love his wife as he should, his problem is in his understanding of justification by faith alone. Only pastors who practice such sanctification as justified men themselves will find persevering grace to minister to Christ's wayward sheep.

So, you see, personal work has a theological foundation rooted in justification by faith and sanctification by faith in Christ exercised as you obey His commandments. Make sure that you understand it for yourself so that you will be gracious in your ministrations and as persevering as God is toward you. To "rejoice in the Lord always" is to believe in God's grace toward you at all times in Christ's justification while you pursue sanctification. This alone will enable you effectively to understand the spiritual condition of those to whom you minister personally so that you may straighten out their misunderstandings of the motive and power of Christian living—God's unconditional grace in Christ.

Personal Work Has Biblical Examples

Timothy, dare I presume to remind you that our Lord Jesus did personal work? Read the gospels and see Him teaching multitudes the Word of God. But do not fail to notice that He made time for a woman at a well, a rich young ruler, a thieving Zacchaeus, a betraying Peter. He evangelized the lost, visited the sick, ate with sinners, loved those who turned away.

Even now, being infinite God, He gives His miraculous, full attention every moment to each of His sheep as if they were the only one for whom He died, arose and reigns. He has not ceased His personal work simply because He is exalted in the heavens. Rather, He has increased it. Is not heaven a place where the Bridegroom once again girds Himself and serves individually His loved ones (Luke 12:37)?

Also, remember the personal work of Paul as an apostle and pastor in Ephesus. For three years he did not shrink from declaring to them anything that was profitable and teaching them publicly and from house to house (Acts 20:20). He taught them the whole counsel of God (20:27).

He did not cease to admonish each one with tears. Indeed, to the Corinthians he wrote: "Who is weak without my being weak? Who is led into sin without my intense concern?" (2 Corinthians 11:29). He labored to present each man complete in Christ, admonishing and teaching every man (Colossians 1:28). This is sufficient to reveal the pastoral heart of Paul, not only as an apostle to the whole church, but as a servant of all. Paul exemplified personal work.

How sad it is to hear pastors say, "I am sticking to my preaching and teaching publicly; all else will come in time—I don't have time to nursemaid every stubbed toe of the saints." Do they not know, Timothy, that every weakness and sin in the saints reveals a misunderstanding of God's grace and justification by faith? That sin cannot be master over you, for you are not under law but grace? That pastoral work is a theological work, transforming minds to think from the viewpoint of grace in which every true Christian stands? That only as we clear up our peoples' understanding of the gospel will they keep the law under grace?

The ministries both of Jesus and Paul were filled with personal work in busier schedules than we have. They saw each soul as made in the image of God now condemned to eternal hell under the law covenant in Adam. Only a move under the grace covenant in Christ, the last Adam, could free them from eternal condemnation and the daily power of sin. They saw eternal souls with shepherd's eyes. They never thought of the inconvenience of dying to self, using up one's time and energy and life, to infuse eternal life in others (2 Corinthians 4). They were selfless men who sacrificed self for the salvation and sanctification of others. They still are biblical examples and models of the pastorate.

Timothy, study Christ, not just *about* Christ. Study Paul, not just *his theology*. You have two biblical examples calling you to do personal work. Others who have followed in their train are Richard Baxter in *The Reformed Pastor*,[2] Charles Bridges in *The Christian Ministry*, D. Martyn Lloyd-Jones in *Preaching and Preachers*[3] and Charles Haddon Spurgeon in *An All-Around Ministry*.[4] These all learned how to apply the law and the gospel properly to each individual's need: the agnostic, the atheist, the new Christian, the young Christian, the mature Christian, the hypocrite, the false convert, those falsely assured, those who should be assured, etc. They understood that all men live out their real theology. To bring lasting change means that the pastor must teach, correct and apply sound theology to their faulty theology so that they may live godly lives and grow in grace. Jesus and Paul are our examples.

Personal Work Requires That You Be Personal

Let me conclude, Timothy, with some specific exhortations. First, set regular hours to visit the flock. There are a thousand things worthy to do with your time. However, the

---

[2] Richard Baxter, *The Reformed Pastor* (reprint, Edinburgh: The Banner of Truth Trust, 1979).
[3] Martyn Lloyd-Jones, *Preaching and Preachers* (Grand Rapids, MI: Zondervan Publishing House, 1971).
[4] C. H. Spurgeon, *An All-Around Ministry* (reprint, Edinburgh: The Banner of Truth Trust, 2000).

pastor's work is an impossible work. You cannot do everything perfectly, but you must try to do everything, living under grace. Therefore, you must discipline yourself for the purpose of godliness. Set regular hours to visit the widows, the sick, the dying, the confused, the lonely, the ignorant, as well as the mature who may grow weary in well-doing. Do not let "squeaky wheels" keep you from oiling the quiet ones. If Christ spends all day, every day, with you, is it too much for Him to ask you to spend some regular time with His loved ones?

Second, study your own heart in light of justification and sanctification. Will this not become a reservoir of counseling Christ's sheep in the byways of sin and the comforts of the gospel? Do not let book study and sermon preparation become a sterile work. Bridges instructs us:

> As an old divine used to say, that a preacher had three books to study—the Bible, himself, and his people. Gillies' Hist. Coll. Bishop Burnet remarks it, as "the capital error in men's preparing themselves for the sacred Ministry, that they study books more than themselves."—History of his Own Times.[5]

---

[5] Ibid., 350. This statement is why the author believes that pastors should be teaching ministerial students in preparation for the ministry, whether by mentoring in the church or instructing in the seminary classroom. Pastors of significant experience can apply book knowledge to students' hearts in every coursework better than those who may be fine academics. We need Pauls in the classroom, not Gamaliels. How can we prepare pastors equipped to think pastorally in all theological subjects if pastors do not model such thinking in each subject? To study books without studying one's heart pastorally will result in an academic mind that has difficulty applying God's Word pastorally in the pulpit and in private.

If Bunyan "preached smartingly what I did feel," should not you do the same?

Third, spend time with individuals. Jesus ate, slept with, walked with, fished with, ate breakfast with and individually applied His teachings to each disciple. We are not pragmatic CEO's. We are not theological ivory towers of truth. We are not commanders of the troops. We are pastors, shepherds, fathers of the faith, mothers in childbirth, brothers in a family and servants of all (Matthew 20:28). Practice hospitality. Fish with men while you fish for men. Wash dirty feet individually, even Judas's. Love as you have been loved. Forgive as you have been forgiven. Serve as you have been served.

Fourth, read biographies of great Christians to flesh out your personal work with encouraging examples of the faith, thus encouraging your people to read of God's work in others lives. All theology and no biography makes pastor and people dull boys.

Fifth, ask great questions of your people. "How does Christ's life and redeeming work help you to live as a husband, a wife, a parent, a child, a church member? What do you think is God's great goal for your life? What does heaven mean to you today? What does Christ think and feel about you when you sin? Do you think God enjoys you?" Such questions give you a clue to their understanding of justification and sanctification and of law and gospel. They get Christ's sheep to thinking. They cause them to look for answers in your teaching. And they give you knowledge of their true spiritual condition that will focus your pulpit ministry and its applications to their real need.

Finally, be yourself. Do not put on the "professional garment." Rather, put on the robe of a walking Christian who is honest about your own spiritual warfare and the comforts you find in Jesus Christ. Such sincerity attracts the sincere to the Savior and gives hope that Christ is enough. In other words, to do personal work you must be personal. You must first feel and then smartingly preach.

In conclusion, dear Timothy, love Christ's sheep as He has loved you and loves them. You only have to do as much personal work as He did and still does. You must get over self and selfishness. You must live in Christ and rejoice in the Lord always. You must remember that He bore you back from lostness on His wide shoulders—rejoicing. Memorize 2 Corinthians 4 and pray that God will use the truth of this passage to grow you shoulders wide enough to bear the sheep of Christ into His glorious presence and present each one under your care complete in Christ. Timothy, *do* personal work.

Your lesser Paul,
Fred A. Malone

PS—Again, Timothy, I encourage you to secure for your library and read the books mentioned earlier in this letter:

1. *The Reformed Pastor* by Richard Baxter (Reprint, Edinburgh: The Banner of Truth Trust, 1979).
2. *The Christian Ministry* by Charles Bridges (Reprint, Edinburgh: The Banner of Truth Trust, 1980).

3. *Preaching and Preachers* by Dr. Martyn-Lloyd Jones (Grand Rapids, MI: Zondervan, 1971).
4. *An All-Around Ministry* by Charles Spurgeon (Reprint, Edinburgh: The Banner of Truth Trust, 2000).

Chapter 11

Watch Your Doctrine
Raymond Perron

Dear Timothy,

Warmest greetings in our Lord Jesus Christ, the only Savior of God's elect! I trust you and your little family are doing well in body and soul. You are always in my thoughts and prayers. It is easy for me to imagine how your hands must be full with your family responsibilities, especially with Mary's pregnancy, your two year-old boy and all the demands of your fresh pastoral ministry.

When you accepted this pastoral position, a new mission, a new work, even a new life began for you. Along with new responsibilities came new promises. But these new promises will be fulfilled through perseverance. I understand that you are still in a period of adjustment in your ministry. You must feel overwhelmed with the immensity of the task that lies before you. Beyond a shadow of a doubt, working with human souls represents the most difficult labor of all. Indeed, it is complex beyond calculation, defying analysis as it is made up of the entire spectrum of crisis, countless impulses, passions and emotions. This is why "beloved, while I was very diligent to write to you concerning our common salvation, I found it necessary to write to you exhorting you to contend earnestly for the faith which was once for all delivered to the saints" (Jude 1:3). My heartfelt appeal to you, my beloved friend and brother, is: Watch your doctrine! As I use the word *doctrine* you understand, of course, that I am referring to the wider meaning of teaching, namely the manner as well as the matter of the instruction conveyed.

If I were to ask you to write a list of the most important things in your life and ministry, what would your list look like? What categories would emerge as your list grew? The apostle Paul's list expressed two categories, core values and doctrinal values: "Take heed to yourself and to the doctrine" (1 Timothy 4:16).

Today, we have come to a place where doctrine is no longer an issue, even among many professing followers of Christ. The time when hard and fast lines were drawn between people on the basis of their particular brand of doctrine is past, having been replaced by an emphasis on experience. But experience that is not given meaning by truth is of a most dangerous fabric. So let me draw your attention to the primacy of doctrine and, consequently, the utmost duty of watching it.

First, consider the importance of doctrine (teaching) in the life and ministry of our Lord Jesus Christ. "And so it was, when Jesus had ended these sayings, that the people were astonished at His teaching [doctrine]" (Matthew 7:28). "Then they understood that He did not tell them to beware of the leaven of bread, but of the doctrine of the Pharisees and Sadducees" (Matthew 16:12). "And the scribes and chief priests heard it and sought how they might destroy Him; for they feared Him, because all the people were astonished at His teaching [doctrine]" (Mark 11:18; cf. Matthew 22:33; Mark 1:27, 4:2, 12:38; Luke 4:32, 18:19). What do these verses say? Our dear Lord was not trying to play up the requirements of His time by turning His sermons into philosophical, moral or aesthetic dissertations; nor was He limiting His presentation of the truth in order to meet the individual views or fancies of His hearers. Truth remains truth in as much as it is in agreement with what God says is true. Only the Almighty has the authority to define doctrine because it originated in His mind. So when the Son of God came to earth, He practiced and taught His Father's doctrine: "My doctrine is not mine, but His who sent me" (John 7:16). "For I have not spoken on My own authority; but the Father who sent Me gave Me a command, what I should say and what I should speak. And I know that His command is everlasting life. Therefore, whatever I speak, just as the Father has told Me, so I speak" (John 12:49–50).

Your mission, dear brother, is to be a prophet of the Lord Jesus Christ. A prophet doesn't make up his message but faithfully delivers the message he has received. The very same doctrine that was so dear to our Lord's heart must be dear to ours as well. So watch your doctrine and be faithful to teach all that God has delivered to us in His Word.

Second, consider the importance of doctrine in the Early Church. Let me, beloved brother, quote just one text that shows the place of doctrine in the first days of Christ's church. "And they continued steadfastly in the apostle's doctrine and fellowship, in the breaking of bread, and in prayers" (Acts 2:42, cf. 5:28). The very first thing in which they were persevering was the apostles' doctrine, this set of beliefs, "this system of truth" that is now contained in Scripture. When we look at all the exhortations that the apostle Paul addresses to Timothy and Titus, we cannot escape the conclusion that doctrine was the main weapon in the fight for truth and against falsehood. For example, ". . . holding fast the faithful word as he has been taught, that he may be able, by sound doctrine, both to exhort and convict those who contradict" (Titus 1:9). This is the very same weapon you have been given. So, keep it sharp, watch your doctrine!

Third, consider the importance of doctrine for your own life. Life is a most eventful pilgrimage during which we experience an unending succession of seasons. My dear friend, let me confess to you that I have tasted a plethora of the soul's states, from the greatest joy to the deepest despair, from the most blazing enthusiasm to the darkest and most morbid passivism consequent to a loss of motivation. In every single circumstance, doctrine proved to be a safeguard. How I cherish the words of the apostle: "For me to write the same things to you is not tedious, but for you it is safe" (Philippians 3:1). How much we need to remain in sound doctrine, avoiding the snare of always looking for new things!

I have known you since your teenage years—your constancy and steadfastness have always been of a great blessing to my soul. Nevertheless, let me remind you that time is able to erode the highest mountains. Watch your doctrine to make sure it will not suffer the erosion that can be caused by the passage of undisciplined years.

The pressure of life, the ever increasing responsibilities of a growing family on top of the endless demands of the pastoral ministry, the daily decision making obligations, could lead you to the temptation of neglecting the cultivation of your doctrine. Take heed to yourself and to your doctrine!

Fatigue and discouragement form a powerful destructive team. It will happen many times that the circumstances of your life and ministry will be at loggerheads with your doctrine. Be prepared to stand firm—watch your doctrine. Look where the apostle finds comfort in the midst of life's most abrasive situations:

> Therefore, since we have this ministry, as we have received mercy, we do not lose heart. But we have renounced the hidden things of shame, not walking in craftiness nor handling the word of God deceitfully, but by manifestation of the truth commending ourselves to every man's conscience in the sight of God. But even if our gospel is veiled, it is veiled to those who are perishing, whose minds the god of this age has blinded, who do not believe, lest the light of the gospel of the glory of Christ, who is the image of God, should shine on them. For we do not preach ourselves, but Christ Jesus the Lord, and ourselves your bondservants for Jesus' sake. For it is the God who commanded light to shine out of darkness, who has shone in our hearts to give the light of the knowledge of the glory of God in the face of Jesus Christ. But we have this treasure in earthen vessels, and the excellence of the power may be of God and not of us. We are hard pressed on every side, yet not crushed; we are perplexed, but not in despair; persecuted, but not forsaken; struck down, but not destroyed—always

carrying about in the body the dying of the Lord Jesus, that the life of Jesus also may be manifested in our body. For we who live are always delivered to death for Jesus' sake, that the life of Jesus also may be manifested in our mortal flesh. So then death is working in us, but life in you. And since we have the same spirit of faith, according to what is written, "I believed and therefore I spoke," we also believe and therefore speak, knowing that He who raised up the Lord Jesus will also raise us up with Jesus, and will present us with you. For all things are for your sakes, that grace, having spread through the many, may cause thanksgiving to abound to the glory of God. Therefore we do not lose heart. Even though our outward man is perishing, yet the inward man is being renewed day by day. For our light affliction, which is but for a moment, is working for us a far more exceeding and eternal weight of glory, while we do not look at the things which are seen, but the things which are not seen. For the things which are seen are temporary, but the things which are not seen are eternal (2 Corinthians 4:1–18).

We find the apostle facing counterfeit gospels, being involved in a hot spiritual battle, feeling his human weakness, being hard pressed by all kinds of troubles, even seemingly defeated. But he does not lose heart! Why? Because he finds comfort in his sound doctrine.

Fourth, consider the importance of doctrine for your ministry. My dear young friend, God has called you to the loftiest task of all, namely taking care of His flock. Indeed, "if a man desires the position of a bishop, he desires a good work." Sound doctrine represents the essence of your care for those who are under your ministry: "Therefore take heed to yourselves and to all the flock, among which the Holy Spirit has made you overseers, to shepherd the church of God which He purchased with His own blood" (Acts 20:28). The apostle next writes about the wolves, even from within the church, who will come and not spare the flock. Let me remind you, Timothy, that the most efficient way of keeping the flock safe against the cunning and craftiness of wolves and against the various winds of deadly doctrines is to build a fortress of sound doctrine. "Take heed to yourself and to the doctrine. Continue in them, for in doing this you will save both yourself and those who hear you" (1 Timothy 4:16).

Consider the value of a human soul! The soul—"the life of the life," as someone called it—is capable of an eternity of good or woe. A soul possesses incalculable potentialities of good and evil extending in a boundless eternity. Consider the importance of your care to such a soul and the consequences of neglecting it. It has been said that the value of a thing is measured by the price paid for it. The cost of the souls that our Lord committed to your care was nothing less than the blood of the Eternal Son of God Himself. So, when you appraise the souls committed to you, you must not only reflect on what they are and what they should be but also appreciate the value that God Himself has set upon them.

You will certainly understand, beloved friend, that if I insist so much on the necessity to watch your doctrine, it is because so many circumstances and foes are going to try to prevent you from doing so. Let me remind you of two of them, namely peer pressure and rampant relativism.

I begin with the latter, relativism. This heinous vice is nowadays considered a virtue. Indeed, to be dogmatic today is the unforgivable sin but to be "open" is the supreme grace, though it is done at the expense of truth. Be prepared to hear all kinds of devastating statements such as: "It doesn't make any difference what you believe as long as you are sincere" or "We are all going to the same place anyway, we just have different roads." Nothing could be further away from God's revelation than these insipid clichés. One Christian leader has rightly warned, "Where the Scriptures are ignored, God is 'the unknown God'" (Acts 17:23). You will also meet people saying, "It doesn't matter what you believe as long as you have a personal relationship with Jesus Christ." You certainly agree with me that we would not challenge the need of such a relationship with our Lord; nevertheless, the existence of this relationship as well as its quality rests upon doctrine. A relationship grounded on falsehood is most deceitful. A true relationship with Jesus must be based upon the truth. Only when we know the truth are we set free (John 8:32).

As you look around you will quickly recognize that the main concern of our contemporary evangelical churches is feelings. This concern manifests itself most often in a church's music and preaching (often mistakenly identified as "praise and worship"). Thus, after a service when you have sung traditional hymns, some people may ask you why you do not have praise and worship in your church. For them, if they did not experience strong feelings of wellbeing, there was no praise and worship—as if worship should consist of exciting each other instead of proclaiming God's virtues and work. Second, it is common today to see people willing to pay lip service to the importance of theology but whose pulpit "has in large measure succumbed to the triumph of the therapeutic," as one contemporary theologian has aptly put it. Indeed, my dear friend, be prepared to face the fact that in many ways psychology has taken the evangelical mind captive. How important it is to remember that real "psychology" (science of the "psyche" [soul] is the Word of God!

You will also have to deal with falsely pietistic people who divorce true spirituality from theology. Theology is simply what we know about God. How then can one have an authentic spirituality without a true knowledge of God? As you aim at developing a deep spirituality in the people to whom you are ministering, give heed to your doctrine!

Let me share a few thoughts with you on the second hindrance to sound doctrine, peer pressure. The apostle Paul warns us of what is awaiting every preacher of the glorious gospel of our Lord Jesus Christ:

> For the time will come when they will not endure sound doctrine, but according to their own desires, because they have itching ears, they will heap up for themselves teachers; and they will turn their ears away from the truth, and be turned aside to fables. But you be watchful in all things, endure afflictions, do the work of an evangelist, fulfill your ministry (2 Timothy 4:3–5).

My dear brother, those of this world will not endure sound teaching. They will not want to hear it when you preach it. They will tell you it is outdated and unappealing.

In the world of business, when you have a product no one wants, you are told to change it and adapt it to the tastes of the consumer. But that is not the rule of the kingdom; truth is not a product that can be adapted according to the consumer's fantasy. The Word of God is not a product developed through research; it is God's revelation. Messengers don't edit and adapt a revelation; they proclaim it. So the apostle's argument is this: the very fact that people don't want to hear the message is an unmistakable indication that they need it. So preach it!

Let me warn you from my own experience that you are going to be enticed to adapt the message of the gospel in order to attract more people. You will find in your own heart the subtle desire to be successful in the eyes of people. After all, it looks so good in our monthly reports to have impressive figures of numeric growth. And you will be tempted to spiritualize your wrong motivation by saying that you are looking for the best way of furthering God's kingdom. Now, there is no shortage of would-be counselors who will invite you to look at how fast the church down the road is growing. Why shouldn't you adopt the same strategy? "Here is the way to do ministry, in a manner that will be more agreeable to the wishes of the majority of the people." "We are not talking about changing the message, but just smoothing it a little bit, just telling people what they want to hear so that you can win them for Christ." Isn't it subtle? Doesn't it sound good? But following this counsel would represent a denial of what the Bible teaches about our methods of evangelism. It would be adopting the old sophist creed: *homo mensura*—man is the measure of all things. Bear in mind, dear friend, that it is the Word of God that does the work of God. The power is not in the sower but in the seed. Look at our gracious Lord Himself. He was never concerned with figures but was obsessed by truth. Be His imitator! Never forget that the church is not a gathering of people whom we have convinced with human arguments or attracted by worldly means. The church of the living God is the pillar and foundation of truth. So watch your doctrine!

Bear these last words of exhortation from an old friend who has already walked many miles down the road you are just beginning. Make your teaching visible for others to comprehend and emulate by being right in your personal life! Be careful in the cultivation of your own spiritual life, giving yourself to prayer and to diligent and regular study of the Word of God. May the words of the Psalmist be the testimony of your own heart: "Oh, how I love Your law! It is my meditation all the day . . . How sweet are Your words to my taste, sweeter than honey to my mouth!" (Psalm 119:97, 103). All kinds of important and urgent activities will constantly try to compete with these first duties that are yours as a minister of the Word. Be on your guard and get prepared for a daily, hot struggle in this matter! Cultivate a constant and systematic companionship with the Bible! Refresh your thinking through confessions of faith and books on systematic theology! Take frequent opportunities to fellowship with people of like mind.

Oh my dearest young co-laborer, preach the Word! Preach it in a sound way; preach it in a faithful way; preach it in a systematic way; preach it in an expository way; preach it doctrinally! Doctrine elucidates the text and guides in the exposition of it. Moreover, doctrine will help you in measuring the rectitude of your exegetical conclusions. Watch your doctrine! Live it and preach it!

Rest assured of my deepest affection. Convey my love to Mary and to your dear son. There are no words to tell you how precious you are to my heart. May our Covenant God keep pouring upon you His richest blessings.

Coram Deo,
Raymond Perron

PS—Let me recommend you three books that have been very precious in my own ministry:

1. *The Precious Things of God* by Octavius Winslow (reprint, Pittsburgh, PA: Soli Deo Gloria, 1993).
2. *The Christian Pastor's Manual* edited by John Brown (reprint, Pittsburgh, PA: Soli Deo Gloria, 1991).
3. *The Christian Ministry* by Charles Bridges (Carlisle, PA: The Banner of Truth Trust, reprint edition 1997).

Chapter 12

Keep Studying
Ligon Duncan

Dear Timothy,

I've been meaning to write you for some time now. I trust that you and your dear Mary are well. News has come to me that you are expecting again. This delights my heart, because the Lord is bringing another child into this world under the charge and care of two wonderful Christian parents. May this little one come to know, love and profess the Lord early and walk with Him always.

Timothy, I have also heard reports of your ministry and God's hand of blessing on it. This is an answer to prayer, and we thank the Lord for His prospering of your labors. One of my petitions for you was that the Lord would grant that your people would esteem and embrace your ministry. In His mercy, He has heard and answered.

Please know that there is a Presbyterian minister (and his congregation) interceding for you and rejoicing that God has placed a faithful, young, Bible-believing, gospel-preaching, Baptist minister, who delights in God's sovereign grace and loves His people, in a congregation of believers to be their shepherd.

Now Timothy, I'm writing with an agenda today. I've been wanting to speak with you about this for some time now, but perhaps writing it down will force me to organize my thoughts. I want to exhort you regarding your personal study. You were always a good student at school and in seminary, and your preaching bears all the marks of a man who is devoted to study. Even so, the pressures of the pastorate will challenge this commitment and so I want to urge you to keep studying.

The Importance of Study

Very frankly, Timothy, most Protestant pastors don't read or study very much these days, and most churches don't encourage them to do so. Church members and even officers sometimes have a hard time appreciating how much time a good message from God's Word takes to develop, and furthermore don't see the importance of the pastor studying anything else other than for preaching and devotions. There is a strong dose of anti-intellectualism in our circles and it doesn't encourage a man to do the hard work of developing the mind and expanding his knowledge.

But precisely because our people are bathed in trivial information in this day and age, they need a shepherd with real knowledge, much discernment and a nose for truth. This knowledge must be acquired and those qualities cultivated, and both require that you become a permanent student. This call to study is, of course, entirely biblical.

The Bible emphasizes the importance of pursuit of sound learning for the wise in general, and for pastors in particular. Proverbs 15:14 says that "The mind of the intelligent seeks knowledge, but the mouth of fools feeds on folly." Proverbs 18:15 reiterates the principle when it says "The mind of the prudent acquires knowledge, and the ear of the wise seeks knowledge." Proverbs 24:5: "A wise man is strong, and a man of knowledge increases power," reminds us of the old dictum "knowledge is power." I don't need to tell you that the wisdom literature of the Bible is replete with calls to the believer to pursue knowledge. But the Bible says more than this. It emphasizes that ministers need to pursue study of the truth.

Ezra 7:10 describes this great Old Testament leader in this way: "Ezra had set his heart to study the law of the LORD and to practice *it*, and to teach *His* statutes and ordinances in Israel." Hosea laments the lack of spiritual leaders like Ezra when it says "My people are destroyed for lack of knowledge. Because you have rejected knowledge, I also will reject you from being My priest. Since you have forgotten the law of your God, I also will forget your children" (4:6). The same aspiration and complaint can be found in the last book of the Old Testament: "For the lips of a priest should preserve knowledge, and men should seek instruction from his mouth; for he is the messenger of the LORD of hosts" (Malachi 2:7).

But it is in the Pastoral Epistles that we find some of the most direct words of instruction and exhortation regarding ministerial study. Paul can say to his Timothy, "Be diligent to present yourself approved to God as a workman who does not need to be ashamed, accurately handling the word of truth" (2 Timothy 2:15). Here we have an apostolic directive for a young minister to study with the equivalent exertion and effort of a tireless day-laborer. The true minister is a workman (Paul really likes this metaphor!). He works hard at his task. The true minister is to work hard at study so as to know and preach the truth rightly.

Furthermore, Paul gives Timothy a sterling example of studiousness from his own practice and priorities. Think of his astonishing request in 2 Timothy 4:13 where he asks, "When you come bring the cloak which I left at Troas with Carpus, and the books, especially the parchments." Now think of it. Paul is only months away from death. He has written the bulk of the letters of the New Testament. He has a lifetime of ministry behind him. And what does he want to do? Study! Winter is approaching and so Paul asks for his cloak, but more importantly he asks for books and parchments. Though almost at the end of his course, Paul aims to keep learning and growing by spiritual reading.

Nobody has ever uttered a more poignant pastoral meditation on this little verse than C. H. Spurgeon:

> How rebuked are they by the apostle! He is inspired, and yet he wants books! He has been preaching at least for thirty years, and yet he wants books! He had seen the Lord, and yet he wants books! He had had a wider experience than most men, and yet he wants books! He had been caught up into the third heaven, and had heard things which it was unlawful for a man to utter, yet he wants books! He had written the major part of the New Testament, and yet he wants books! The apostle says to Timothy and so he says to every preacher, "GIVE THYSELF UNTO READING."

The man who never reads will never be read; he who never quotes will never be quoted. He who will not use the thoughts of other men's brains, proves that he has no brains of his own. Brethren, what is true of ministers is true of all our people. YOU need to read. Renounce as much as you will all light literature, but study as much as possible sound theological works, especially the Puritanic writers, and expositions of the Bible. We are quite persuaded that the best way for you to be spending your leisure, is to be either reading or praying. You may get much instruction from books which afterwards you may use as a true weapon in your Lord and Master's service. Paul cries, "Bring the books"—join in the cry.

Paul herein is a picture of industry. He is in prison; he cannot preach: WHAT will he do? As he cannot preach, he will read. As we read of the fishermen of old and their boats. The fishermen were gone out of them. What were they doing? Mending their nets. So if providence has laid you upon a sick bed, and you cannot teach your class—if you cannot be working for God in public, mend your nets by reading. If one occupation is taken from you, take another, and let the books of the apostle read you a lesson of industry.[1]

Paul was a life-long learner, and you should be too, my Timothy. As my PhD supervisor once said to me, with an impish grin and a twinkle in his eye, "time not spent reading, is wasted time—well almost!"

---

[1] C. H. Spurgeon, Sermon #542: "PAUL—His Cloak And His Books" in *Metropolitan Tabernacle Pulpit*, vol. 9 (London, England: Passmore & Alabaster, 1882), 668–669.

What to Study

Now what to study is of vital importance in a day when so much of the literature peddled on the Christian market is drivel. So you need to purpose to read wisely. Life is too short to waste on insubstantial reading. Naturally, you are going to be reading Bible commentaries in preparation for preaching, but you need to plan to read more than just commentaries. The following kinds of books ought to be a regular part of your diet. The emphasis here is on biblical piety, the doctrines of grace, a biblical view of church and ministry, and the challenge to consecrate the whole heart (not just the mind) to ministerial study: Sam Waldron's *A Modern Exposition of the 1689 Baptist Confession of Faith*[2]; B. B. Warfield, *The Religious Life of Theological Students*,[3] which continues to be relevant for ministers; J. I. Packer, *Knowing God*,[4] a devotional classic that ought to be plundered often; Richard Baxter, *The Reformed Pastor*,[5] foundational for thinking about pastoral care; John Bunyan, *Pilgrim's Progress*,[6] no intelligent Protestant minister should have not read this book; William

---

[2] Sam Waldron, *A Modern Exposition of the 1689 Baptist Confession of Faith* (Darlington, England: Evangelical Press, 1989).

[3] Benjamin B. Warfield, *The Religious Life of Theological Students* (reprint, Phillipsburg, NJ: P&R, 2001).

[4] J. I. Packer, *Knowing God* (Downers Grove, IL: InterVarsity Press, 1973).

[5] Richard Baxter, *The Reformed Pastor*, abridged (1862, reprint, Edinburgh: The Banner of Truth Trust, 1974).

[6] John Bunyan, *The Pilgrim's Progress* (reprint, Edinburgh: The Banner of Truth Trust, 1977).

Hendriksen, *Survey of the Bible*,[7] a gem that will greatly aid your outlining, summarizing, organizing and memorizing; J. I. Packer, *A Quest for Godliness*,[8] a brilliant set of essays on the Puritan vision of the Christian life; John Murray, *Redemption Accomplished and Applied*,[9] the classic popular treatment of the *ordo salutis*; J. Gresham Machen, *Christianity and Liberalism*,[10] a must for all modern evangelicals; J. C. Ryle, *Holiness*,[11] one of the great modern devotional books; and David F. Wells, *No Place for Truth*,[12] a disturbing but important tome.

In other words, you want to be reading soul-fattening books—works that will increase your knowledge, your love for the Lord and your confidence in Scripture. You will, of course, from time to time read things that are not soul-fattening, but you must never allow this best kind of book to be entirely absent from your normal plan of reading. Additionally, you will want to listen to CDs/tapes (Mark Dever's Center for Church Reform interviews are superb, Ken Myers' Mars Hill Tape Library is stimulating and informative, our own "First Things" interviews available through

---

[7] William Hendriksen, *Survey of the Bible* (reprint, Darlington, England: Evangelical Press, 1995).

[8] J. I. Packer, *A Quest for Godliness: The Puritan Vision of the Christian Life* (Wheaton, IL: Crossway Books, 1990).

[9] John Murray, *Redemption Accomplished and Applied* (Grand Rapids, MI: Eerdmans, 1955).

[10] J. Gresham Machen, *Christianity and Liberalism* (Grand Rapids, MI: Eerdmans, 1923).

[11] J. C. Ryle, *Holiness* (reprint, Darlington, England: Evangelical Press, 1979).

[12] David F. Wells, *No Place for Truth* (Grand Rapids, MI: Eerdmans, 1993).

LifeAudio.com may be helpful. Get "The Teaching Company" catalog and listen to the best undergraduate lecturers from across the country on important subject areas). You can listen while you take your daily exercise, or as you are driving to the church or on the way home or heading out on a visit. Go to conferences—not "how to" conferences, but conferences that feed your soul or make you think—Banner of Truth conferences, Founders Conferences, the Evangelical Theological Society and such. Keep up with current events (glance at the *New York Times*, read *World* magazine and *Atlantic Monthly*, then visit the *Arts and Letters Daily* website, or *Ars Disputandi* or the *Access Research Network*—all of which can be found easily with a Google search on the Internet) and think hard about the culture (Phil Ryken charts a helpful course for this in *This Is My Father's World*).[13]

But above all, determine to read and master the great books of your Reformation heritage. Luther's *Bondage of the Will*, Calvin's *Institutes of the Christian Religion*, Turretin's *Institutes of Elenctic Theology*, Ames' *Marrow of Theology*, Heppe's *Reformed Dogmatics* as well as works by John Bunyan, John Owen, John Gill, John Dagg, C. H. Spurgeon and Carl Henry. Read the classics and read primary sources. You may well have come across C. S. Lewis's famous comments on this in his "On the Reading on Old Books" (which was originally composed as an introduction to Athanasius' *On the Incarnation*). His counsel is wise. Lewis says:

---

[13] Phil Ryken, *This Is My Father's World* (Phillipsburg, NJ: P&R, 2002).

There is a strange idea abroad that in every subject the ancient books should be read only by the professionals, and that the amateur should content himself with the modern books. Thus I have found as a tutor in English Literature that if the average student wants to find out something about Platonism, the very last thing he thinks of doing is to take a translation of Plato off the library shelf and read the Symposium. He would rather read some dreary modern book ten times as long, all about "isms" and influences and only once in twelve pages telling him what Plato actually said. The error is rather an amiable one, for it springs from humility. The student is half afraid to meet one of the great philosophers face to face. He feels himself inadequate and thinks he will not understand him. But if he only knew, the great man, just because of his greatness, is much more intelligible than his modern commentator. The simplest student will be able to understand, if not all, yet a very great deal of what Plato said; but hardly anyone can understand some modern books on Platonism. It has always therefore been one of my main endeavours as a teacher to persuade the young that firsthand knowledge is not only more worth acquiring than secondhand knowledge, but is usually much easier and more delightful to acquire.

This mistaken preference for the modern books and this shyness of the old ones is nowhere more rampant than in theology. Wherever you find a little study circle of Christian laity you can be almost certain that they are studying not St. Luke or St. Paul or St. Augustine or Thomas Aquinas or Hooker or Butler, but M. Berdyaev or M. Maritain or M. Niebuhr or Miss Sayers or even myself.

Now this seems to me topsy-turvy. Naturally, since I myself am a writer, I do not wish the ordinary reader to read no modern books. But if he must read only the new or only the old, I would advise him to read the old. And I would give him this advice precisely because he is an amateur and therefore much less protected than the expert against the dangers of an exclusive contemporary diet. A new book is still on its trial and the amateur is not in a position to judge it. It has to be tested against the great body of Christian thought down the ages, and all its hidden implications (often unsuspected by the author himself) have to be brought to light. Often it cannot be fully understood without the knowledge of a good many other modern books. If you join at eleven o'clock a conversation which began at eight you will often not see the real bearing of what is said. Remarks which seem to you very ordinary will produce laughter or irritation and you will not see why—the reason, of course, being that the earlier stages of the conversation have given them a special point. In the same way sentences in a modern book which look quite ordinary may be directed *at* some other book; in this way you may be led to accept what you would have indignantly rejected if you knew its real significance. The only safety is to have a standard of plain, central Christianity ("mere Christianity" as Baxter called it) which puts the controversies of the moment in their proper perspective. Such a standard can be acquired only from the old books. It is a good rule, after reading a new book, never to allow yourself another new one till you have read an old one in between. If that is too much for you, you should at least read one old one to every three new ones.

Every age has its own outlook. It is specially good at seeing certain truths and specially liable to make certain mistakes. We all, therefore, need the books that will correct the characteristic mistakes of our own period. And that means the old books. All contemporary writers share to some extent the contemporary outlook—even those, like myself, who seem most opposed to it. Nothing strikes me more when I read the controversies of past ages than the fact that both sides were usually assuming without question a good deal which we should now absolutely deny. They thought that they were as completely opposed as two sides could be, but in fact they were all the time secretly united—united with each other and against earlier and later ages—by a great mass of common assumptions. We may be sure that the characteristic blindness of the twentieth century—the blindness about which posterity will ask, "But how could they have thought that?"—lies where we have never suspected it, and concerns something about which there is untroubled agreement between Hitler and President Roosevelt or between Mr. H. G. Wells and Karl Barth. None of us can fully escape this blindness, but we shall certainly increase it, and weaken our guard against it, if we read only modern books. Where they are true they will give us truths which we half knew already. Where they are false they will aggravate the error with which we are already dangerously ill. The only palliative is to keep the clean sea breeze of the centuries blowing through our minds, and this can be done only by reading old books. Not, of course, that there is any magic about the past. People were no cleverer then than they are now; they made as many mistakes as we. But not the same mistakes. They will not flatter us in the errors we are already committing; and their own errors, being now open and palpable, will not endanger us. Two heads are better than one, not because either is infallible, but because they are unlikely to go wrong in the same direction. To be sure, the books of the future would be just as good a corrective as the books of the past, but unfortunately we cannot get at them.[14]

So, one way you can avoid being caught up in the banalities, trivialities and fads of current "learning" is to interact with the best thinkers of the past. Against the backdrop of my call to reading though, remember the wise counsel of Thomas Brooks: "Christ, the Scripture, your own hearts, and Satan's devices, are the four prime things that should be first and most studied and searched. If any cast off the study of these, they cannot be safe here, or happy hereafter. It is my work as a Christian, but much more as I am a Watchman, to do my best to discover the fullness of Christ, the emptiness of the creature, and the snares of the great deceiver."

How You Study

My comments so far obviously indicate that reading will be a major aspect of your ongoing study as a minister. That is wholly appropriate, especially in light of our evangelical doctrine of revelation: God communicates to us in propositions. But let me add just a little to this. There are five

---

[14] C.S. Lewis, *God in the Dock* (reprint, Grand Rapids, MI: William B. Eerdmans Publishing, 1994), 200–207.

main ways in which your ongoing study will be aided: reading, reflection, writing, teaching and living. I'll say no more here about reading, my emphasis on it is already apparent. On the subject of reflection, I will only say that you need to go to the Puritans to learn their practice of Christian reflection, or meditation, in order to gain the most from your reading. Regarding writing, let me simply say that there is no discipline more suited to force the mind to organize and communicate the truth than that of writing. If you can't communicate a truth, you don't understand it. If you can't communicate it in more than one way, you don't understand it. If you can't communicate it clearly you don't understand it. Writing helps in all these areas. A perfect forum to practice this skill is in your church publications. In regard to teaching, it—like writing—is a tremendous boon to self-education. When you have venues to try your hand at it, take them. I'm not just talking about your regular preaching (which will naturally contain a component of teaching in it) or simply speaking of Sunday School opportunities. I'm talking about settings that push you to understand and convey truth at a higher level—lectures before undergraduates, seminary classes, public addresses and the like. When you have those opportunities, take them.

But the thing I want to emphasize here, precisely because it is so often overlooked among those who are devoted to study, is the importance of living to learning. By that I mean on the one hand that one ought to be constantly asking how one's learning is playing out in one's life. Because of my learning am I loving God more, loving Scripture more, more devoted to Christ, more committed to kingdom ministry, more Christlike, a better Christian husband and father, more loving of my neighbor, more just, merciful and humble and growing in grace? Jesus regularly emphasized in His teaching that our doing shows what we really love and believe. Hence our attitudes, actions and priorities in living reveal the secrets of the heart. If your learning is not helping you in your living and pastoring according to biblical standards and emphases, then it is learning gone bad.

By the importance of living to learning, on the other hand, I mean that it is the school of Christian experience under the hand of providence that is the testing ground of all true learning. Especially God's dark providences—suffering, trials, tests, disappointments, "losses and crosses," as the Puritans called them—reveal the extent of our learning. Benjamin Disraeli once said, "Seeing much, suffering much, and studying much, are the three pillars of learning." He was simply echoing a dictum that can be found from Luther all the way back to the Bible that "Prayer, meditation and temptation [meaning trials and testings] make the Christian." Indeed, Luther put it more provocatively than this, when he said that a preacher is not made by reading books, but by "living and dying and being damned." In other words, God makes preachers in the crucible. Never forget that. God makes a minister of the gospel by breaking his heart. Isn't that one thing that Jesus meant when He beckoned us to take up our cross and follow Him?

When You Study

Now, if we can return to a relatively mundane subject, having just penetrated some fairly sober regions, when your study is liable to be a challenge. Today's minister, by definition, is something of a jack-of-all-trades. He is often viewed as the chief administrative officer, the chief executive officer, the staff hand-holder, the chief visitor, the head preacher/teacher/counselor, the public relations liaison, the key denominational representative of the local congregation and more. It is flatly impossible to do a good job at all of this. When one tries to do so, study usually gets squeezed out by the tyranny of the urgent. So, you are going to have to plan carefully when to study and then how to protect that time.

The three main challenges will be how to deal with your officers, members and family in regard to the timing and protection of your study. You will need to devote some time to cultivating in your officers a sense of the prime importance of your study time (if they do not already appreciate its significance). I am blessed with officers who fully appreciate how important it is for me to have time to study, but not all ministers are so fortunate. If your officers are unsupportive in this way, or just unaware of the importance of it, start with those most sympathetic to you and begin to explain how you understand your calling and what things are necessary to the accomplishment of it. Compare what they have to do in their workday (including the unglamorous but essential behind-the-scenes work) to what you have to do. Help them appreciate the ways they benefit from your having adequate study time. Then explain and solicit their support for the ways you are going about setting and protecting that time. They need to be your champions with the people on this.

With regard to members, when they call for an appointment and ask to speak with you, I have found only a few very sanctified souls gracious enough to be satisfied by a secretary responding with "he's unavailable right now, he's studying." People naturally think that their crisis of the moment is more important than a dusty old book the pastor is reading. They take offense at being put off for your study time. So, I would suggest that your assistant protect your study time by simply saying "he's unavailable at this time." That way the caller doesn't have the opportunity to personally judge whether his issue outweighs your need to study.

Now family is a different matter. My wife is extremely supportive of my ministry. Especially when it comes to pastoral duties like emergency counseling or hospital visits, she is unfailingly accommodating of my taking the time to do them, no matter how disruptive they are to the family schedule. But she has a harder time when it comes to study. So balancing family time and study can be a challenge for us. You will need to work through this issue so that your wife can become comfortable with the rhythm and amount of your study time and thus support what this means for the family schedule.

Needless to say, study time should not be wasted on e-mail, chat rooms, discussion rings (which usually simply pool ignorance), meandering on the Internet or taken to the neglect of other important pastoral duties. This is a problem with many ministers, especially those who are more introverted and shy away from the "people-responsibilities" of ministry. But I do not see that problem in you, so I pass over it here with a fleeting mention.

Why You Study

You will need to be self-conscious about your personal motivations for study. Many a good man has fallen prey to false motivations and thus has lost the real benefit of ongoing study. For one thing, your ongoing study should not be motivated by the desire to gain a certain status. Many seminaries and institutions of higher learning appeal to pastors to do "advanced" course work that is hardly advanced by any realistic standard because they offer an impressive sounding but vacuous degree title to those who complete the course. Don't fall prey to that. The goal of learning is knowledge, not status.

The British have had a much healthier attitude about academic degree titles than we have here in America (although I think we are finally having a baneful effect upon even them in this area). The great F. F. Bruce, for instance, had the equivalent of an American undergraduate degree (he had a Scottish MA) and yet was rightly recognized as a first order scholar in his field. His lack of a PhD didn't matter. He knew more than a roomful of PhDs. I, personally, don't give a hoot about what title a man has. If he does not possess right, useful knowledge and good judgment, he is of little value to the church as a teacher.

One motivation that ought to impel your study is simply the desire to learn—to learn the truth and to acquire true and useful knowledge. There are very few times when it is okay to be greedy in life; but in learning we ought to be "greedy" to learn, because truth is God's and we ought to want to know it. Furthermore, we ought to be motivated to learn in order to be a help to the church. Not infrequently have I encountered Christian ministers who, by much study, considered themselves very sophisticated and "above" the average churchgoer. Such an attitude is unbecoming in the extreme (and, interestingly, is not often found in those who have truly first-order minds). The minister studies precisely to be a help to the people of God, however humble they may be. We want to learn in order to be serviceable to the church.

Along the same lines, you ought to be motivated to learn in order to be helpful to other ministers and churches. Become an expert at something so that you can help fellow ministers grappling with a specialized area of knowledge that they don't know so well as you. Maybe you'll become very familiar with the best academic literature about Islam, not only so that you can teach your people and bear witness yourself, but also to help other ministers who don't know as much about what is now the chief organized religious rival to global Christianity. Or maybe you'll become an expert in the Puritans, not only so that you can be edified through that excellent material, but also so that you can disabuse others of the considerable and negative mythology which surrounds this whole field of study. You get my point. Be motivated to learn in order that your learning may bless the larger church.

There are most certainly more motivations to study than these. But take these as suggestive.

What You Aim At in Studying

Now as to your goals in study, obviously among them will be God's glory, your personal growth in grace, the edification of others and the increase of your own capacities to teach and preach. In this connection it would be good to remember the three famous *dicta* of Herman Witsius (the famous seventeenth-century Dutch theologian and pastor) who said, "No one teaches well unless he has first learned well," "No one learns well unless he learns in order to teach" and "Both learning and teaching are vain and unprofitable, unless accompanied by practice." These words are well worth pondering, as is Witsius little classic *On the Character of a True Theologian* (Greenville, SC: Reformed Academic Press, 1994).[15]

Additionally, let me mention these as proper goals for your study. One appropriate goal in study is to acquire true and useful information or knowledge. Primarily, of course, you will be concerned to get knowledge that consists of the knowledge of God revealed in the Scriptures. But you will also properly want knowledge of God's creation, including ourselves, our times, the world and our flock. The major source of this knowledge will of course be special revelation, but our study will of necessity include basic insights from general revelation.

---

[15] Herman Witsius, *On the Character of a True Theologian* (reprint, Greenville, SC: Reformed Academic Press, 1994).

A second aim of your study will be the acquisition of the ability to employ the right use of that knowledge, which you gain in study. The sort of knowledge of God that can be gained by book study is not an end in itself but a means to an end. That end is the glory of God and union with Him, from which flows the benefit of communion with Him. We learn about God in order that we might know Him, that is, enter into relationship or fellowship with Him. To repeat this idea another way—saving knowledge is covenant knowledge—the knowledge of communion and fellowship with the living God. Propositional knowledge is an essential element of that saving knowledge and hence imperative in all Christians' spiritual walks. But it is neither the only element of saving knowledge, nor the end/goal of our study. May God grant you not only a firm grasp of saving truth but also a right understanding and employment of its proper uses.

A third goal of your study will be the development of your analytical skills. You need to develop your abilities of discernment to the point that you are capable of synthesizing knowledge, able to engage in critical thought and possessed of good judgment. For you will be a walking reference point for your flock. Moreover, every sermon or lesson that you prepare will require you to be discerning and analytical of the text (in the original and translation), the tools (dictionaries, commentaries, lexicons and other literature), the context (when and where the lesson is being taught, what are the burning trends, issues, sins and worries of the day) and the congregation (where they are spiritually, what they need, etc.).

A fourth aim of study ought to be an ongoing refreshment of our desire to learn, obey, worship and pastor. We should be thirsty for knowledge of the Word of God and of His world (including His people and their context). Not all of us will be equally interested in the same things, but each of us should be hungry for commanding knowledge of something. We must also be hungry to put this knowledge to work in the service of obedience. True, some more "practically" oriented folk want to skip the thinking and get to the doing, but that kind of zeal without knowledge is prideful and potentially destructive. We ought to burn in our hearts to worship and most of all to pastor. But all these desires need stoking. Study can help add fuel to the fires of our devotion.

A fifth aspect of our aim in learning ought to be to enable our capacity for self-criticism and to increase our ability to exercise appropriate repentance. It is a sober work to which we are called and the dangers to our souls (and those of our congregations) are many, should we be careless in our vocation. We are called to be stewards of the mysteries of God, and one day we will give an account of our conduct to the Almighty. Spiritual self-examination and self-criticism (evidences of a repentant spirit) and openness to rebuke from others are absolutely essential if we are to avoid pitfalls in the Christian ministry.

Finally, we ought to aim in our study for the cultivation of a warm, full, natural, practical piety or godliness. This piety should be characterized by reverence to God, love of neighbor, seriousness of purpose in one's calling and determination to holiness. My desire is that you will be (to borrow an apt summarization from David Wells) "God-centered in your thoughts, God-fearing in your heart, and God-honoring in your life."

What You Do With Your Study

True gospel study ought to be turned into prayer. When we study something that causes us to realize the greatness of God and His saving work, it ought to move us to adoration, thanksgiving and praise. We should not resist the impulse of prayer in our study. When we read something that convicts us, we ought to be impelled to confession of sin in prayer. When we read something that reminds us of the plight of others, we ought to be moved to intercession. When we read something soul-killing or potentially harmful to the spiritual well-being of others, we ought to beg God to squelch the poison, to spare unwary sheep, to rebuke the false shepherd, to protect faithful pastors and to spare our own souls from the contagion of falsehood.

All our study ought to be turned into prayer and made to serve the interests of sanctification—ours and that of others. This just reminds us again of the importance of an experiential knowledge of God to our theological learning. Without a true, saving, covenantal knowledge of God, study is bound to go wrong on us. This alone urges upon us the importance of prayer and the Holy Spirit in our study. In prayer we show our utter dependence on God for the attainment of true knowledge. And only by the Teacher, the Holy Spirit, do we get true knowledge and the true knowledge of God. Both of these realities must permeate our whole approach to study. This is one reason for the profound statement of Proverbs 1:7, "The fear of the LORD is the beginning of knowledge."

Timothy, may God raise you up as a "mighty man" in our day, committed to the authority of Scripture, firmly persuaded of its great doctrines, masterful in your grasp of gospel truth and on fire to proclaim it, characterized by warm-hearted godliness and steady holiness, prayerful and careful in your pastoral duties and diligent to keep studying to show yourself approved, that the church would be built up, her walls enlarged and Christ glorified.

Your friend,
Ligon Duncan

PS—Timothy, I've already mentioned a number of books to you in this overly long letter, but let me suggest just a few that would be especially helpful in your thinking through the issue of study.

1. *On the Character of a True Theologian* by Herman Witsius (reprint, Greenville, SC: Reformed Academic Press, 1994). I've already mentioned this little classic but it is superb.
2. *The Religious Life of Theological Students* by B.B. Warfield (reprint, Phillipsburg, NJ: P&R, 2001). Written for seminarians but with lifelong applications for pastors.
3. *An Introduction to Theological Studies* by William Cunningham (reprint, Greenville, SC: Reformed

Academic Press, 1994). A classic that alerts us to hidden traps in study and guides us toward more fruitful learning. Cunningham, among other things, (1) reminds us of the importance of an experiential knowledge of God to theological work; (2) sets forth the different branches of theological studies, their significance and relation to one another; (3) urges upon us the importance of prayer and the Holy Spirit to the attainment of true knowledge of God; (4) shows us the importance of meditation—considered, prayerful, reflection—to our growth in grace; (5) suggests to us the vital role of Christian experience in our formation for ministry; (6) counsels us on the absolute importance of mastering the biblical languages and being thoroughly familiar with our English Bibles and (7) exhorts us in the necessity of resting from our professional studies on the Lord's Day.

4. *Patterns in History* by David Bebbington (Downer's Grove, IL: Inter-Varsity Press, 1990). Will introduce you to the practice of historiography, important for your ongoing study but rarely broached in seminary.

5. *The Study of Theology* by Richard Muller (Grand Rapids, MI: Zondervan, 1991). Something of a modern classic—will be a boon to your continued reflections in the arena of Systematics.

Chapter 13

Learn from the Puritans I
Joel Beeke

Dear Timothy,

You asked me in your last letter, "As you look back over twenty-five years of ministry, what was the most helpful, optional spiritual discipline that you maintained for your own spiritual life and for your preaching and pastoral ministry?" I answer without hesitation: maintaining a steady diet of Puritan literature.

Reading Puritan literature has been a major boon for me spiritually for thirty-five years. When the Holy Spirit began to convict me of the seriousness of sin and the spirituality of the law at age fourteen, I searched the Scriptures and devoured Puritan literature from my father's bookcase. My mother would call upstairs each evening at 11:00 P.M., "Lights out!" After my parents' lights went out, I would turn mine back on and read until 12:30 or 1:00 A.M. I read all the Puritan titles published by Banner of Truth Trust with relish, started a church library, then founded a non-profit organization called Bible Truth Books and later, as a minister, Reformation Heritage Books. I have spent thousands of hours with Puritan writers in my life and sold tens of thousands of Puritan books over the spread of the last thirty-five years. Why?

First, let me tell you briefly what I mean by "the Puritans," then show you how reading the Puritans can be so profitable for you. Simply put, my use of the word *Puritan* includes not only those people who were ejected from the Church of England by the Act of Uniformity in 1662, but also those in Britain and North America who, for several generations after the Reformation, worked to reform and purify the church and to lead people toward biblical, godly living consistent with the Reformed doctrines of grace.[1]

---

[1] Richard Mitchell Hawkes, "The Logic of Assurance in English Puritan Theology," *Westminster Theological Journal* 52 (1990): 247. For the difficulties in, and attempts at, defining Puritanism, see Ralph Bronkema, *The Essence of Puritanism* (Goes: Oosterbaan and LeCointre, 1929); Leonard J. Trinterud, "The Origins of Puritanism," *Church History* 20 (1951):37–57; Jerald C. Brauer, "Reflections on the Nature of English Puritanism," *Church History* 23 (1954):98–109; Basil Hall, "Puritanism: The Problem of Definition," in G. J. Cumming, ed., *Studies in Church History*, vol. 2 (London: Nelson, 1965), 283–96; Charles H. George, "Puritanism as History and Historiography," *Past and Present* 41 (1968):77–104; William Lamont, "Puritanism as History and Historiography: Some Further Thoughts," *Past and Present* 42 (1969):133–46; Richard Greaves, "The Nature of the Puritan Tradition," in R. Buick Knox, ed., *Reformation, Conformity and Dissent: Essays in Honour of Geoffrey Nuttall* (London: Epworth Press, 1977), 255–73; D.M. Lloyd-Jones, "Puritanism and Its Origins," *The Puritans: Their Origins and Successors* (Edinburgh: Banner of Truth Trust, 1987), 237–59; James I. Packer, "Why We Need the Puritans," in *A Quest for Godliness: The Puritan Vision of the Christian Life* (Wheaton, IL: Crossway Books, 1990), 21–36; Joel R. Beeke, *The Quest for Full Assurance: The Legacy of Calvin and His Successors* (Edinburgh: Banner of Truth Trust, 1999), 82ff.

Puritanism grew out of at least three needs: (1) the need for biblical preaching and the teaching of sound, Reformed doctrine; (2) the need for biblical, personal piety that stresses the work of the Holy Spirit in the faith and life of the believer and (3) the need for a restoration of biblical simplicity in liturgy, vestments and church government, so that a well-ordered church life would promote the worship of the triune God as prescribed in His Word.[2] Doctrinally, Puritanism was a kind of broad and vigorous Calvinism; experientially, it was a warm and contagious kind of Christianity; evangelistically, it was tender as well as aggressive.[3] J. I. Packer wrote, "Puritanism was, at its heart, a movement of spiritual revival."[4]

I want to write two letters to you, Timothy, about how, with the Spirit's blessing, the Puritans can profit you. This first letter will focus on how they can profit you personally, and the second, on how they can profit you in your preaching and teaching.[5]

---

[2] Peter Lewis, *The Genius of Puritanism* (Hayward Heath, Sussex: Carey, 1975), 11ff.
[3] Sidney H. Rooy, *The Theology of Missions in the Puritan Tradition: A Study of Representative Puritans: Richard Sibbes, Richard Baxter, John Eliot, Cotton Mather, and Jonathan Edwards* (Grand Rapids, MI: Eerdmans, 1965), 310–28.
[4] Cf. Packer's introduction in Leland Ryken, *Worldly Saints: The Puritans As They Really Were* (Grand Rapids, MI: Zondervan, 1990), xv.
[5] Some of my advice is being adapted from my *Puritan Evangelism: A Biblical Approach* (Grand Rapids, MI: Reformation Heritage Books, 1999).

SHAPE YOUR LIFE BY SCRIPTURE

More than any other group of writers in church history, the Puritans show us how to shape our entire lives and ministries by the Holy Scriptures.

The Puritans were people of the living Book. They loved, lived and breathed Scripture, relishing the power of the Spirit that accompanied the Word.[6] They regarded the sixty-six books of Scripture as the library of the Holy Spirit that was graciously bequeathed to them. They viewed Scripture to be God speaking to them as a father speaks to his children. They saw the Word as truth they could trust in and rest upon for all eternity. They saw it as Spirit-empowered to renew their minds and transform their lives.

The Puritans searched, heard and sang the Word with delight and encouraged others to do the same. Puritan Richard Greenham suggested eight ways to read Scripture: with diligence, wisdom, preparation, meditation, conference, faith, practice and prayer.[7] Thomas Watson provided numerous guidelines on how to listen to the Word. Come to the Word with a holy appetite and a teachable heart. Sit

---

[6] See Joel R. Beeke and Ray B. Lanning, "The Transforming Power of Scripture," in *Sola Scriptura: The Protestant Position of the Bible*, ed. Don Kistler (Morgan, PA: Soli Deo Gloria, 1995), 221–76.

[7] "A Profitable Treatise, Containing a Direction for the reading and understanding of the holy Scriptures," in H[enry] H[olland], ed., *The Works of the Reverend and Faithfvll Servant of Iesvs Christ, M. Richard Greenham* (1599; reprint New York: Da Capo Press, 1973), 389–97. Cf. Thomas Watson, "How We May Read the Scriptures with Most Spiritual Profit," in *Heaven Taken by Storm: Showing the Holy Violence a Christian Is to Put Forth in the Pursuit After Glory*, ed. Joel R. Beeke (1669; reprint, Pittsburgh, PA: Soli Deo Gloria, 1992), 113–129.

under the Word attentively, receive it with meekness and mingle it with faith. Then retain the Word, pray over it, practice it and speak to others about it.[8] "Dreadful is their case who go loaded with sermons to hell," Watson warned. By contrast, those who respond to Scripture as a "love letter sent to you from God" will experience its warming, transforming power.[9]

"Feed upon the Word," the Puritan preacher John Cotton exhorted his congregation.[10] The preface to the Geneva Bible contains similar advice, saying the Bible is "the light to our paths, the key of the kingdom of heaven, our comfort in affliction, our shield and sword against Satan, the school of all wisdom, the glass wherein we behold God's face, the testimony of his favor, and the only food and nourishment of our souls."[11]

The Puritans sounded a clarion call to become intensely Word-centered in faith and practice. Richard Baxter's *Christian Directory* shows how the Puritans regarded the Bible as a trustworthy guide for all of life. Every case of conscience was subjected to Scripture's directives. Henry Smith preached to his congregation, "We should set the Word of God always before us like a rule, and believe nothing but that which it teacheth, love nothing but that which it

---

[8] Ibid., 16–18, and Thomas Watson, *A Body of Divinity* (1692; reprint, London: Banner of Truth Trust), 377–79.
[9] Ibid., 379. "There is not a sermon which is heard, but it sets us nearer heaven or hell" (John Preston, *A Pattern of Wholesome Words*, quoted in Christopher Hill, *Society and Puritanism in Pre-Revolutionary England*, 2nd ed. (New York: Schocken, 1967), 46.
[10] *Christ the Fountain of Life* (London: Carden, 1648), 14.
[11] *Geneva Bible* (1599; reprint Ozark, MO: L.L. Brown, 1990), 3.

prescribeth, hate nothing but that which it forbiddeth, do nothing but that which it commandeth."[12] Perhaps John Flavel said it best, "The Scriptures teach us the best way of living, the noblest way of suffering, and the most comfortable way of dying."[13]

Pray Without Ceasing

The Puritans show us the need to be praying men of God. They were truly "men of the closet." In their closets—their special, private place dedicated to prayer, be it in the bedroom, the attic or the open field—they would lift up their voices and cry aloud to the God of heaven for divine benediction upon themselves and their ministries, their families, churches and nations.

Unlike many modern ministers, the quality of the spiritual life of Puritan ministers seems to have been uniformly high.[14] I believe that the Puritans were great preachers first and foremost because they were also great petitioners who wrestled with God for divine blessing upon their preaching. Richard Baxter said, "Prayer must carry on our work as well as preaching; he preacheth not heartily to his people,

---

[12] "Food for New-Born Babes," in *The Works of Henry Smith*, ed. Thomas Smith (Edinburgh: James Nichol, 1866), 1:494.

[13] Quoted in I.D.E. Thomas, *The Golden Treasury of Puritan Quotations* (Chicago, IL: Moody Press, 1975), 33.

[14] See Benjamin Brook, *The Lives of the Puritans*, 3 vols. (1813; reprint, Pittsburgh, PA: Soli Deo Gloria, 1994); William Barker, *Puritan Profiles* (Fearn, Ross-shire: Christian Focus, 1996).

that prayeth not earnestly for them. If we prevail not with God to give them faith and repentance, we shall never prevail with them to believe and repent."[15] And Robert Traill wrote, "Some ministers of meaner gifts and parts are more successful than some that are far above them in abilities; not because they preach better, so much as because they pray more. Many good sermons are lost for lack of much prayer in study."[16]

Timothy, your private prayers must season your pulpit messages. Take to heart Richard Sibbes's admonition: "A minister of Christ is often in the highest honor with men for the performance of one half of his work [the public ministry], while God is regarding him with displeasure for the neglect of the other half [prayer]" (cf. Acts 6:4). Like the Puritans, jealously guard your personal devotional time. Set your priorities on spiritual, eternal realities. Be persuaded that as soon as you cease to watch and pray, you court spiritual disaster. Be painfully aware, as John Flavel said, "that a man may be *objectively* a *spiritual [man]*, and all the while *subjectively* a *carnal* man."[17] Believe, as John Owen noted, that "no man preacheth that sermon well that doth not first preach it to his own heart . . . . If the word do not dwell with power *in* us, it will not pass with power *from* us."[18]

---

[15] Baxter, *The Reformed Pastor*, 123.
[16] *The Works of the late Reverend Robert Traill* (1810; reprint, Edinburgh: Banner of Truth Trust, 1975), 1:246.
[17] *The Works of John Flavel* (1820; reprint, London: Banner of Truth Trust, 1968), 5:568.
[18] *Works of John Owen*, 9:455, 16:76.

Learn How to Meditate

Perhaps nowhere are the Puritans so helpful as in offering guidelines for the process of spiritual, biblical meditation. They said to begin by asking the Holy Spirit for assistance. Pray for the power to harness your mind and to focus the eyes of faith on this task. As Edmund Calamy wrote, "I would have you pray unto God to enlighten your understandings, to quicken your devotion, to warm your affections, and so to bless that hour unto you, that by the meditation of holy things you may be made more holy, you may have your lusts more mortified, and your graces more increased, you may be the more mortified to the world, and the vanity of it, and lifted up to Heaven, and the things of Heaven."[19]

Next, the Puritans said to read the Scriptures, then select a verse or doctrine upon which to meditate. Be sure to pick out relatively easy subjects to meditate on at the beginning, they advised. For example, begin with the attributes of God rather than the doctrine of the Trinity. And consider subjects one at a time.

In addition, select subjects that are most applicable to your present circumstances and that will be most beneficial for your soul. For example, if you're spiritually dejected, meditate on Christ's willingness to receive poor sinners and to pardon all who come to Him. If your conscience troubles you, meditate on God's promises to give grace to the peni-

---

[19] Edmond Calamy, *The Art of Divine Meditation* (London: for Tho. Parkhurst, 1680), 172.

tent. If you're financially afflicted, meditate on God's wonderful providences to those in need.[20]

Now, memorize the selected verse(s), or some aspect of the subject, to stimulate meditation, to strengthen faith and to serve as a means of divine guidance.

Next, fix your thoughts on the Scripture or a scriptural subject without prying further than what God has revealed. Use your memory to focus on all that Scripture has to say about your subject. Consider past sermons and other edifying books.

Use "the book of conscience, the book of Scripture, and the book of the creature"[21] as you consider various aspects of your subject: its names, causes, qualities, fruits and effects. Like Mary, ponder these things in your heart. Think of illustrations, similitudes and opposites in your mind to enlighten your understanding and enflame your affections. Then let judgment assess the value of what you are meditating upon.

Here's an example from Calamy. If you would meditate on the subject of sin, "Begin with the description of sin; proceed to the distribution of sin; consider the original and cause of sin, the cursed fruits and effects of sin, the adjuncts and properties of sin in general and of personal sin in particular, the opposite of sin—grace, the metaphors of sin, the titles given to sin, [and] all that the Scripture saith concerning sin."[22]

---

[20] Ibid., 164–68.
[21] *The Works of George Swinnock* (reprint, Edinburgh: Banner of Truth Trust, 1998), 2:417.
[22] Calamy, *The Art of Divine Meditation*, 178–84. Cf. Thomas Gouge, *Christian Directions, shewing How to walk with God All the Day long* (London: R. Ibbitson and M. Wright, 1661), 70–73.

Two warnings are in order. First, as Thomas Manton wrote, "Do not bridle up the free spirit by the rules of method. That which God calleth for is religion, not logic. When Christians confine themselves to such rules and prescriptions, they straiten themselves, and thoughts come from them like water out of a still, not like water out of a fountain."[23] Second, if your mind wanders, rein it in, offer a short prayer for forgiveness, ask for strength to stay focused, read a few appropriate Scriptures again and press on. Remember, reading Scripture, meditation and prayer belong together. As one discipline wanes, turn to another. Persevere; don't surrender to Satan by abandoning your task.

Next, stir up affections, such as love, desire, hope, courage, gratitude, zeal and joy,[24] to glorify God.[25] Hold soliloquies with your own soul. Include complaints against yourself because of your inabilities and shortcomings, and spread before God your spiritual longings. Believe that He will help you.

Paul Baynes, in discussing meditations as a "private means" of grace, compared it first with the power of sight to affect the heart, then with the process of conception and birth: "Now look as after conception, there is a travell to bring forth & a birth in due season: so when the soule by thought hath conceived, presently the affections are [moved], for the affections kindle on a thought, as tinder

---

[23] *The Works of Thomas Manton* (London: James Nisbet & Co., 1874), 17:281.
[24] Richard Baxter, *The Saints' Everlasting Rest* (unabridged reprint, Ross-shire, Scotland: Christian Focus, 1998), 579–90.
[25] Jonathan Edwards, *Religious Affections* (reprint, London: Banner of Truth Trust, 1959), 24.

doth, when a sparke lighteth on it. The affections moved, the will is stirred and inclined."[26]

Now, following the arousal of your memory, judgment and affections, apply your meditations to yourself, to arouse your soul to duty and comfort and to restrain your soul from sin.[27] As William Fenner wrote, "Dive into thy own soul; anticipate and prevent thy own heart. Haunt thy heart with promises, threatenings, mercies, judgments and commandments. Let meditation trace thy heart. Hale thy heart before God."[28]

Examine yourself for your own growth in grace. Reflect on the past and ask, "What have I done?" Look to the future, asking, "What am I resolved to do, by God's grace?"[29] Do not ask such questions legalistically but out of holy excitement and opportunity to grow in Spirit-worked grace. Remember, "Legal work is our work; meditation work is sweet work."[30]

Follow Calamy's advice, "If ever you would get good by the practice of meditation, you must come down to *particulars*; and you must so meditate of Christ, as to apply Christ to thy soul; and so meditate of Heaven, as to apply Heaven to thy soul."[31] Live out your meditation (Joshua 1:8). Let

---

[26] Paul Baynes, *A Help to True Happinesse* (London, 1635).
[27] *The Works of William Bates* (reprint, Harrisonburg, VA: Sprinkle, 1990), 3:145.
[28] William Fenner, *The Use and Benefit of Divine Meditation* (London: for John Stafford, 1657), 16–23.
[29] James Ussher, *A Method for Meditation* (London: for Joseph Nevill, 1656), 39.
[30] *The Works of William Bridge* (reprint, Beaver Falls, PA: Soli Deo Gloria, 1989), 3:153.
[31] Calamy, *The Art of Divine Meditation*, 108. [90] *The Sermons of Thomas Watson* (reprint, Morgan, PA: Soli Deo Gloria, 1995), 269, 271.

meditation and practice, like two sisters, walk hand in hand. Meditation without practice will only increase your condemnation.[32]

Next, turn your applications into resolutions. "Let your resolutions be firm and strong, not [mere] wishes, but resolved purposes or Determinations," wrote Thomas White.[33] Make your resolutions commitments to fight against your temptations to sin. Write down your resolutions. Above all, resolve that you will spend your life "as becomes one that hath been meditating of holy and heavenly things." Commend yourself, your family and everything you own to the hands of God with "sweet resignation."

Conclude with prayer, thanksgiving and Psalm singing. "Meditation is the best beginning of prayer, and prayer is the best conclusion of meditation," wrote George Swinnock. Watson said, "Pray over your meditations. Prayer sanctifies every thing; without prayer they are but unhallowed meditations; prayer fastens meditation upon the soul; prayer is a tying a knot at the end of meditation that it doth not slip; pray that God will keep those holy meditations in your mind for ever, that the savour of them may abide upon your hearts."[34]

Thank the Lord for assistance in meditation or else Richard Greenham warned, "we shall be buffeted in our next meditation."[35]

---

[32] *The Sermons of Thomas Watson* (reprint, Morgan, PA: Soli Deo Gloria, 1995), 269, 271.
[33] *A Method and Instructions for the Art of Divine Meditation* (London: for Tho. Parkhurst, 1672), 53.
[34] Ibid, 269.
[35] *The Works of the Reverend and Faithfvll Servant of Iesvs Christ M. Richard Greenham* (London: Felix Kingston, 1599), 41.

The metrical versions of the Psalms are a great help in meditation. Their metrical form facilitates memorization. As God's Word, they are a proper subject for meditation. As a "complete anatomy of the soul" (Calvin), they afford abundant material and guidance for meditation. As prayers (Psalm 72:20) and as thanksgiving (Psalm 118:1), they are both a proper vehicle for meditation and a fitting way to conclude it. Joseph Hall wrote that he found much comfort in closing his meditations by lifting up his "heart and voice to God in singing some verse or two of David's Psalms—one that answers to our disposition and the matter of our meditation. In this way the heart closes up with much sweetness and contentment."[36] John Lightfoot added, "Singing God's praise is a work of the most meditation of any we perform in public. It keeps the heart longest upon the thing spoken. Prayer and hearing pass quick from one sentence to another; this sticks long upon it."

Finally, don't shift too quickly from meditation to engagement with things of this world, lest, as Thomas Gouge advised, "thereby thou suddenly quench that spiritual heart which hath in that exercise been kindled in thine heart."[37] Remember that one hour spent in such meditation is "worth more than a thousand sermons," Ussher said, "and this is no debasing of the Word, but an honour to it."[38]

---

[36] *The Art of Meditation* (reprint, Jenkintown, PA: Sovereign Grace Publishers, 1972), 26–27.
[37] *Christian Directions, shewing How to walk with God All the Day long*, 70.
[38] Ussher, *A Method for Meditation*, 43.

Handle Trials Christianly

The Puritans show us how to handle trials. Consider the Scottish brothers, Ebenezer and Ralph Erskine. In addition to the religious controversies that dampened their joy in ministry for twenty-five years, they endured much domestic grief. Ebenezer Erskine buried his first wife when she was thirty-nine; his second wife, three years before his own death. He also lost six of fifteen children. Ralph Erskine buried his first wife when she was thirty-two and nine of thirteen children. The three sons who reached maturity all entered the ministry, but one helped to depose his own father.

The Erskines well understood that God has "only one Son without sin but none without affliction," as one Puritan put it. Their diaries, so typical of the Puritans, are filled with Christ-centered submission in the midst of affliction. When his first wife was on her deathbed and he had just buried several children, Ebenezer Erskine wrote:

> I have had the rod of God laying upon my family by the great distress of a dear wife, on whom the Lord hath laid his hand, and on whom his hand doth still lie heavy. But O that I could proclaim the praises of his free grace, which has paid me a new and undeserved visit this day. He has been with me both in secret and public. I found the sweet smells of the Rose of Sharon, and my soul was refreshed with a new sight of him in the excellency of his person as Immanuel, and in the sufficiency of his everlasting righteousness. My sinking hopes are revived by the sight of him. My bonds are loosed, and my bur-

dens of affliction made light, when he appears.... "Here am I, let him do to me as seemeth good unto him." If he call me to go down to the swellings of Jordan, why not, if it be his holy will? Only be with me, Lord, and let thy rod and staff comfort me, and then I shall not fear to go through the valley of trouble, yea, through the valley of the shadow of death.[39]

We can learn from the Puritans that we need affliction to humble us (Deuteronomy 8:2), to teach us what sin is (Zephaniah 1:12) and to bring us to God (Hosea 5:15). "Affliction is the diamond dust that heaven polishes its jewels with," wrote Robert Leighton. Timothy, view God's rod of affliction as His means to write Christ's image more fully upon you so that you may be a partaker of His righteousness and holiness (Hebrews 12:10–11). Let your hardships move you to walk by faith and wean you from the world. As Thomas Watson wrote, "God would have the world hang as a loose tooth which, being easily twitched away, doth not much trouble us." Strive for grace to allow affliction to elevate your soul to heaven and pave your way to glory (2 Corinthians 4:7).

If you are presently undergoing profound trials, learn from the Puritans not to overestimate those trials. Read William Bridge's *A Lifting Up for the Downcast,* Thomas Brooks's *A Mute Christian Under the Rod* and Richard Sibbes's *A Bruised Reed.* Remember that life is short and eternity is forever. You are young, but to you too, the Puritans would

---

[39] Donald Fraser, *The Life and Diary of the Reverend Ebenezer Erskine* (Edinburgh: William Oliphant, 1831), chap. 6.

rightly advise: Think more of your coming crown and your eternal communion with the Triune God, saints and angels than of temporal tribulations. As John Trapp wrote, "He that rides to be crowned need not think much of a rainy day."

You are merely a renter here; a mansion awaits you in glory. Don't despair. The Shepherd's rod is held by a fatherly hand of love, not a punitive hand of judgment. Consider Christ in your afflictions—were not His much more than yours, and was not He wholly innocent? Consider how He perseveres for you, how He prays for you, how He helps you toward the goals He has for you. In the end, He will be glorified through your afflictions. As John Bunyan quaintly said, "God's people are like bells; the harder they are hit, the better they sound."

God will use your trials to make you a better preacher, too, just as He did the Puritans. George Whitefield wrote:

> Ministers never write or preach so well as when under the cross; the Spirit of Christ and of glory then rests upon them. It was this, no doubt, that made the Puritans . . . such burning and shining lights. When cast out by the black Bartholomew-act [the 1662 Act of Uniformity] and driven from their respective charges to preach in barns and fields, in the highways and hedges, they in an especial manner wrote and preached as men having authority. Though dead, by their writings they yet speak; a peculiar unction attends them to this very hour.[40]

---

[40] *Works* (London: for Edward and Charles Dilly, 1771), 4:306–307.

That "peculiar unction" Whitefield refers to is an experimental, Christ-centered unction that derives from learning the art of contentment in the school of affliction. Under affliction, the Puritans experienced rich spiritual contentment and consolations in Christ. So must we, Timothy. Read *The Rare Jewel of Christian Contentment* by Jeremiah Burroughs. He'll teach you how to turn trial into contentment. Then, the next time you're buffeted in the ministry by others, Satan or your own conscience, instead of complaining, carry those buffetings to Christ and ask Him, by His Spirit, to sanctify them so that you may model spiritual contentment for your flock.

Rebuke Pride

The Puritans show us how to handle pride in the ministry. God hates pride (Proverbs 6:16–17). He hates the proud with His heart, curses them with His mouth and punishes them with His hand (Psalm 119:21; Isaiah 2:12, 23:9). Pride was God's first enemy. It was the first sin in paradise and the last we will shed in death. "Pride is the shirt of the soul, put on first and put off last," writes George Swinnock.[41]

As a sin, pride is unique. Most sins turn us away from God, but pride is a direct attack upon God. It lifts our hearts above God and against God, Henry Smith said. Pride seeks to dethrone God and enthrone itself.

The Puritans did not consider themselves immune to this sin. Twenty years after his conversion, Jonathan

---

[41] Thomas, *Puritan Quotations*, 224.

Edwards groaned about the "bottomless, infinite depths of pride" left in his heart.

Pride spoils our work. As Richard Baxter says, "When pride has written the sermon, it goes with us to the pulpit. It forms our tone, it animates our delivery, it takes us off from that which may be displeasing to the people. It sets us in pursuit of vain applause from our hearers. It makes men seek themselves and their own glory."[42]

Pride is complex. Jonathan Edwards said that it takes many forms and shapes and encompasses the heart like the layers of an onion—when you pull off one layer, there is another underneath.

We ministers, always in the public eye, are particularly prone to the sin of pride. As Richard Greenham writes, "The more godly a man is, and the more graces and blessings of God are upon him, the more need he hath to pray because Satan is busiest against him, and because he is readiest to be puffed up with a conceited holiness."[43]

Pride feeds off nearly anything: a fair measure of ability and wisdom, a single compliment, a season of remarkable prosperity, a call to serve God in a position of prestige—even the honor of suffering for the truth. "It is hard starving this sin, when it can live almost upon anything," writes Richard Mayo.[44]

---

[42] Baxter, *The Reformed Pastor* (New York: Robert Carter & Brothers, 1860), 212–26.
[43] *The Works of Greenham*, 62.
[44] Cf. William Greenhill, *Puritan Sermons: 1659–1689: The Morning Exercises at Cripplegate*, (Wheaton, IL: Richard Owen Roberts, 1981), 3:378–93.

The Puritans said, If we think we are immune to the sin of pride, we should ask ourselves: How dependent are we on the praise of others? Are we caring more about a reputation for godliness than about godliness itself? What do gifts and rewards from others say to us about our ministry? How do we respond to criticism from people in our congregation?

A godly minister fights against pride, whereas a worldly one feeds pride. Cotton Mather confessed that when pride filled him with bitterness and confusion before the Lord, "I endeavoured to take a view of my pride as the very image of the Devil, contrary to the image and grace of Christ; as an offense against God, and grieving of His Spirit; as the most unreasonable folly and madness for one who had nothing singularly excellent and who had a nature so corrupt."[45] Thomas Shepard also fought pride. In his diary entry for November 10, 1642, Shepard wrote, "I kept a private fast for light to see the full glory of the Gospel . . . and for the conquest of all my remaining pride of heart."[46]

Can you identify with these Puritan pastors in your struggle against pride? Do you care enough about your brothers in the ministry to admonish them about this sin? When John Eliot, the Puritan missionary, noticed that a colleague thought of himself too highly, he would say to him, "Study mortification, brother; study mortification."[47]

---

[45] Charles Bridges, *The Christian Ministry* (1830 reprint, London: Banner of Truth Trust, 1959), 152.

[46] *God's Plot: Puritan Spirituality in Thomas Shepard's Cambridge,* ed. Michael McGiffert (Amherst: University of Massachusetts Press, 1994), 116–17.

[47] Cited in Bridges, The Christian Ministry, 128.

How do we fight against pride? Do we understand how deeply rooted it is in us—and how dangerous it is to our ministry? Do we ever remonstrate ourselves like the Puritan Richard Mayo: "Should that man be proud that has sinned as thou hast sinned, and lived as thou hast lived, and wasted so much time, and abused so much mercy, and omitted so many duties, and neglected so great means?—that hath so grieved the Spirit of God, so violated the law of God, so dishonoured the name of God? Should that man be proud, who hath such a heart as thou hast?"[48]

Timothy, if you would kill worldly pride and live in godly humility, look at your Savior, whose life, as Calvin says, "was naught but a series of sufferings." Nowhere is humility so cultivated than at Gethsemane and Calvary. When pride threatens you, consider the contrast between a proud minister and our humble Savior. Sing with Isaac Watts:

When I survey the wondrous cross,
On which the Prince of glory died;
My richest gain I count but loss,
And pour contempt on all my pride.

Here are some other ways to subdue pride, learned from the Puritans and their successors:

- View each day as an opportunity to forget yourself and serve others. As Abraham Booth writes, "Forget not, that the whole of your work is ministerial; not

---

[48] *Puritan Sermons 1659–1689*, 3:390.

legislative—that you are not a lord in the church, but a servant."⁴⁹ The act of service is innately humbling.
- Seek a deeper knowledge of God, His attributes and His glory. Job and Isaiah teach us that nothing is so humbling as knowing God (Job 42, Isaiah 6).
- Read the biographies of great saints, such as Whitefield's *Journals*, *The Life of David Brainerd* and Spurgeon's *Early Years*. As Dr. Lloyd-Jones says, "If that does not bring you to earth, then I pronounce that you are just a professional and beyond hope."⁵⁰
- Remember daily that "pride goeth before destruction, and a haughty spirit before a fall" (Proverbs 16:18).
- Pray for humility. Remember how Augustine answered the question, "What three graces does a minister need most?" by saying, "Humility. Humility. Humility."
- Meditate much on the solemnity of death, the certainty of Judgment Day and the vastness of eternity.

Rely on the Spirit

The Puritans show us our profound reliance upon the Holy Spirit in everything they said and did. They keenly felt their inability to bring anyone to Christ as well as the magnitude of conversion. "God never laid it upon thee to convert those he sends thee to. No; to publish

---

[49] Abraham Booth, "Pastoral Cautions," in *The Christian Pastor's Manual*, ed. John Brown (reprint Pittsburgh, PA: Soli Deo Gloria, 1990), 66.
[50] Martyn Lloyd-Jones, *Preaching and Preachers* (Grand Rapids, MI: Zondervan, 1971), 256.

the gospel is thy duty," William Gurnall said to ministers.[51] And Richard Baxter wrote, "Conversion is another kind of work than most are aware of. It is not a small matter to bring an earthly mind to heaven and to show man the amiable excellencies of God, to be taken up in such love to him that can never be quenched; to make him flee for refuge to Christ and thankfully embrace him as the life of his soul; to have the very drift and bent of his life change so that a man renounces that which he took for his happiness, and places his happiness where he never did before."[52]

The Puritans were convinced that both preacher and listener are totally dependent on the work of the Spirit to effect regeneration and conversion when, how and in whom He will.[53] The Spirit brings God's presence into human hearts. He persuades sinners to seek salvation, renews corrupt wills and makes scriptural truths take root in stony hearts. As Thomas Watson wrote, "Ministers knock at the door of men's hearts, the Spirit comes with a key and opens the door."[54] And Joseph Alleine said: "Never think you can convert yourself. If ever you would be savingly converted, you must despair of doing it in your own strength. It is a resurrection from the dead (Ephesians 2:1), a new creation

---

[51] William Gurnall, *The Christian in Complete Armour* (1662; reprint, London: Banner of Truth Trust, 1964), 574 (second pagination).

[52] Cf. Richard Baxter, *Reformed Pastor*, abridged (1862; reprint, London: Banner of Truth Trust, 1974), 94–96, 114–16.

[53] Packer, *A Quest for Godliness*, 296–99.

[54] *The Select Works of Rev. Thomas Watson* (New York: Robert Carter & Brothers, 1856), 154.

(Galatians 6:15; Ephesians 2:10), a work of absolute omnipotence (Ephesians 1:19)."[55]

Especially as a young minister, Timothy, you need to be persuaded that the Spirit's regenerating action is, as John Owen wrote, "infallible, victorious, irresistible, and always efficacious"; it "removeth all obstacles, overcomes all oppositions, and infallibly produces the effect intended."[56] All modes of action which imply another doctrine are unbiblical. Packer writes: "All devices for exerting psychological pressure in order to precipitate 'decisions' must be eschewed, as being in truth presumptuous attempts to intrude into the province of the Holy Ghost." Such pressures may even be harmful, he goes on to say, for while they "may produce the outward form of 'decision,' they cannot bring about regeneration and a change of heart, and when the 'decisions' wear off those who registered them will be found 'gospel-hardened' and antagonistic." Packer concludes in a Puritan vein: "Evangelism must rather be conceived as a long-term enterprise of patient teaching and instruction, in which God's servants seek simply to be faithful in delivering the gospel message and applying it to human lives, and leave it to God's Spirit to draw men to faith through this message in his own way and at his own speed."[57]

Remember, Timothy, the Holy Spirit must and will also bless faithful preaching both to the conversion of unbelievers

---

[55] Joseph Alleine, *An Alarm to the Unconverted* (Charlestown: Samuel Etheridge, 1807), 29–30.
[56] *Works of John Owen* (1850; reprint, Edinburgh: Banner of Truth Trust, 1976), 3:317ff.
[57] Packer, *A Quest for Godliness*, 163–64.

and to the growth in grace of believers. Be encouraged. God's Word will accomplish its purpose by His Spirit (Isaiah 55:10–11; John 3:8). The *Westminster Larger Catechism* (Q. 155) says that the Spirit of God makes "especially the preaching of the word an effectual means of enlightening, convincing, and humbling sinners; of driving them out of themselves, and drawing them unto Christ; of conforming them to his image, and subduing them to his will; strengthening them against temptations and corruptions; of building them up in grace, and establishing their hearts in holiness and comfort through faith unto salvation."

Live in Two Worlds

The Puritans show us how to live from a two-worldly point of view. Richard Baxter's *The Saint's Everlasting Rest* is a magnificent demonstration of the power that the hope of heaven should have for the directing, controlling and energizing of your life here on earth. Despite being 800+ pages, this classic became household reading in Puritan homes, exceeded only by John Bunyan's *Pilgrim's Progress,* which, by the way, is an allegorical proof of my point. Bunyan's pilgrim is heading for the Celestial City, which he never has out of his mind except when he is betrayed by some form of spiritual malaise.

The Puritans believed that you ought to have heaven "in your eye" throughout your entire earthly pilgrimage. They took seriously the two-worldly, now/not yet dynamics of the New Testament, stressing that keeping the "hope of glory" before our minds helps guide and keep our lives straight here on earth. Living in the light of eternity for the Puritans often necessitated radical self-denial. Timothy, refuse to become a self-seeking, spiritually careless minister, and instead, deny indulging in anything you cannot pray about or pursue in light of the immense value of eternity. Like the Puritans, live in terms of the settled judgment that the joy of heaven will make amends of any losses and crosses, strains and pains that we must endure on earth if we are going to follow Christ faithfully. Regard preparedness to die as the first step in learning to live. View this earth as God's dressing-room and gymnasium that prepares you for heaven.

When visiting Robert Murray M'Cheyne's church in Dundee a few years ago, I couldn't help but notice a large flat stone, perhaps 8' x 8,' placed at the entrance of the graveyard adjacent to the church. I got down on my hands and knees to wipe away the dust and dirt that was clouding a single word carved into the center of that large stone. I traced the word with my fingers: "Eternity" is all it said. I have little doubt that M'Cheyne, permeated by the Puritan spirit, had it placed there, so that no one could visit that graveyard without considering the solemn reality of their future state.

When Jonathan Edwards was thirteen years old, he wrote in his diary, "God, stamp eternity upon my eyes." Dear Timothy, make it your daily prayer: "O Triune God, stamp eternity on my eyes, my conscience, my soul, my hands and feet, my family and public worship, yes, my entire being and ministry—every sermon I preach and class I teach, every pastoral visit I make and every article I write. Help me to preach as a dying man to dying people. Help me to always live on the edge of eternity—with shod feet, girt loins, and ready staff—prepared to meet the living God every day."

Conclusion: Emulate Puritan Spirituality

There's so much more to learn from the Puritans, Timothy—how they promoted the authority of Scripture, biblical evangelism, church reform, the spirituality of the law, spiritual warfare against indwelling sin, the filial fear of God, the dreadfulness of hell and the glories of heaven—but this letter is already too long. In a word, Timothy, I advise you, as I advise myself: Emulate Puritan spirituality. Let's ask ourselves questions like these: Are we, like the Puritans, thirsting to glorify the triune God? Are we motivated by biblical truth and biblical fire? Do we share the Puritan view of the vital necessity of conversion and of being clothed with the righteousness of Christ? It is not enough to just read the Puritans. A stirring of interest in the Puritans is not the same thing as a revival of Puritanism. We need the inward disposition of the Puritans—the authentic, biblical, intelligent piety they showed in our hearts, lives and churches.

Let me challenge you, Timothy! Will you live godly in Christ Jesus like the Puritans? Will you go beyond studying their writings, discussing their ideas, recalling their achievements and berating their failures? Will you practice the degree of obedience to God's Word for which they strove? Will you serve God as they served Him? Will you live with one eye on eternity as they did? "Thus saith the

LORD, Stand ye in the ways, and see, and ask for the old paths, where is the good way, and walk therein, and ye shall find rest for your souls" (Jeremiah 6:16).

Warmly, in the Master's bonds,
Joel R. Beeke

PS—If you are just starting to read the Puritans, Timothy, begin with Thomas Watson's *Heaven Taken By Storm,* John Bunyan's *The Fear of God,* John Flavel's *Keeping the Heart* and Thomas Brooks's *Precious Remedies Against Satan's Devices,* then move on to the works of John Owen, Thomas Goodwin, and Jonathan Edwards. You can find out the basics about Puritan books by reading a forth coming book, *Meet the Puritans: A Guide to Modern Reprints.* In that book, Randall Pederson and I give a brief summary of each Puritan title that has been reprinted since the resurgence of Puritan literature in the 1950s and provide you with a biographical summary of each Puritan author's life. You should also get Robert P. Martin's *A Guide to the Puritans* (Edinburgh: Banner of Truth Trust, 1997), which indexes most of the Puritan reprints, so that you can quickly find what the Puritans have to say on any major subject.

For secondary sources that introduce you to the Puritans lifestyle and theology, begin with Leland Ryken, *Worldly Saints: The Puritans As They Really Were* (Grand Rapids, MI: Zondervan, 1990), Peter Lewis, *The Genius of Puritanism* (Morgan, PA: Soli Deo Gloria, 1997) and Erroll Hulse, *Who are the Puritans? and what do they teach* (Darlington, England: Evangelical Press, 2000). Then move on to James I. Packer's *A Quest for Godliness: The Puritan Vision of the*

Christian Life (Wheaton, IL: Crossway Books, 1990). For a bibliography that contains numerous Puritan works not yet reprinted, see my *The Quest for Full Assurance: The Legacy of Calvin and His Successors* (Edinburgh: Banner of Truth Trust, 1999).

A good source for purchasing Puritan titles at discount prices, including all of the above, is Reformation Heritage Books (www.heritagebooks.org). *Tolle lege!*

Chapter 14

Learn from the Puritans II
Joel Beeke

Dear Timothy,

I hope you profited from my last letter on learning from the Puritans. Here's my promised second letter on what you can learn from the Puritans for your preaching and teaching ministry. May God graciously bless you and make you an able expositor of His precious Word.

PREACH THE WORD

Learn from the Puritans to shape the content and method of all your preaching by Scripture. *The Westminster Directory of Public Worship* says of ministers, "Ordinarily, the subject of his sermon is to be some text of scripture, holding forth some principle or head of religion, or suitable to some special occasion emergent; or he may go on in some chapter, psalm, or book of holy scripture, as he shall see fit."[1] Edward Dering put it succinctly, "The faithfull Minister, like unto Christ, [is] one that preacheth nothing but the word of God."[2] John Owen agreed: "The first and principal duty of a pastor is to feed the flock by diligent preaching of the word."[3] As Miller Maclure noted, "For the Puritans, the sermon is not just hinged to Scripture; it quite literally exists inside the Word of God; the text is not in the sermon, but the sermon is in the text . . . . Put summarily, listening to a sermon is being in the Bible."[4]

Puritan preaching allowed Scripture to dictate the emphasis for each message. The Puritans did not preach sermons that were a kind of balancing act between various doctrines. Rather, they let the biblical text determine the content and emphasis of each message. When Jonathan Edwards preached on hell, for example, he didn't make a single reference to heaven, and when he preached on heaven, he didn't speak about hell.[5]

The Puritans preached a Bible text completely whatever its theme, so in time they would be sure to address every major theme of Scripture and thereby every major doctrine of Reformed theology. Nothing was left unbalanced in the total range of their many and lengthy sermons. In

---

[1] *The Westminster Confession of Faith* (Inverness: The Publications Committee of the Free Presbyterian Church of Scotland, 1985), 379.
[2] M. *Derings Workes* (1597; reprint, New York: Da Capo Press, 1972), 456.
[3] *The Works of John Owen*, ed. William H. Goold (1853; London: Banner of Truth Trust, 1965), 16:74.
[4] Miller Maclure, *The Paul's Cross Sermons, 1534–1642* (Toronto: University of Toronto Press, 1958), 165.
[5] Cf. *The Wrath of Almighty God: Jonathan Edwards on God's Judgment against Sinners*, ed. Don Kistler (Morgan, PA: Soli Deo Gloria, 1996); *The Works of Jonathan Edwards*, 2:617–41; John H. Gerstner, *Jonathan Edwards on Heaven and Hell* (Grand Rapids, MI: Baker, 1980).

theology proper, they proclaimed God's transcendence as well as His immanence. In anthropology, they preached about the image of God in its narrower as well as its wider sense. In Christology, they exhibited Christ's state of humiliation as well as exaltation. In soteriology, they focused both on God's work and on man's response and knew when to accent each. In ecclesiology, they acknowledged the high calling of special offices (ministers, elders and deacons) as well as the equally high calling of the general office of all believers. In eschatology, they declared both the glories of heaven and the horrors of hell.

Timothy, learn from the Puritans, in your lifestyle and your preaching, to show wholehearted allegiance to the Bible's entire message. Be a man of the living Book. Believe in preaching. Never forget that when you proclaim the Scriptures as a lawfully ordained preacher, Christ speaks through you, so that, by His Spirit, the preached Word is a living Word. That makes your calling so significant, that Henry Smith could preach to his flock, "If ye did consider, my beloved, that ye cannot be nourished unto eternal life but by the milk of the word, ye would rather desire your bodies might be without souls, that your churches without preachers."[6]

Marry Doctrine and Practice

Timothy, let the Puritans be your mentors in marrying doctrine and practice in our preaching. Follow their example in these three ways:

---

[6] *The Works of Henry Smith*, ed. Thomas Smith (Edinburgh: James Nichol, 1866), 1:495.

- *Address the mind with clarity.* Puritan preaching addressed man as a rational creature. The Puritans loved and worshipped God with their minds. They refused to set mind and heart against each other but taught that knowledge was the soil in which the Spirit planted the seed of regeneration. They viewed the mind as the palace of faith. "In conversion, reason is elevated," John Preston wrote. And Cotton Mather said, "Ignorance is the mother not of devotion but of heresy." Puritans thus preached that we need to *think* in order to be holy. They challenged the idea that holiness is only a matter of emotions. They reasoned with sinners through what they called "plain preaching," using biblical logic to persuade each listener that it was foolish not to seek and serve God because of the value and purpose of life and the certainty of death and eternity.

God gave us minds for a reason, the Puritans taught. It is crucial that we ministers become like Christ in the way we think. Our minds must be enlightened by faith and disciplined by the Word, then put into God's service in the world. Timothy, be challenged by the Puritans to use your intellect to further God's kingdom. Without clear thinking, you will never be able to feed God's people nor evangelize and counter the culture in which you live, work and minister. You will become empty in yourself, non-productive and narcissistic, lacking a developing interior life.

The Puritans preached that a flabby mind is no badge of honor. They understood that a mindless Christianity fosters a spineless Christianity. An anti-intellectualistic gospel will spawn an irrelevant gospel that doesn't get beyond "felt needs." That's what is happening in our churches today. We have lost our Christian mind, and for the most part we don't see the necessity of recovering it. We do not understand that where there is little difference between the Christian and non-Christian in what we think and believe, there will soon be little difference in how we live.

- *Confront the conscience pointedly.* The Puritans worked hard on the consciences of sinners as the "light of nature" in them. Plain preaching named specific sins, then asked questions to press home the guilt of those sins upon the consciences of men, women and children. As one Puritan wrote, "We must go with the stick of divine truth and beat every bush behind which a sinner hides, until like Adam who hid, he stands before God in his nakedness." They believed this was necessary because until the sinner gets out from behind that bush, he will never cry to be clothed in the righteousness of Christ. So the Puritans preached *urgently*, believing that many of their listeners were still on their way to hell. They preached *directly*, confronting their hearers with law and gospel, with death in Adam and life in Christ. They preached *specifically*, taking Christ's command seriously "that repentance and remission of sins should be preached in his name" (Luke 24:47).

Today, modern evangelism is, for the most part, afraid to confront the conscience pointedly. Learn from the Puritans, Timothy, who were persuaded that the friend who loves you most will tell you the most truth about yourself. Like Paul and the Puritans, we need to testify, earnestly and with tears, of the need for "repentance toward God, and faith toward our Lord Jesus Christ" (Acts 20:21).

- *Woo the heart passionately.* Puritan preaching was affectionate, zealous and optimistic. It is unusual today to find a ministry that both feeds the mind with solid biblical substance and moves the heart with affectionate warmth, but this combination was commonplace with the Puritans. They did not just reason with the mind and confront the conscience; they appealed to the heart. They preached out of love for God's Word, love for the glory of God and love for the soul of every listener. They preached with warm gratitude for the Christ who had saved them and made their lives a sacrifice of praise. They set forth Christ in His loveliness, hoping to make the unsaved jealous of what the believer has in Christ.

STRESS PRACTICING PIETY

Like Augustine and Calvin, the Puritans stressed the practice of piety (*praxis pietatis*), or practical godliness, flowing out of sound doctrine. "The Directory for Public Worship" in the *Westminster Confession of Faith* summarizes the Puritans' commitment to sanctified application:

> He (the preacher) is not to rest in general doctrine, although never so much cleared and confirmed, but to bring it home to special use, by application to his hearers: which albeit it prove a work of great difficulty to himself, requiring much prudence, zeal, and meditation, and to the natural and corrupt man will be very unpleasant; yet he is to endeavour to perform it in such a manner, that his auditors may feel the word of God to be quick and powerful, and a discerner of the thoughts and intents of the heart; and that, if any unbeliever or ignorant person be present, he may have the secrets of his heart made manifest, and give glory to God.[7]

Believing that God's way to the heart and life was through the mind, the Puritan preachers saw how Scripture and theology relate to the problems of daily life. They did not disjoin the sacred from the secular. That's why their books contain so many "uses," by which they show how to apply their text for practical good. The "Directory of Public Worship" identifies six types of application: instructions in true doctrines, refutations of false doctrines, exhortations to perform duties, admonitions to repentance, consolations to the troubled and self-examinations for every hearer.[8] To pursue only one type, "uses" of exhortations embrace such primary virtues as intense personal and family exercises in godliness, wholehearted commitments to goodness and truth, diligence in work, exercise of brotherly love, responsible use of gifts and time, strict observance of the Sabbath and, most importantly, experiential dealings with

---

[7] *Westminster Confession of Faith*, 380.
[8] Ibid.

God. The Puritans loved the application of biblical texts to the full range of life, focusing both on God's promises and on man's duties.

Let the Puritans teach you how to employ a few of these "uses" in each sermon to various kinds of hearers. William Perkins distinguishes seven kinds of hearers—four of whom are unsaved (the ignorant and unteachable, the ignorant but teachable, those who have knowledge but are not humbled and those who are humbled but are not yet brought to freedom in Christ) and three who are saved (those who believe, those who are fallen, and the "mixed"—i.e. fathers, young men and children in grace). He shows us in less than twenty pages how to apply our sermons to each of these kinds of hearers. Read these pages often and examine your sermons by them.[9]

In short, preaching and theology are means to an end—the goal being sanctification. The Puritans saw theology as essentially practical. William Perkins called theology "the science of living blessedly for ever";[10] William Ames, "the doctrine or teaching of living to God."[11] As Sinclair Ferguson writes, "To them, systematic theology was to the pastor what a knowledge of anatomy is to the physician. Only in the light of the whole body of divinity (as they liked to call it) could a minister provide a diagnosis of,

---

[9] William Perkins, *The Art of Prophesying* (1606; edited and reprinted, Edinburgh: Banner of Truth Trust, 1996), 56–73.
[10] *The Works of William Perkins* (London: John Legate, 1609), 1:10.
[11] William Ames, *The Marrow of Theology*, ed. John D. Eusden (1629; Boston, MA: Pilgrim Press, 1968), 77.

prescribe for, and ultimately cure spiritual disease in those who were plagued by the body of sin and death."[12]

The Puritans, therefore, rejoiced to preach the whole counsel of God. Their all-embracing Christianity was integrated well into their daily lives. Their lifestyle was holistic, reflecting a whole gospel for the whole of personal and corporate life. Their biblical worldview—which embraced work and leisure, duties and pleasures—aimed for "holiness to the Lord" and to "do all to the glory of God" (1 Corinthians 10:31). Go and stress likewise, Timothy.

PREACH EXPERIENTIALLY

The Puritans show us how to promote the experiential dimension of Reformed preaching. Puritan preaching explained how a Christian experiences biblical truth in his life. The term *experimental* comes from the Latin word *experimentum*, which is derived from the verb that means to "try, test, prove or put to the test." The same verb can also mean "to find or know by experience" and so gives rise to the word *experientia*, meaning "trial, experiment" and "the knowledge gained by experiment." Calvin used experiential and experimental interchangeably, since both words, from the perspective of biblical preaching, indicate the need for examining or testing experienced knowledge by the touchstone of Scripture (Isaiah 8:20).[13]

---

[12] Sinclair Ferguson, "Evangelical Ministry: The Puritan Contribution" in *Compromised Church,* John Armstrong, ed. (Wheaton, IL: Crossway Books, 1998), 266.
[13] Willem Balke, "The Word of God and *Experientia* according to Calvin," in *Calvinus Ecclesiae Doctor,* ed. W. H. Neuser (Kampen: J.H. Kok, 1978), 20–21; cf. Calvin's *Commentary* on Zechariah 2:9.

Experimental preaching stresses the need to know the truths of the Word of God by experience. Experimental preaching seeks to explain in terms of biblical truth, how matters *ought to go* and how they *do go* in the Christian life and aims to apply divine truth to the whole range of the believer's experience: in his walk with God as well as his relationship with family, the church and the world around him. We can learn much from the Puritans about this type of preaching. As Paul Helm writes:

> The situation calls for preaching that will cover the full range of Christian experience, and a developed experimental theology. The preaching must give guidance and instruction to Christians in terms of their actual experience. It must not deal in unrealities or treat congregations as if they lived in a different century or in wholly different circumstances. This involves taking the full measure of our modern situation and entering with full sympathy into the actual experiences, the hopes and fears, of Christian people.[14]

Puritan preaching was marked by a discriminating application of truth to experience. Discriminatory preaching defines the difference between the non-Christian and the Christian. Discriminatory preaching pronounces the wrath of God and eternal condemnation upon the unbelieving and impenitent. It likewise offers the forgiveness of sins

---

[14] Paul Helms, "Christian Experience," *Banner of Truth*, No. 139 (Apr. 1975):6.

and eternal life to all who embrace by true faith Jesus Christ as Savior and Lord. Such preaching teaches that if our religion is not experiential, we will perish—not because experience itself saves, but because Christ who saves sinners must be experienced personally as the Rock upon whom our eternal hope is built (Matthew 7:22–27; 1 Corinthians 1:30, 2:2).

The Puritans were very aware of the deceitfulness of the human heart. Consequently, Puritan evangelists took great pains to identify the marks of grace that distinguish the church from the world, true believers from merely professing believers and saving faith from temporary faith.[15] Thomas Shepard in *The Ten Virgins,* Matthew Mead in *The Almost Christian Discovered,* Jonathan Edwards in *Religious Affections* and other Puritans wrote dozens of works to differentiate imposters from true believers.[16]

Puritan preachers knew, in Thomas Boston's words, "the art of manfishing." They aimed for both initial and ongoing conversion among their hearers. They believed that the sermon was a means of grace and would be used by the Spirit to accomplish conversion and growth in grace. Hence they aimed to deal meaningfully with inner spiritual struggles. As Sydney Ahlstrom writes, "Without denying the objective, purely gracious character of God's redemptive acts, they

---

[15] Thomas Watson, *The Godly Man's Picture* (1666; reprint, Edinburgh: Banner of Truth Trust, 1992), 20–188, sets forth twenty-four marks of grace for self-examination.

[16] Thomas Shepard, *The Parable of the Ten Virgins* (1660; reprint, Ligonier, PA: Soli Deo Gloria, 1990); Matthew Mead, *The Almost Christian Discovered; Or the False Professor Tried and Cast* (1662; reprint, Ligonier, PA: Soli Deo Gloria, 1988); Jonathan Edwards, *Religious Affections* (New Haven, CT: Yale University Press, 1959).

wished also to make a place for the willing, knowing, repenting, thanking, loving acts of the human person . . . they sought to make a place in the economy of salvation for *subjectivity*, for the acts of human consciousness."[17] This accounts for the impression one receives that their sermons are both solidly founded on Calvinistic theology and simultaneously packed with the imperatives of the biblical gospel and its urgings to repent and believe.

How different this is from most contemporary preaching! The Word of God is often preached today in a way that will never transform anyone because it never discriminates and never applies. Preaching is reduced to a lecture, a catering to the wishes and needs of people or a form of experientialism removed from the foundation of Scripture. Such preaching fails to expound from Scripture what the Puritans called vital religion: how a sinner is stripped of all his own righteousness, driven to Christ alone for salvation, finds joy in obedience and reliance upon Christ, encounters the plague of indwelling sin, battles against backsliding and gains the victory through Christ.[18]

Timothy, when God's Word is preached experimentally, the Holy Spirit uses it to transform men, women and nations. Such preaching transforms because it corresponds to the vital experience of the children of God (Romans 5:1–

---

[17] "Theology in America," *The Shaping of American Religion*, ed. James Ward Smith and A. Leland Jamison (Princeton, NJ: Princeton University Press, 1961), 240.
[18] Joel R. Beeke, *Jehovah Shepherding His Sheep* (Grand Rapids, MI: Eerdmans, 1982), 164–203, and *Backsliding: Disease and Cure* (Grand Rapids, MI: Eerdmans, 1982), 17–32.

11), clearly explains the marks of saving grace in the believer (Matthew 5:3–12; Galatians 5:22–23), proclaims the high calling of believers as the servants of God in the world (Matthew 5:13–16) and shows the eternal destination of believers and unbelievers (Revelation 21:1–9).[19]

Focus on Christ

The experimental preaching of the Puritans focused on the preaching of Christ. As Scripture clearly shows, evangelism must bear witness to the record God has given of His only begotten Son (Acts 2:3, 5:42, 8:35; Romans 16:25; 1 Corinthians 2:2; Galatians 3:1). The Puritans thus taught that any preaching in which Christ does not have the preeminence is not valid preaching. William Perkins said that the heart of all preaching was to "preach one Christ by Christ to the praise of Christ."[20] According to Thomas Adams, "Christ is the sum of the whole Bible, prophesied, typified, prefigured, exhibited, demonstrated, to be found in every leaf, almost in every line, the Scriptures being but as it were the swaddling bands of the child Jesus."[21] "Think of Christ

---

[19] See the *Heidelberg Catechism* for a Reformed confessional statement that facilitates experimental preaching. This is evidenced by (1) the Catechism's exposition of an outline (misery, deliverance and gratitude) that is true to the experience of believers, (2) its application of most doctrines directly to the believer's conscience and spiritual profit, and (3) its warm, personal character in which the believer is regularly addressed in the second person.
[20] *Works of Perkins*, 2:762.
[21] *The Works of Thomas Adams* (1862; reprint Eureka, CA: Tanski, 1998), 3:224.

as the very substance, marrow, soul, and scope of the whole Scriptures," Isaac Ambrose said.[22]

Like Paul, the Puritans preached Christ crucified. Packer says, "Puritan preaching revolved around 'Christ, and him crucified'—for this is the hub of the Bible. The preachers' commission is to declare the whole counsel of God; but the cross is the center of that counsel, and the Puritans knew that the traveler through the Bible landscape misses his way as soon as he loses sight of the hill called Calvary."[23]

The Puritans were lovers of Christ and wrote much about His beauty. Listen to Samuel Rutherford: "Put the beauty of ten thousand thousand worlds of paradises, like the Garden of Eden in one; put all trees, all flowers, all smells, all colors, all tastes, all joys, all loveliness, all sweetness in one. O what a fair and excellent thing would that be? And yet it would be less to that fair and dearest well-beloved Christ than one drop of rain to the whole seas, rivers, lakes, and foundations of ten thousand earths."[24] Thomas Goodwin concluded, "Heaven would be hell to me without Christ."[25]

---

[22] *Works of Isaac Ambrose* (London: for Thomas Tegg & Son, 1701), 201.
[23] Packer, *A Quest for Godliness*, 286.
[24] Quoted by Don Kistler, *Why Read the Puritans Today* (Morgan, PA: Soli Deo Gloria, 1999), 4.
[25] Ibid., 3.

Maintain Biblical Balance

The Puritans show us how to maintain proper biblical balance in our preaching. Let me just mention three important ways:

- By maintaining the objective and subjective dimensions of Christianity. The objective is the food for the subjective; thus the subjective is always rooted in the objective. For example, the Puritans stated that the primary ground of assurance is rooted in the promises of God, but those promises must become increasingly real to the believer through the subjective evidences of grace and the internal witness of the Holy Spirit. Without the Spirit's application, the promises of God lead to self-deceit and carnal presumption. On the other hand, without the promises of God and the illumination of the Spirit, self-examination tends to introspection, bondage and legalism. Objective and subjective Christianity must not be separated from each other.
We must seek to live in a way that reveals Christ's internal presence based on His objective work of active and passive obedience. The gospel of Christ must be proclaimed as objective truth, but it must also be applied by the Holy Spirit and inwardly appropriated by faith. We therefore reject two kinds of religion: one that separates subjective experience from the objective Word, thereby leading to man-centered

mysticism; and one that presumes salvation on the false grounds of historical or temporary faith.[26]

- By maintaining the sovereignty of God and the responsibility of man. Nearly all of the Puritans stressed that God is fully sovereign and man is fully responsible. How that can be resolved logically is beyond our finite minds. When Charles Spurgeon was asked how these two grand, biblical doctrines could be reconciled, he responded as a real heir of the Puritans: "I didn't know that friends needed reconciliation." He went on to compare these two doctrines to the rails of a track upon which Christianity runs. Just as the rails of a train, which run parallel to each other, appear to merge in the distance, so the doctrines of God's sovereignty and man's responsibility, which seem separate from each other in this life, will merge in eternity. The Puritans would wholeheartedly concur. Our task, they said, is not to force their merging in this life but to keep them in balance and to live accordingly. We must thus strive for experiential Christianity that does justice both to God's sovereignty and to our responsibility.
- By rejecting Arminianism and hyper-Calvinism. False converts are multiplied today through shallow Arminian and decisionistic methods, which has given birth to the carnal Christian theory in order to accommodate non-fruitbearing "Christians." The Puritans combated shallow Arminianism through

---

[26] Joel R. Beeke, *Quest for Full Assurance: The Legacy of Calvin and His Successors* (Edinburgh: Banner of Truth Trust, 1999), 125, 130, 146.

their sovereign grace soteriology. John Owen's *A Display of Arminianism* and his *The Death of Death in the Death of Christ* powerfully underscore that the fallen will of man is in bondage.

On the other hand, a growing number of Reformed conservatives today, moving beyond Calvin, are espousing that God does not sincerely offer grace unconditionally to every hearer of the gospel. The result is that the preaching of the gospel is hampered and man's responsibility is dismissed, if not denied. Happily, we are freed from such rationalistic, hyper-Calvinistic conclusions about the doctrines of grace when we read Puritan writings such as John Bunyan's *Come and Welcome to Jesus Christ,* John Howe's *The Redeemer's Tears Shed Over Lost Souls* or William Greenhill's sermon, "What Must and Can Persons Do Toward Their Own Conversion."[27]

Timothy, if you preach with a true Reformed balance, some of your parishioners may call you a hyper-Calvinist and others may call you an Arminian, but the majority will view you as being solidly biblical and Reformed.

---

[27] John Bunyan, *Come and Welcome* (reprint, Choteau, MT: Gospel Mission, 1999); John Howe, *Redeemer's Tears* (Grand Rapids, MI: Baker, 1989); William Greenhill, *Puritan Sermons: 1659–1689: The Morning Exercises at Cripplegate,* (Wheaton, IL: Richard Owen Roberts, 1981), 1:38–50.

Persevere in Catechizing

The Puritans show us the importance of persevering in catechizing your own church people and your neighbors. Like the Reformers, the Puritans were catechists. They believed that pulpit messages should be reinforced by personalized ministry through *catechesis*—the instruction in the doctrines of Scripture using catechisms. Puritan catechizing was important in several ways:

- Scores of Puritans reached out to children and young people by writing catechism books that explained fundamental Christian doctrines via questions and answers supported by Scripture.[28] For example, John Cotton titled his catechism, *Milk for Babes, drawn out of the Breasts of both Testaments*.[29] Other Puritans included in the titles of their catechisms such expressions as "the main and fundamental points," "the sum of the Christian religion," the "several heads" or "first principles" of religion and "the ABC of Christianity." Ian Green shows the high level of

---

[28] See George Edward Brown, "Catechists and Catechisms of Early New England" (D.R.E. dissertation, Boston University, 1934); R.M.E. Paterson, "A Study in Catechisms of the Reformation and Post-Reformation Period" (M.A. thesis, Durham University, 1981); P. Hutchinson, "Religious Change: The Case of the English Catechism, 1560–1640" (Ph.D. dissertation, Stanford University, 1984); Ian Green, *The Christian's ABC: Catechisms and Catechizing in England c. 1530–1740* (Oxford: Clarendon Press, 1996).

[29] John Cotton, *Milk for Babes, drawn out of the Breasts of both Testaments* (London, 1646).

continuity that exists in Puritan catechism books in their recurring formulae and topics such as the Apostles' Creed, the Ten Commandments, the Lord's Prayer and the sacraments. He goes on to suggest that there was no substantial discrepancy even between the simple message of many elementary works and the more demanding content of more sophisticated catechisms.[30] At various levels in the church as well as in the homes of their parishioners, Puritan ministers catechized in order to explain the fundamental teachings of the Bible, to help young people commit the Bible to memory, to make sermons and the sacraments more understandable, to prepare covenant children for confession of faith, to teach them how to defend their faith against error and to help parents teach their own children.[31]

- Catechizing was related to both sacraments. When the *Westminster Larger Catechism* speaks of "improving" one's baptism, it refers to a task of lifelong instruction in which catechisms such as the *Shorter Catechism* play an important role.[32] William

---

[30] Ian Green, *The Christian's ABC* (Oxford: Claredon Press, 1996), 557–70.

[31] Cf. W.G.T. Shedd, *Homiletics and Pastoral Theology* (1867; reprint, London: Banner of Truth Trust, 1965), 356–75.

[32] The Westminster Assembly desired to establish one catechism and one confession of faith for both England and Scotland, but a spate of catechisms continued to be written after the Westminster standards were drafted. See J. Lewis Wilson, "Catechisms, and Their Use Among the Puritans," in *One Steadfast High Intent* (London: Puritan and Reformed Studies Conference, 1966), 41–42.

Perkins said that the ignorant should memorize his catechism, *The Foundation of Christian Religion*, so they would be "fit to receive the Lord's Supper with comfort." And William Hopkinson wrote in the preface to *A Preparation into the Waie of Life* that he labored to lead his catechumens "into the right use of the Lord's Supper, a special confirmation of God's promises in Christ."[33]

- Catechizing enhanced family worship. The more their public efforts to purify the church were crushed, the more the Puritans turned to the home as a bastion for religious instruction and influence. They wrote books on family worship and the "godly order of family government." Robert Openshawe prefaced his catechism with an appeal "to those who were wont to ask how you should spend the long winter evenings, [to] turn to singing of psalms and teaching your household and praying with them."[34] By the time of the Westminster Assembly in the 1640s, the Puritans considered a lack of family worship and catechizing to be an evidence of an unconverted life.[35]

---

[33] William Hopkinson, *A Preparation into the Waie of Life, with a Direction into the righte use of the Lordes Supper* (London, 1583), sig. A.3.
[34] Robert Openshawe, *Short Questions and Answeares* (London, 1580), A.4.
[35] Wilson, "Catechisms, and Their Use Among the Puritans," 38–39.

- Catechizing was a follow-up to sermons and a way to reach neighbors with the gospel. Joseph Alleine reportedly followed up his work on Sunday five days a week by catechizing church members as well as reaching out with the gospel to people he met on the streets.[36] Richard Baxter, whose vision for catechizing is expounded in *The Reformed Pastor*, said that he came to the painful conclusion that "some ignorant persons, who have been so long unprofitable hearers, have got more knowledge and remorse of conscience in half an hour's close disclosure, than they did from ten years' public preaching."[37] Baxter thus invited people in his home every Thursday evening to discuss and pray for blessing upon the sermons of the previous Sabbath.
- Catechizing was helpful for purposes of examining people's spiritual condition and for encouraging and admonishing them to flee to Christ. Baxter and his two assistants spent two full days each week catechizing parishioners in their homes. Packer concludes: "To upgrade the practice of personal catechizing from a preliminary discipline for children to a permanent ingredient in evangelism and pastoral care for all ages was

---

[36] C. Stanford, *Joseph Alleine: His Companions and Times* (London, 1861).

[37] Richard Baxter, *Gidlas Salvianus: The Reformed Pastor: Shewing the Nature of the Pastoral Work* (1656; reprint New York: Robert Carter, 1860), 341–468.

Baxter's main contribution to the development of Puritan ideals for the ministry."[38]

Puritan churches and schools considered catechism instruction so important that some even offered official catechists. At Cambridge University, William Perkins served as catechist at Christ's College and John Preston at Emanuel College. The Puritan ideal, according to Thomas Gataker, was that a school be a "little church" and its teachers "private catechists."[39]

The Puritan ministry, carried on by preaching, pastoral admonition and catechizing, took time and skill.[40] The Puritans were not looking for quick and easy conversions; they were committed to building up lifelong believers whose hearts, minds, wills and affections were won to the service of Christ.[41]

The hard work of the Puritan catechist was greatly rewarded. Richard Greenham claimed that catechism teaching built up the Reformed church and did serious damage to Roman Catholicism.[42] When Baxter was installed at

---

[38] Packer, *A Quest for Godliness*, 305.
[39] Thomas Gataker, *David's Instructor* (London, 1620), 18; see also B. Simon, "Leicestershire Schools 1635–40," *British Journal of Educational Studies* (Nov. 1954):47–51.
[40] Thomas Boston, *The Art of Manfishing: A Puritan's View of Evangelism*, intro. J. I. Packer (reprint Fearn, Ross-shire: Christian Focus, 1998), 14–15.
[41] Thomas Hooker, *The Poor Doubting Christian Drawn to Christ* (1635; reprint Worthington, PA: Maranatha, 1977).
[42] Richard Greenham, *A Short Forme of Catechising* (London: Richard Bradocke, 1599).

Kidderminster in Worcestershire, perhaps one family in each street honored God in family worship; at the end of his ministry there, there were streets where every family did so. He could say that of the six hundred converts that were brought to faith under his preaching, he could not name one that had backslidden to the ways of the world.

Timothy, I trust I've given you sufficient reasons to persevere in reading the Puritans. I'd advise you to always be reading at least one Puritan book in your devotional or free reading time. Let the Puritans persuade you by example and precept to persevere in piety, in preaching and in catechizing, even when you cannot find fruit. "Cast thy bread upon the waters: for thou shalt find it after many days" (Ecclesiastes 11:1).

Warmly, in the Master's bonds,
Joel R. Beeke

Chapter 15

Preach the Word
Roger Ellsworth

Dear Timothy,

I trust all is well with you. These are certainly exciting and challenging days for you and Mary with a rambunctious two-year-old and another child on the way. Enjoy these years of parenting little ones. They will pass before you know it.

And here you are in the early months of a new pastorate! That is both exciting and challenging. I look upon you now with a great deal of satisfaction. I have felt, since I met you as a teenager, that God had His hand upon you and would use you in a wonderful way. I continue to believe that and will certainly pray for you to that end.

I do not pretend to be able to offer you words of wisdom on every aspect of the pastorate. There is so much about it that I have not mastered. I am still learning even after all these years. I would, however, emphasize for you the importance of the words of the apostle Paul to his Timothy:

"Preach the Word." No task is more important. Fail here and you will have failed in your central task.

Sadly enough, many are failing at this point. There is among pastors these days such a desire to see their churches grow that they are even willing to set aside the true preaching of God's Word. In its place is a "life-management" preaching that focuses on how to cope with life and the challenges it has to offer. This type of preaching does not confront the hearers with sin and cannot, therefore, bring them to faith in the God who saves from sin.

I certainly have nothing against church growth, but it is my firm conviction that the thing that produces real and lasting growth is the Word of God. I hope this will be your conviction as well.

Many assure themselves that they are preaching the Word. They are, after all, finding texts in the Bible, reading those texts to their people and building their sermons around them. But the mere presence of these elements does not produce biblical preaching.

The sermons we preach must not merely use the Bible as a springboard. It is not even enough to simply draw points from the text. Our sermons must seek to lay before our people the message that God Himself intended when He inspired the authors of Scripture. As God gives us light and ability to discern His Word, it is our responsibility to draw out and expound the truth of the text.

Because preaching the Word is so very vital and because there is such a scarcity of it, I venture to offer you some principles that have been helpful to me.

First, to preach the Word of God you must be convinced that it is the Word of God. The man who doubts the divine inspiration of Scripture cannot preach with authority. There can be no "Thus saith the Lord" in his preaching because he cannot be sure that the Lord has said anything.

To preach well, you must be a man of great faith. You must be a great believer. Your people must be able to see in your preaching that the teachings of Scripture are the delight of your soul. Charles Spurgeon used to say, "Brethren, be great believers. Little faith will bring your souls to heaven, but great faith will bring heaven to your souls."[1]

Learn to delight in the Word of God in such a way that it will be apparent to all that you have heaven in your soul. You will soon find that many of your hearers will desire to have the same.

Second, to preach the Word of God you must be ruthless with yourself in allowing it to speak. So many preachers are willing to pay lip service to the authority of God's Word until they come to a passage that says something they themselves do not like to hear. At that point, they tell themselves that it cannot possibly mean what it appears to mean. Suddenly they are engaged in making the text say what they think it should say. This is especially true with those texts that affirm the sovereignty of God, the holiness of God, the reality of sin, the certainty of judgment and the exclusivity of Christ as Savior and Lord.

One example of this is the potter and the clay in Jeremiah 18:1–10. Because they do not like the teaching that God is sovereign and can do with us as He pleases, preachers have even been known to resort to speaking of the clay as being

---

[1] Ernest W. Bacon, *Spurgeon: Heir of the Puritans* (Grand Rapids, MI: William B. Eerdmans Publishing Co., 1968), 114.

"willing" to be molded. The point of the passage is just the opposite. The clay is in the hands of the potter who does with it as he wills. And the people of Judah were in the hands of God in exactly the same way.

Preachers who refuse to let the Bible speak its own message often do so because they fear being out of step with popular opinion. They are too concerned about the findings of the latest survey and not enough concerned about being faithful to God and His Word. Having a mortal dread that they will be out of step with the times, they come to their Bibles with a preconceived mental "grid" in place. And they come away from them with messages that are influenced by that grid and ones that reflect the politically correct dogmas of the day.

While I am on this matter of being ruthless with yourself, I would caution you about the common practice of alliteration. It is possible to so fall in love with this that we become more focused on it than we are on dealing honestly with the text. If we are not careful, we can distort what the text actually says in order to get from it another point that fits our alliterative scheme. I am not opposed to the use of alliteration if it is natural and not contrived, but our primary concern must be what the text says. Truth carries its own appeal.

Third, to preach the Word of God you must keep in mind that its theme is God's gracious redemption of sinners through the saving work of His Son. We do not truly preach if we do not preach Christ. As we prepare to preach, we must keep in mind that each passage of Scripture has both an immediate context and a larger context. The immediate context can be any one of a wide variety of things, but the larger context is always God's plan of redemption. We must, therefore, even when addressing such practical matters as the gifts of the Spirit, Christian stewardship or family living, always do so from the perspective of redemption. J. I. Packer rightly says, "If the expositor finds himself out of sight of Calvary, that shows that he has lost his way."[2]

I commend for your careful consideration the words of Michael Horton:

> I advocate the "redemptive-historical" approach to preaching, which treats the Bible as an unfolding drama of redemption rather than as a handbook of timeless principles. . . . Instead of trying to make the Bible relevant for "today's busy Christian," I suggest that we allow the Bible to arrest us, condemn us, justify and free us. We need more preaching that focuses on God and what he has done, is doing, and will do in history, and less on ourselves and how we can be happier with God's help.[3]

I also urge you to carefully consider these words from J. I. Packer:

> The key that unlocks the biblical outlook is the perception that the real subject of Holy Scripture is not man and his religion, but God and his glory; from which it follows that God is the real subject of every text, and

---

[2] J. I. Packer, *Collected Shorter Writing of J. I. Packer,* vol. 3 (United Kingdom: Paternoster Press, 1999), 274.

[3] "An Interview with Michael Horton," no.8, in *The Discerning Reader*, ed. David Barrett, et al. (Grand Rapids, MI: Baker Book House, 1995), 4.

must therefore be the real subject of every expository sermon, . . . [4]

Such wise words from such wise men will help us to remember that we are not called to be "life technocrats" who tinker with the nuts and bolts of better living in this world. We are called by the eternal God to preach to eternity-bound people the timeless gospel of Jesus Christ. Many church-goers these days can sit through weeks of sermons without hearing anything about the cross of Christ and the glories of redemption. Make sure your hearers cannot say this about you.

I also want to urge you to preach Christ who is mighty to save His people from their sins. Reject the modern Christ who went to the cross to simply demonstrate His love for sinners and preach the Christ who actually made atonement for sinners by receiving in His own person the penalty for their sins.

I might add just one thing more. It is not enough to keep the theme of redemption ever in view. We must speak about it in such a way as to convey to our people the glory and grandeur of redemption. We must never speak of redemption as if we were reading our grocery list. Packer writes of Martyn Lloyd-Jones: ". . . his sense of spiritual reality told him that great things must be said in a way that projected their greatness."[5]

Fourth, to preach the Word of God you must study diligently. The modern pastorate is such that you will find it

---

[4] Packer, *Shorter Writing*, 3:274–5.
[5] Ibid., 3:282.

necessary to fight for time to study. You will find that the demands on your time are legion. You will be expected to preach two riveting sermons each week and to provide an equally riveting Bible study in the midweek service. You will have to officiate at funerals and weddings. You will have to make frequent visits to hospitals and nursing homes as well as making visits in the homes of prospects, inactive members and those in crisis.

In addition to all these things, you will be expected to participate in denominational activities and community events. No matter how hard you try to meet all these obligations, you may rest assured that someone in your flock will register his or her view that you should have been somewhere you weren't.

And in those times when you feel that you cannot possibly spare another moment, some well-meaning soul will stick his head in the door and breezily say, "Are you busy? I'll only take a minute."

You must not allow the multitude of your responsibilities to keep you from your main responsibility, which is to feed the flock of God with the Word of God. This requires time and you must find it. You may find it necessary, as many pastors do, to block out certain times of the week during which you will not be available except in emergency. You may find it necessary to go to your study very early in the morning for study and sermon preparation.

The temptation to take shortcuts will be frequently before you. Many pastors yield to that temptation and regularly offer their people "Internet" sermons or sermons they have heard on tape from well-known preachers. I urge you to resist this temptation with all your might. God has not placed you before your congregation to deliver the sermon John MacArthur preached to his congregation.

When your sermon is the product of your own diligent study, it carries with it an authentic ring, and it brings a satisfaction to you and your hearers that "shortcut" sermons can never bring.

You must not, however, take the serious responsibility of preparation to be a license to lock yourself in your study. You must study the Word, but you must also study your people. That type of study can only be done as you mingle with them and minister to them.

Fifth, to preach well you must have a clear theme that is supported by equally clear points. A sermon is not just a running commentary on a passage of Scripture. It is rather finding the main theme of the particular passage and showing how that passage develops the theme. I always try to ask myself two questions about the Scripture with which I am dealing: "What is the passage talking about?" and "What does it say concerning this matter about which it is talking?" My answer to the first question is my theme, and my answers to the second are my points and sub-points.

J. I. Packer goes to the heart of this matter with these words:

> A sermon is a single utterance; therefore it must have a single subject, its divisions (which should be clearly marked, to help the listener follow and remember) should act like the joints of a telescope: "each successive division . . . should be as an additional lens to

bring the subject of your text nearer, and make it more distinct."[6]

One of my joys is my teenagers who fill two or three of the front pews and sit, with pens and paper, eagerly waiting for me to announce the points of the sermon. I hope the Lord will be pleased to give you the same joy.

That joy, however, puts the pressure on me to make sure the points are there, that they truly develop the theme and that they are understandable and memorable. I can always tell from the faces of those teenagers if the theme is interesting and if they are looking forward to each of the points.

Sixth, to preach the Word of God well you must use language that your people can understand. We may impress our congregations by referring to an *a priori* or an *ad hominem* argument, but most of them will not have the slightest idea what we are talking about.

Geoffrey Thomas observes:

> The Word of God is not a sword in the hands of a circus performer to be thrown up and caught again and again in a dazzling display of virtuosity so that after twenty minutes the performance is over and the crowds go home saying how good a show it was. That sword is more akin to the surgeon's scalpel, and the physicians of the Word must cut deep.[7]

---

[6] Ibid., 3:271.
[7] Samuel T. Logan, Jr., ed., *The Preacher and Preaching* (Phillipsburg, NJ: Presbyterian and Reformed Publishing Co., 1986), 377.

We can only cut deep if we are understood. Being understood is far better than being impressive.

Seventh, to preach the Word of God you must employ the element of persuasion. Preachers who are reformed in their doctrine seem to be more inclined to approach preaching as the mere sharing of information. Some preachers give me the impression that exposition means going into detail about every nuance of every word in the text. This turns preaching into an academic exercise. True preaching not only lays truth before people but seeks to show them the glory of that truth and bring them to embrace it.

The greatest preachers in history have been persuaders and pleaders. They do not simply lay the truth on the plates of their hearers and say, "There it is." They show them how vital it is and urge them to accept it. I suggest reading the sermons of Charles Spurgeon and Martyn Lloyd-Jones to learn the art of wooing.

In his biography of Lloyd-Jones, Iain Murray shares these helpful words:

> To expound is not simply to give the correct grammatical sense of a verse or passage, it is rather to set out the principles or doctrines which the words are intended to convey. True expository preaching is, therefore, doctrinal preaching, it is preaching which addresses specific truths from God to man. The expository preacher is not one who "shares his studies" with others, he is an ambassador and a messenger, authoritatively delivering the Word of God to men. Such preaching presents a text, then, with that text in sight throughout, there is deduc-

tion, argument and appeal, the whole making up a message which bears the authority of Scripture itself.[8]

Eighth, to preach the Word of God you must trust God to use His Word to do His work. God has promised that His Word will not return to Him void but will accomplish what He pleases (Isaiah 55:10–11). He tells us that His Word is "the sword of the Spirit" (Ephesians 6:17). It is, in fact, "living and powerful, and sharper than any two-edged sword, piercing even to the division of soul and spirit, and of joints and marrow" (Hebrews 4:12). Furthermore, it is "a discerner of the thoughts and intents of the heart" (Hebrews 4:12).

What wonderful teachings these are! How distressing it would be to preach without them! But with them, we can preach with confidence. It may oftentimes appear that our preaching is accomplishing nothing—that it is falling on deaf ears—but these verses assure us that this is not the case. God accomplishes His will through biblical preaching. He uses it to put a song in troubled hearts, grit in wavering hearts, faith in unbelieving hearts and renewed faith in straying hearts. We cannot see all this happening, but it happens nonetheless, and when we finally come into His presence, the Lord will be pleased to show us all that He was pleased to do through our preaching.

Ninth, to preach well you must pray well. My years in the ministry have convinced me that while true preaching is hard, genuine praying is harder. I think Satan, knowing

---

[8] Iain Murray, *D. M. Lloyd-Jones*, vol. 2 (Edinburgh: The Banner of Truth Trust, 1990), 261.

far better than we the value of prayer, opposes us at this point more than any other. But pray we must. Prayer fetches strength from God against Satan. It takes us away from our preoccupation with ourselves and points us to God who alone can give us sufficiency for preaching. Prayer is the pipeline God has established between His sufficiency and our woeful inadequacy.

Tenth, to preach the Word of God well you must think about what you are doing. After we are in the ministry for a while, the danger of professionalism sets in. By this, I simply mean that we can get to the place where we can churn out sermons with a fair amount of ease. We can preach these sermons without realizing the enormity of what we are doing. The preacher must, therefore, constantly remind himself that he is, in the well-worn words of Richard Baxter, preaching "as never sure to preach again and as a dying man to dying men."[9]

If that reminder does not free us from being professional sermon-producers and bring a sharp edge of urgency to us, we may be beyond help.

Lloyd-Jones used to say that the worst thing that can happen to a preacher is to preach simply because he has been announced to preach.[10] May God deliver us from that trap!

Much more could be said, but I will stop. I do not want you to be discouraged by the magnitude of the task. It is a task for which no one is sufficient. But the Lord is suffi-

---

[9] Cited in Martyn Lloyd-Jones, *Preaching and Preachers* (Grand Rapids, MI: Zondervan Publishing House, 1971), 86.
[10] Ibid., 253.

cient for us, and He is pleased to bless us and use us although we are nothing but frail earthen vessels.

As I prepare my sermons, I try to keep in mind one particular moment that occurs each time I stand before my congregation. This is what I call, "the moment of the upturned face." I notice it each time I take my place at my pulpit—that wonderful and awful moment when the people look up at me with anticipation. It is wonderful because the people are telling me that they are ready to listen to God's message for the hour. It is awful because it makes me conscious of my enormous responsibility.

There toward the back is the face of that one who often attends but does not yet know Christ and, immediately in front of him, the face of that one who is grieving over the loss of a loved one. Over there is the face of that teenager who is trying to determine what really matters. Halfway back on my right is the face of that person who has never been to church before but has come just this one time to see what it is all about. And there in front is that faithful member who is trying to find strength to go on.

All week long these people have heard what the myriad voices of our society have to say. Now they have come to church to find out what God says. I stand there with them looking at me and I tremble as I realize that I stand between heaven and earth. I breathe a prayer for God to help me and I begin. With God's help, the sermon takes life and those faces continue to be upturned. Some begin to nod in agreement and some begin to shine. And, as I leave my pulpit, I am aware that this was God's message and His moment. I know these people have heard from heaven, and I thank God that He made me a preacher.

My prayer for you is that you will have many such experiences. May God so endue you with power in preaching that your people would sooner be without food for their bodies than without your food for their souls.

Sincerely,
Roger Ellsworth

PS—I believe you will find the following titles on preaching to be very helpful:

1. *Preaching and Preachers* by Martyn Lloyd-Jones (Grand Rapids, MI: Zondervan Publishing Co., 1971).
2. *Between Two Worlds* by John R. W. Stott (Grand Rapids, MI: William B. Eerdmans Publishing Co., 1982).
3. *The Preacher and Preaching* by Samuel T. Logan, ed. (Phillipsburg, NJ: Presbyterian and Reformed Publishing Co., 1986).
4. *The Supremacy of God in Preaching* by John Piper (Grand Rapids, MI: Baker Book House, 1990).

Chapter 16

Worship in Spirit and Truth

Terry Johnson

Dear Timothy,

Leading the church in its worship is the single most important responsibility that you will have as a minister of the gospel. Keep this in mind throughout your time of preparation and however many years of active ministry that the Lord should give you. You are a "minister of the Word and sacraments," previous generations of Protestants would have said. Your primary task is to lead the people of God when they gather publicly to hear the written Word of God read, preached, sung and prayed and the "visible word" (Augustine's designation)—the sacraments—administered.

You will find that the pastorate is a busy place. Competition for you time will be intense. Fight off the temptation to become absorbed in other work, even other important work. Worship comes first not only because God comes first but also because nearly everything else, including the public perception of your effectiveness, rides on your ability to lead the worship services. Do not turn this responsibility over to others. Worship "teams" and worship "leaders" finally will not do for the people of God what can only be done through the preaching and praying of one called, trained, examined and ordained to do so. Your reading and preaching of the Scriptures will feed the flock. Your prayers will model piety and teach your people how to address God and relate to Him. Your song selections will expose your people to the words and phrases with which to offer praise to God and respond to the vicissitudes of life.

But I am getting ahead of myself. We are in the midst of "worship wars" today. Churches, denominations, mission agencies and even families are being divided by the question of *how* we are to worship God. The trends are clear enough—novelty is in, tradition is out. Contemporary expressions of worship draw crowds, classic forms draw dust, or so the champions of innovation would have us to believe.

I urge you to think through the implications of the whole biblical witness regarding God and His worship and in particular John 4:7–24. Jesus provides the Christian community with the basic outline of its worship: "God is Spirit, and those who worship Him must worship in spirit and truth" (John 4:24).

Because of who God is ("God is Spirit") we are obligated to worship God (we "must worship") in a manner consistent with two fundamental principles ("spirit and truth"). We are *not at liberty* to worship God in any other way than this that He has commanded. God determines the worship that is pleasing to Him and *is at liberty* to require of us that which *is* rather than that which *isn't*. I sometimes get the impression that decisions are being made in worship today based on someone's perception of what might be "neat" or "special" or make the loudest bang or evoke the biggest tears. These are not the questions that you should be addressing. As a minister of the Word and sacrament you should be asking two fundamental questions—what is it to worship God in spirit? And what is it to worship God in truth? These provide the framework for God-pleasing worship.

Worship in Spirit

The meaning of the first of these, worship "in spirit" is clear enough. The Samaritan woman is arguing about geography, isn't she? (John 4:20). The debate between Jews and Samaritans was over the *place*—which mountain, which building, which altar? "Spirit" is contrasted with place. Place, of course, *was* important in the Old Testament. Jerusalem was *the* place because located there was *the* temple and *the* altar and *the* priests who offered *the* sacrifices, all by divine command and institution. This is why the words of Jesus in verse 21 are perhaps the most revolutionary in the whole Bible. "Jesus said to her, 'Woman, believe Me, an hour is coming when neither in this mountain, nor in Jerusalem, shall you worship the Father.'"

Jesus indicates radical discontinuity with the Old Testament at this point. All of the external factors mentioned above were important *then* in the ways that they are not *now* in the New Testament era. This has important implications for your worship services.

Lead worship that is spiritual. God has always been primarily concerned with the spirit or heart of worship. "All that is within me" is to "bless His holy name." Wholehearted worship has always been required (Psalm 103:1). "Clean hands and a pure heart" and a "broken and contrite heart" are the norm for Old Testament and New Testament worship (Psalm 24:4; Psalm 51:17). Jesus' point must be seen as one of emphasis. This is *especially* the case in the New Testament. The city, the temple, the altars, the sacrifices, the priests, the incense all had symbolic importance. They were all types of Christ whose usefulness ceased with the arrival of the antitype to whom they all pointed, the Lord Jesus Christ (Hebrews 7–10). Do not reintroduce symbols in worship. Do not try to enliven your services with external props like candles and incense and pictures and statues and crosses or whatever other holy hardware liturgists might urge. The whole history of the Old Testament proves the propensity of highly symbolic worship toward mechanical worship on the one hand ("formalism") and idolatry on the other (the worship of the symbols). Each element of worship should be spiritual, aiming at the heart through the conscience.

Keep it simple. Have you noticed that there is no book of Leviticus in the New Testament? There is no ritual by which to approach God (e.g. begin facing the east, bow, repeat the Lord's Prayer, genuflect, etc.). There are no ceremonies excepting the Lord's Supper and Baptism. Your service should be simple, employing what the Puritans called a "plain style." Your reading, preaching, praying and singing should all partake of the ordinary. The apostle Paul gives this some emphasis in his writing. He tells the Corinthians, for example:

> And when I came to you, brethren, I did not come with superiority of speech or of wisdom, proclaiming to you the testimony of God. For I determined to know nothing among you except Jesus Christ, and Him crucified. And I was with you in weakness and in fear and in much trembling. And my message and my preaching were not in persuasive words of wisdom, but in demonstration of the Spirit and of power, that your faith should not rest on the wisdom of men, but on the power of God (1 Corinthians 2:1–5).

A plain style, devoid of rhetorical ornamentation or excess was important to the apostle Paul. "Cleverness of speech" would contradict the message and the cross of Christ would be "made void" (1 Corinthians 1:17). The manner of presentation must be straightforward and simple, authentic in its "weakness and in fear and in much trembling," devoid of "persuasive words of wisdom." Earnestness, sincerity and purity—close cousins of simplicity—are crucial in leading worship services. As the apostle Paul says again, "For we are not like many, peddling the word of God, but as from sincerity, but as from God, we speak in Christ in the sight of God" (2 Corinthians 2:17). A straightforward, unadorned presentation of the truth is the only "style" (if we must speak of styles) that is compatible with a simple gospel. "Therefore, since we have this ministry, as we received mercy, we do not lose heart, but we have renounced the things hidden because of shame, not walking in craftiness or adulterating the word of God, but by the manifestation of truth commending ourselves to every man's conscience in the sight of God" (2 Corinthians 4:1–2). There it is! Simply "manifest" the truth and thereby appeal "to every man's conscience."

In other words, Jesus is concerned with the internal spirit of worship not the external form, except that the form must be simple because simplicity reinforces spirituality. He insists that the *heart,* or spirit, of worship, not the place, the ritual, the ceremony, the theatrics, the technology or the professionalism is crucial. Our worship should be spiritual, simple, straightforward, unadorned, sincere and pure. Do not clutter it with symbols, rituals, ceremonies, complexity or sophistication not authorized in God's Word.

This spirituality and simplicity is also the basis of worship's *catholicity.* Because it is so simple, consisting of Scripture, prayer, singing and the sacraments, it can be conducted anywhere, whether in Alaska or the Amazon. This is also the basis of *the communion of the saints* in worship. Our communion is built upon what we hold in common. Wherever we go in the world we should know essentially what we will encounter when we enter a Christian assembly. Shun the novel, the idiosyncratic, the particular, the unprecedented and aim at the tried and true, the universal and transcendent.

Keep it reverent. The spirit of worship, its tone, its mood, its atmosphere, is that of reverence. God is to be worshipped with "reverence and awe" (Hebrews 12:28). Conduct the service in a mood suitable to the serious business of worshipping Almighty God. Even when you rejoice, let it be "with trembling" (Psalm 2:11).

Worship in Truth

Are you with me so far? Let me move ahead. Second, Jesus says that we must worship in "truth." It seems to me that this means two things.

Worship God as He has commanded. We must worship according to God's truth. Too many people are doing whatever *they* want in worship. What we should be doing is what *God* wants. The sourcebook for finding out what God wants is the Bible. The Samaritan woman thinks that it's acceptable to worship God in the mountains of Samaria according to the ways of the Samaritans. She is wrong about that. Jesus says the Samaritans worship "that which (they) do not know" whereas the Jews worship "that which we know" (verse 22). The whole passage assumes that God can and does tell us what we "must" do in worship (verse 24). Perhaps I've said enough about this already.

Worship must be filled with truth. Not only is worship *ordered* by God's truth, it is also *filled* with God's truth. The content of each element is the Bible. We may follow the simple formula mentioned above—read the Word, preach the Word, sing the Word, pray the Word and administer the visible Word. This is the way to honor God, save sinners, sanctify the saints and worship in truth.

Here is what I want to ask all ministers of the gospel:

- Do you believe that the gospel is the power of God for salvation (Romans 1:16)?
- Do you believe that we are born again by the Word (1 Peter 1:23–25)?

- Do you believe that faith comes by hearing the Word of God (Romans 10:17)?
- Do you believe that we are sanctified by the truth (John 17:17)?
- Do you believe that the Scriptures are living and active and sharper than any two edged sword (Hebrews 4:12)?

If you do (and I know that you do), then you must be alarmed by the trends of the last one hundred years and especially the last thirty. We have seen the Scriptures gradually, and now rapidly, take a reduced role in Christian worship. Less is read (a few verses versus a chapter or more). Less is preached (witness the shift from expository preaching to topical messages). Less is sung (metrical Psalms and theologically rich hymnody have been replaced first by gospel songs and then choruses). Less is prayed (with little praying going on at all).

Indisputably these are the trajectories of modernized worship. They represent an unmitigated disaster in American evangelicalism if we accept the supposition that the Word plays the primary role in converting sinners and sanctifying saints. Resist these trends, Timothy. God "must" be worshipped "in truth," Jesus says. Trust that He will bless His Word as you read, preach, sing and pray it. It will not return void, He has promised (Isaiah 55:11).

Mechanics

I hope that you haven't minded the somewhat dense biblical and theological opening comments that I have made. But I thought they were necessary preliminaries for the practical advice I wish to give now.

First, remain God-centered throughout. You are there to help lead the people into the presence of God. Do not distract them. Do not let your ambition to be liked, beloved and admired get in the way. Do not try to be cute or funny or clever. In short, the services you lead are not about you. Am I stating the obvious? Oh that I were! A few moments viewing Christian TV or a short visit to a typical mega-church will confirm that evangelicalism is not above the cult of personality. Flee from it. You will keep people from God if you draw them to yourself. Let all that you do be God-centered—your opening of the service, your closing of the service, your song selections, your prayers, your preaching.

Second, be Christ-centered in your worship. This means that the great themes of sin and redemption must be prominent throughout and even made to give broad structure to your services.

- Begin with praise for the God of the Bible, Father, Son and Holy Spirit, Creator, Sustainer and Redeemer. "Enter His gates with thanksgiving, and His courts with praise" (Psalm 100:4). This praise can be expressed through a call to worship, a hymn of praise, and a prayer of invocation and praise and a confessional affirmation.

- Move from the vision of God's glory expressed in your praise to a time of confession of sin (cf. Isaiah 6:1–6). This is a logical and gospel-driven order for worship.[1] As we see God's praiseworthiness we naturally become aware of our sin and need of forgiveness. A view of the infinite One reminds us that we are finite. A view of the Holy One reminds us that we are corrupt. You might use the Ten Commandments as preparation for confession. In your prayer lead your people from the full acknowledgement of their sin to the cross and the Christ who died "the just for the unjust" (1 Peter 3:18), who "bore our sin in His body on the cross (1 Peter 2:24), who became a curse for us (Galatians 3:13), who gave His life as a "ransom" for ours (Matthew 20:28) and in whom we have "redemption, the forgiveness of sins (Colossians 1:14).
- Humbly lead your worshippers from confession of sin to the means of grace that God has provided for forgiven but needy disciples.

  - Read the Word
  - Preach the Word
  - Administer the living Word, the sacraments
  - Pray the Word

---

[1] For more on a gospel-driven order of worship see my *Leading in Worship* (Oak Ridge, TN: Covenant Foundation, 1996), 15; and my *The Pastor's Public Ministry* (Greenville, SC: Reformed Academic Press, 2001), 10–15.

- Conclude with thanksgiving and a blessing, giving thanks in Jesus' name for all that is ours in Christ, as we abide in Him (John 15:1 ff.). Our approach to God in worship is like our approach to God in conversion. Seeing who God is in all His grandeur leads to repentance and faith in Christ and eager supplication for sustaining grace mediated through the Word and Spirit.

Third, be Bible-centered. This means certain things about your choices. You have a finite amount of time in worship, typically from an hour to an hour and a half. Think through the amount of time that ought to be given to each element—announcements and preliminaries, prayer, Bible reading, preaching, singing and administration of the sacraments. Just as important, given the five to ten minutes that you intend to sing, what shall you sing? Given the thirty to forty-five minutes that you intend to preach, what shall you preach? Given what I reminded you about above, that we are sanctified by the truth of God's Word (John 17:17), that faith comes by hearing the Word of God (Romans 10:17), let me elaborate on that to which I have only hinted so far.

- Pray the Bible—study Matthew Henry's *Method For Prayer*,[2] Isaac Watts' *Guide to Prayer*[3] or Samuel Miller's *Thoughts on Public Prayer*[4] and see

---

[2] Matthew Henry, *A Method For Prayer* (1716; reprint, Greenville, SC: Reformed Academic Press, 1994).
[3] Isaac Watts, *A Guide to Prayer* (1715, reprint, Edinburgh: The Banner of Truth Trust, 2001).
[4] Samuel Miller, *Thoughts on Public Prayer* (1844, reprint, Harrisonburg, VA: Sprinkle Publications, 1985).

how previous generations of ministers prayed. Their prayers were rich in biblical language and biblical imagery. They learned the language of confession from the Bible's prayers of confession, the language of praise from the Bible's expressions of praise and so on. Nothing will so move your people as hearing the echo of Scripture in their pastor's praise, confession and petitions. "Faith comes by hearing the word of God" (Romans 10:17).

- Read the Bible. I recommend that you read a chapter of another book of the Bible in addition to the section from which you are going to preach. If you are preaching from the Old Testament, read from the New Testament. If you are preaching from the New Testament, read from the Old Testament. "Give attention to the public reading of Scripture," Paul tells Timothy (1 Timothy 4:13). "Faith comes by hearing the word of God" (Romans 10:17).
- Preach the Bible. By this I mean, preach sequential expository sermons. Preach word-by-word, verse-by-verse, book-by-book through the whole Bible. And don't just read the text and then preach topically from it. Preach the passage itself, finding your message and application in the text. Your best models for this today may be John MacArthur at Grace Community Church in Southern California and the late James Montgomery Boice of Tenth Presbyterian Church in Philadelphia. Their written works and audio recordings are both available. This decision to preach expositionally may be the single most important decision that you have to make. Shall you

preach topically or will you have the discipline to preach sequentially? It is my conviction that since Christ is found in "all the Scriptures," we shall not know the whole Christ unless we preach the whole Bible (Luke 24:27). Moreover the *lectio continua* keeps us honest. We all tend to jump on our hobbyhorses and ride them for all they're worth. Sequential expository preaching forces ministers to preach the next text, whatever it is. Thus we are more likely to preach the "whole counsel of God" through a systematic expository method than if we are picking and choosing topics according to our own perceptions and desires (Acts 20:27).

- Sing the Bible. Sing poetically competent songs that are rich in biblical content. Again, you have a finite amount of time. A decision to sing one thing is at the same time a decision not to sing another. Make the best selections possible to fill that time. I would urge you to reintroduce the singing of metrical Psalms to your congregation. This is a "no-brainer" to me. The Psalms are God's hymnbook. They were written to be sung. We ought to sing them. What could be more obvious? Our Protestant ancestors sang Psalms exclusively for over 200 years and predominately for another 100 years beyond that. Only in the last 125 years or so has Psalm-singing slipped from view to the detriment of the churches. It is time to bring them back. The *Trinity Psalter*[5] with

---

[5] *Trinity Psalter* (Pittsburgh, PA: Crown and Covenant, 1994).

the *Trinity Psalter Music Edition*[6] are invaluable resources, combining the words of every verse of every Psalm with familiar tunes. The *Psalms of the Trinity Psalter*[7] and *Psalms of the Trinity Psalter—II*[8] CD's offer beautifully produced recordings of about sixty of 150 Psalms of the *Trinity Psalter*.

Respecting hymns, the eighteenth century was something of a "golden age" in hymn writing, featuring such giants as Isaac Watts, Charles Wesley, John Newton, Augustus Toplady, William Cowper and Philip Doddridge. They set the bar for future generations. Make generous use of their hymns. Shy away from the superficial, the repetitions and the trite. Remember it doesn't matter when a song was written, but the strength of its content and the suitability of its music. Not every musical genre is appropriate for worship. Ask yourself of the words—are they biblically and theologically sound and mature (1 Corinthians 3:1; Hebrews 5:11–6:2)? Of the music, is it singable? Is it emotionally balanced? Is it appropriate for the worship of the God of the Bible?

Fourth, be church-centered in your worship. The church consists of the whole people of God, young and old, rich and poor, Jew and Gentile. The true church tran-

---

[6] *Trinity Psalter Music Edition* (Pittsburgh, PA: Crown and Covenant, 2000).
[7] *Psalms of the Trinity Psalter CD* (Savannah, GA: IPC Press, 1999).
[8] *Psalms of the Trinity Psalter—II CD* (Savannah, GA: IPC Press, 2002).

scends all of the world's divisions based on culture, race, ethnicity and age (Galatians 3:28). So should its worship. I know that the whole trend and direction of things is contrary to this. The theory today is that each sub-culture needs its own worship expressed in its own style of format, music and speech. Think through with me where this will leave us. Inevitably the church will divide into thousands of affinity groups, each one demanding its own worship in its own preferred cultural style—services presumably for black, white, brown, yellow and red; for teens, singles, gen-xers, boomers, and of course, the "greatest generation"; for those who prefer jazz, rock, swing, classical, country, rap, etc., etc., etc. That which ought to be the time when we all become one in Christ will become that moment in the week when we are the most divided. This is a dead end. Don't go there.

Instead consider that the church has its own culture. It has its own treasure of music which includes contributions from Bach, Handel, Beethoven, Mozart, Haydn and Mendelssohn. It has a treasury of lyrics that includes contributions by Watts, Wesley, Newton, Havergal, Luther, Calvin, St. Bernard, St. Francis and so on. Gradually additions are made to the treasury over time. A bare handful of the hundreds of songs that have appealed to any single generation are still around a hundred years later. Those that endure are added to the treasury. Essentially the treasury consists of the songs and words that have appealed across class, race, culture and generation. They have appeared for Welsh, French, German, Spanish, Greek, Latin and Hebrew sources. Yet they have transcended local taste and instead appealed universally. They have stood the test of time. Who doesn't love "Amazing Grace"? Who doesn't delight to sing "Joy to the World"? What I am saying is, do not select a format, a style of language or style of music that appeals to one group's peculiar tastes and thereby excludes all the others. Rather, stick to the church's own transcendent culture, which no one group can claim as it's own, which boasts a universal aesthetic appeal, and so is owned by all.[9] Don't be deflected by the claim that the issue is communication, as though the gospel can't be understood unless it is wrapped up in each individual's cultural preferences. It's not.

Concluding Issue

Lead worship as I have outlined, and you may be criticized. "You're just an apologist for traditional worship," the objection may be raised. "You don't make any provision for the unchurched, for seekers, for the lost. They will be bored and turned-off by what you describe." This is a serious challenge. But before you and I capitulate, let's see if we have understood the complaint correctly. We've said our worship is to be God-centered, Christ-centered, Word-centered and church-centered. Is this what is thought to be insufficiently evangelistic? What we have described is loaded with the gospel from top to bottom, from start to finish. Frankly, only those who have lost confidence that the gospel (itself) is the "power of God for salvation" (Romans 1:16), that

---

[9] See my *Reformed Worship: Worship That is According to Scripture* (Greenville, SC: Reformed Academic Press, 2000), 9–13.

"faith comes by hearing the word of God" (Romans 10:17), that we are "sanctified by the truth" (John 17:17), could draw such a conclusion. I know not what to think of those who feel the necessity to substitute skits and dances, concerts and talk shows for solid biblical preaching, singing and praying. Unbelief comes to mind. Idolatry suggests itself as well.

When the people of God reverently worship God, we should expect that the result will be a meeting significantly different from anything that the unchurched will have previously experienced. Yet this should not concern us so long as the service is conducted in a known tongue. If it is, the apostle Paul is confident that the unbeliever, in the presence of reverent, God-centered, Christ-centered, Word-filled worship, "is convicted by all, he is called to account by all; the secrets of his heart are disclosed; and so he will fall on his face and worship God, declaring that God is certainly among you" (1 Corinthians 14:24–25).

There is not one church in a hundred (a thousand?) that combines biblical preaching with reverent worship. Some churches have the preaching, but their worship suffers. Some have the worship, but their preaching not just suffers, it is insufferable. There is a slowly building demand for churches that combine both together. Do so and you'll not only worship as Jesus says we "must" but will be ready to meet the need as it rises in the days that are ahead.

Sincerely,
Terry

PS—Here are some books, in addition to those referred in the footnotes that I heartily recommend that you read:

1. *With Reverence and Awe* by D. G. Hart and John R. Muether (Phillipsburg, NJ: P&R Publishing, 2002).
2. *Leading in Prayer* by Hughes Oliphant Old (Grand Rapids, MI: Eerdmans, 1995).
3. *Worship That Is Reformed According to Scriptures— Guides to the Reformed Tradition* by Hughes Oliphant Old (Atlanta, GA: John Knox Press, 1984).
4. *O' Come Let Us Worship* by Robert Rayburn (Grand Rapids, MI: Baker Book House, 1980).

Chapter 17

Train Other Men
Steve Martin

Dear Timothy,

Greetings from Atlanta! It has been a while since I last wrote to you. I trust that you are well and close to Christ. It is a beautiful late winter day here and it makes one glad to be living in Atlanta in January and not Minneapolis! But wherever we are with Christ is the best place. If you are walking with Christ, then you are in the best place for you.

In reflecting upon our interactions over the past months, my thoughts turned to yet another area where I believe you can grow and expand as a pastor. You have labored to be a faithful workman, handling accurately the Word of Truth. You seem to diligently watch over your own heart and your doctrine. May the Lord be praised for keeping you and energizing you to do that. But to be a faithful pastor, you must add to your vision not only the care and feeding of your soul, and that of your family, and that of the church family in general, but you should also target other men in the church to nurture and train in the things of God.

Why train other men? First, some needs of Christ's churches can only be met when we train other men. The need of the hour, in every generation, is for godly men to be raised up to serve at home, in the local church and in the wider work of the kingdom of God.

We need men of God to lead our Christian families. From Genesis to Revelation, the Word of God highlights again and again the importance of the husband and the father in the home. Men who are not good husbands and fathers leave a legacy of spiritual mediocrity and disaster behind them. Pastor after pastor I talk to complains of the lack of godly men, growing men, men who can lead in their homes and then outside their homes. You yourself may have cried out to God, "Where are the men of God?" The need of the hour in family after family, church after church, is for godly men to lovingly lead their wives and children in the things of God. If the husband cares more about making money and advancing his career than he does about the eternal destinies of his wife and children, then the family will soon show the effects of his idolatry of work and success and the so-called "good life."

Our surrounding secular culture has been under the judgment of God, according to Romans 1:18–32, for some time. We have been given over to a graceless condition of moral and spiritual blindness and stupidity. We cannot see let alone solve our true national problems. It depresses biblically sensitive readers to see a national weekly news magazine have as its cover story: "Men and Women—Are They Different?" Yet this is only a recent skirmish in the three decade-long war to obscure or clarify maleness, femaleness and the family. The war has produced millions of marriage and family casualties and brought almost wholesale cultural upheaval and devolution.

As American culture has been in the throes of a battle for marriage and the family, the churches have not been silent. Pastors and theologians have identified the enemies and alerted the churches. But the need still stands to train men to be biblical singles, biblical husbands, biblical fathers and biblical older men. We cannot take it for granted that conversion gives a man all he needs to know about manhood, marriage, child raising and leadership. There may have been a time a few decades ago when a family could begin to attend your church, be converted and hit the ground running. There was then much more common grace in American culture than there is today. We can no longer assume that very much, if any, understanding of biblical manhood, marriage, the Christian nurture of children and aging among our families will come to us from the world. Sadly, many churches have allowed the culture to dictate their views of gender, marriage and the family. We cannot be passive but must become proactive in teaching our people these things. We must be training our men in these areas.

Next, we need men of God to lead our churches. It has always been God's way to use men. As A. W. Tozer pointedly said, "God the Holy Spirit does not fill rabbits." The cry around the world in the churches is for men, godly men, men who will lead at home and then in the church. Too many churches are functionally led by women. Once, when asked why there were such few men in the British churches, London pastor Martyn Lloyd-Jones replied, "That is because there are so many old ladies in the pulpits." If pastors themselves are not truly biblical men, men of God, they will not attract men. A famous evangelist stung the men of one large Baptist church here in Atlanta when he challenged them by saying, "You work and dream and sweat to put Coca Cola and UPS on the map around the world. But you have small visions and little energy for Jesus Christ and to spread His fame around the world!" And this evangelist was right. Too often young business and professional men are far more concerned about pouring their lives into their jobs and careers than they are at pouring themselves into being Christ-like churchmen. South African mission leader Michael Cassidy spoke of men "giving up their small ambitions." There is more to life for the Christian man than money, fame and power. Our family and our church family need Christ-like male leadership. They do not need men of confused gender and pitiful priorities who give Christ, their family and His church the dregs of their lives. The barrenness of so many busy lives today silently preaches that men must change.

And don't be too quick to listen to those who say that life is too hard in our day and time is too precious for men to give up their frantic pursuit of financial security and personal success for serving Christ in His churches. Life has always been hard since the fall. By the sweat of his brow a man must labor amongst the thistles and thorns of farming, business, industry and technology. When was it ever easy and leisurely for men to provide for their families' needs?

But God gives men to the churches as gifts who have enough grace to slake the thirst of their own souls from the wells of salvation and slake the thirst of their families and that of others in their local churches. Our Lord promised His hearers that coming to Christ would enlarge a man, magnify his abilities and multiply his life. The Head of the church cried out to the thirsty crowds on the feast day recorded in John 7:37–38, "If anyone thirsts, let him come to me and drink. Whoever believes in me, as the Scripture has said: 'Out of his heart will flow rivers of living water.'" Verse 39 tells the reader that Jesus was referring to the Holy Spirit who was yet to be given in His fullness at Pentecost. Our Lord was giving a mental picture of the expansive life the Holy Spirit would create within each regenerate heart. He was not promising a drop or a cup or a bucket of the Spirit's living water. He promised a river! Surely such an expansive heart has an overflow to others. Later in John 10:10b, when comparing His ministry to His sheep as the Good Shepherd with the ministry of the hireling shepherds, the Pharisees and Sadducees, our Lord said, "I came that they might have life and have it abundantly." The word *abundantly* means "more than enough." It means that you have more than you need. Men who enter into the new birth have the means to look beyond themselves and give to others. Men who enter into the new birth and are trained to be biblical channel their overflowing lives within the riverbanks set out in God's Word. Regeneration produces life and energy. The Bible provides the guidelines for what the regenerate person is to be and do. Men who are saved and trained are a mighty source for good in the local church.

And third, we need men of God to build up the kingdom of God beyond the local church. In Matthew 9:35–38 our Lord exhorted His disciples (and us) to pray to "the Lord of the Harvest" that He might raise up harvesters for the harvest fields. The harvest is great but the workers are few. For a man to leave his church and his culture and the comforts of the "known," something greater than human persuasion and motivation is needed. Divine authority must call a man and compel a man to go. That is why we must pray for these divinely called men to recognize the call of God upon their lives and to faithfully answer the call with active obedience. Pitifully few good men are coming forth to become pastors to preach the gospel at home. Pitifully few good men are coming forth to become missionary church planters abroad. Women are filling the vacuum in seminaries and on the mission field. Where are the men? We pastors must pray for our men that the Lord of the Harvest might call men from each of our churches to give up their small, self-centered ambitions and become zealous for Christ, the Spirit-anointed preaching of His gospel, the ingathering of His elect and the spread of His glory throughout the earth.

Training men is not optional for a pastor. In Matthew 28:19–20, our Lord commanded His apostles (and through them the churches of all generations) to go into all the world and make disciples. The imperative was "make disciples." The other verbs in the sentence are explanatory. It is by going, baptizing in the name of the Trinity and teaching all things that Jesus taught, that making disciples is accomplished. Taking the initiative and going to the lost with the gospel, baptizing those who respond in repentance and faith and then teaching them "all things whatsoever I have commanded you," rounds out the job description of disciple making. The Lord was not interested in spraying the masses with the gospel before some "secret rapture" occurred, but truly making lasting Christians—biblical disciples.

Jesus wants decisions that become disciples. Timothy, too much evangelism of the past one hundred years has been of the shallow, superficial kind that seeks to induce a decision that is countable but does not take the time to truly make disciples. Sad studies have shown that in nation-wide evangelism strategies in America that targeted the masses with the minimalist approach to evangelism and fulfilling the Great Commission, only nine-tenths of one percent of the so-called decisions are involved in local churches a year later. If we would follow our Lord's command and aim not for decisions but for making disciples, how different our churches would be, how different American Christianity would be.

Paul commanded his young assistant to also make disciples. In his final letter, with all the important issues he wanted to leave clearly focused in Timothy's mind, Paul emphasized making disciples. In 2 Timothy 2:2, Paul wrote, "And what you have heard from me in the presence of many witnesses entrust to faithful men who will be able to teach others also." Herein lies the genius of a faithful ministry: Men discipling men who in turn disciple other men. The torch of truth must be passed on from generation to generation of Christians through the men by means of faithful disciple making. Our Lord saved Paul and uniquely made the message clear to him. He in turn discipled young Timothy, as his spiritual son. Timothy in turn was to pour the truth into faithful vessels, men who would in turn find faithful men to whom to relay the truth. Four generations of faithful men—Paul, Timothy, "faithful men" and "others."

We do not need to jazz up or somehow enhance a weak gospel. We need to faithfully teach and preach the biblical gospel and see to it that identifiably faithful men will take the unadulterated gospel on to the next generation. That is how to grow a church biblically. To end your days as faithful is no small thing. The Pastoral Epistles and indeed the whole of the New Testament hold up "faithfulness" as the model. "Faithfulness" is not blandness nor is it least-common-denominator-Christianity, but rather fidelity to the biblical gospel. The apostle Paul did not fill his final letter to his chosen and loved assistant with fluff or small talk. One of the primary and important things of a pastor who wants to hear the Lord say, "Well done, good and faithful servant," is to disciple faithful men who will in turn be able to teach others the biblical truth without adulteration or pollution or diminution.

Both our Lord's closing command to His church and Christ's great apostle's closing command to his assistant tell us to make disciples in our ministry. And the Scripture also gives us many examples of training men.

The method of God the Son to establish His kingdom upon the earth was to pour His life and teaching into twelve men. He knew His earthly ministry was temporary. He repeatedly talked of His impending departure. The cross and the resurrection, the forty days of appearances and then the ascension would take Him from the scene. What would the church be left with to compensate for the loss of its Leader? Because of His discipling efforts, the church was left with twelve Spirit-filled leaders who would soon fan out and expand the scope of Christ's ministry, thereby doing greater things than Jesus Himself did in His earthly ministry.

In Luke 6:40 Jesus taught an important principle about His ministry with men: "A disciple is not above his teacher, but everyone when he is fully trained will be like his teacher." Christ knew that He had hand-picked and personally trained twelve men, even though one would falter and become the son of perdition. Many people followed our Lord as disciples in the broad sense of the word. From within this larger group, Jesus chose twelve for specialized training and commissioning who would become apostles. Among the twelve, there was the inner circle of three who are most frequently seen with Jesus (Peter, James and John). As you reread the gospel accounts, notice the special time our Lord spent with these three. And even among the three, He was especially close to John, the disciple Jesus loved. But notice too in the gospels that our Lord commissioned seventy more disciples to take the gospel out from their midst preaching and verifying that the kingdom of God had come upon them. If you go through the gospels highlighting the times our Lord was with the twelve, the three or the seventy, it is eye-opening how committed He was to training men as the means to continue and to expand His ministry.

But our Lord's example is not alone in the New Testament. Consider Barnabas. A true "son of encouragement" as his name reads, he seemed to have a special gift for spotting underdeveloped men and bringing them along to be more useful to the Savior. When the churches were initially suspicious of Saul of Tarsus and his recent professed conversion, it was Barnabas who took Saul/Paul under his wing and lent him credibility (cf. Acts 4:36–37, 8:1–3, 9:1–30, and 13:1–13). It is not long in the Acts account until "Barnabas and Saul" becomes "Saul and Barnabas" (cf. 13:2 and 13:13). You may well discover that one of the men you train may exceed you in usefulness to the Master. Regard that not as a threat, but as a token of divine blessing on your ministry.

Barnabas's ministry of training men was not limited to Paul. Remember how he helped John Mark. After Mark deserted the first missionary journey, Barnabas gave him another opportunity, even though it meant splitting with Paul. John Mark was salvaged and would later assist his uncle, Peter, in his ministry. Many scholars, as you know, believe that Mark's gospel is really Simon Peter's gospel filtered through John Mark as his secretary. Later Paul himself would ask for Mark's help, praising his usefulness. So Paul's thirteen letters and Peter's gospel were written by men who were one time viewed as questionable for the ministry but were invaluable when trained by Barnabas. To put it another way, the Holy Spirit inspired over half of our New Testament to be written by men Barnabas had discipled!

Paul also gives us an example of training other men. The New Testament record reveals that Paul took men wherever he went, and the implication becomes clear that he was training them: Silas (Acts 15:40), Timothy (Acts 16:3), Aquila and Priscilla (Acts 18:18), Erastus (Acts 19:22 and Romans 16:23), Sopater of Berea (Acts 20:4), Aristarchus and Secundus from Thessalonica (Acts 20:4), Gaius from Derbe (Acts 20:4), Tychicus and Trophemus from the province of Asia (Acts 20:4) and Luke the physician (note the "we" portions of Luke's book of Acts of the Apostles). Paul was a great preacher of the gospel and teacher of the Scriptures, but he was also a great trainer of men.

So when Paul admonishes Timothy to train men in 2 Timothy 2:2 he is only advocating that which he himself practiced. And notice the content of his training: "what you have heard from me in the presence of many witnesses." He is referring to the gospel. This is what he is to commit to others. Whatever else a faithful disciple may know, he must have a clear knowledge of the contents of the gospel.

Having proven to be faithful himself, Timothy was also to entrust this good deposit of the gospel to "faithful men." One must be faithful. One must train faithful men. Timothy was to make sure that the next level or generation of church leaders was to be made up of faithful men who could "color within the lines" also. "Faithful men" were men who kept the template intact, who did not rub out the edges of the pattern of sound words. It is paramount that each generation of preachers gets the gospel right.

To keep the gospel unadulterated and unchanged and undiluted is very hard. While the word *faithful* may seem old-fashioned and weak, like the Bible word *meek*, it is not. It is required of men entrusted with a sacred charge that they prove faithful (1 Corinthians 4:1–2). Christian pastors want "faithful" written on their tombstone, not "innovative," not "creative," not "he pushed the envelope." Those terms are left for the biographies of the liberals, the heretics and the heterodox. Biblical shepherds want to hear our Lord say on Judgment Day, "Well done, good and faithful servant!"

Some groups in Christendom boast of their "apostolic succession." Well, the true "apostolic succession" is the faithful transmission of the gospel from one man down to another generation of faithful men. The faithfulness of these men is seen in their faithful adherence to the truth of the gospel as well as their faithful depositing the truth in another generation of faithful men "who will be able to teach others also."

The teaching skills referred to here do not necessarily refer to those who have formal training in educational methods. A clear understanding of the truth and a personal desire to preach and teach it to others is what is in view. A man does not necessarily have to go to seminary to gain these truths and have them firmly lodged in his heart and mind. God's "apostolic succession" is faithful men training faithful men in the unadulterated gospel. Multiplying faithful men is God's time-honored method. Before the New Testament had been completed, it was especially crucial that the truth of the gospel and the details of the Scriptures not be lost. The Word of God must remain free from error. Yet today, there is still validity in this process. The gospel is still being lost by faithless men. Impostors and charlatans still plague the churches with their "gospel-lite" and their journey down paths of heresy. The price for keeping the truth and keeping the church in the truth is perpetual vigilance in guarding the gospel and entrusting it to faithful men.

Your primary goal is to train men to be Christ-like men of God. If he is married, then being a man of God involves being a Christ-like husband. If he is a father, then it includes being a loving and faithful nurturer of his children.

Biblical manhood should not be taken for granted. Paul told young Titus to instruct those under his charge with sound doctrine about gender—Christian men, older and younger, are to act like this (Titus 2:1–2, 6–8, 11–14). Paul tells young Timothy to teach those under his charge how Christian men are to conduct themselves in the local assembly (1 Timothy 2:8–15). After a quarter of a century of gender bending by the increasingly graceless and clueless American culture, American churches have assimilated people who do not understand nor strive to be examples of biblical manhood and womanhood. God's Word teaches that Spirit-filled husbands and fathers exhibit identifiable traits according to Ephesians 5:16–6:4. God's Word teaches that Scripture-filled husbands and fathers exhibit identifiable traits, according to Colossians 3:16–21. (Note that the same traits are taught in both passages, revealing two sides of the same coin.) God's Word teaches that Christian men who are single must learn to channel their energy into godly and constructive goals, according to 1 Corinthians 7:6–9. An orthodox church with an orthodox confession and an orthodox pulpit that does not have faithful men incarnating these orthodox truths and in turn ministering out of the overflow of their lives to their wives and children, is not a healthy church. It is a sick and weak church that only has a name for orthodoxy.

If you do not train men to be men and men of God, then you will have failed in entrusting the good deposit to faithful men. If the men of your church and their marriages are biblical (not perfect but faithful to Scriptural norms), then you will have a healthy foundation from which to build faithful men. But men who are derelict at home cannot be entrusted with leadership in the church. Scripture forbids men who are not faithful at home from multiplying their mediocrity. Train your men to be men who know Christ and love Him and who love their wives and children for Christ's sake. Their success at home is their credibility with others. If a man can't handle four people, why entrust to him forty? Biblical wisdom says, "No, let him manage four well first and then we may give him forty."

Some of the men you train to be faithful men of God and husbands and fathers may well become elders for a local church. Faithful men are the spiritual backbone of any congregation. Paul gives simple instructions on who is qualified to be an elder and on what elders do. Paul's Spirit-inspired instruction as to who qualifies to be an elder/overseer/shepherd are clear from comparing 1 Timothy 3:1–7, Titus 1:5–9 and Acts 20:17–35. Elders are to be time-tested men of God who watch over the well-being of God's flock as those who must give an account to God for this sacred trust (Hebrews 13:17). You are seeking to build men who will feed, guard and guide the flock with the Word of God, under the authority of Jesus Christ, the Chief Shepherd.

Some of the men you train may well become deacons. Deacons are seen in the New Testament as assistants to the elders in ministering to the flock of God. Their qualifications are listed by Paul in 1 Timothy 3:8–13. Paul does not believe we should guess or be in the dark as to what qualities are necessary for leadership in the local assembly. He spells them out for us. Luke recorded how the needs of ministry grew in the early church such that an order of local church officers was created to meet physical and fiscal needs. These "proto-deacons" in Acts 6:1–6 freed up the apostles and elders in the church in Jerusalem for teaching and prayer. That is what godly and faithful deacons do today. In this you are seeking to build men who will aid the elders in serving the flock.

The church of Jesus Christ always needs godly pastors and missionary church planters. God alone sovereignly equips and calls them. But He does not do this in a vacuum. He normally does His sovereign work in local congregations where young men first gain knowledge of Christ and the glory of preaching His gospel. As I mentioned earlier, our Lord's commission recorded in Matthew 28:19–20 has never been rescinded. Likewise, when the Master told the apostles in Acts 1:8 to wait for the Holy Spirit, He promised them that the Spirit would enable them to be witnesses "to the uttermost parts of the world." The world still needs the gospel. All of Christ's elect have not been brought into the fold. We have much sacrificial work to do "until all the ransomed church of God be saved to sin no more" (2 Timothy 2:10). God the Holy Spirit still makes men supernaturally empowered witnesses to the truth of Christ and the gospel of "ruin by the fall, ransom by the Son and regeneration by the Holy Spirit." And He still is compelling men to leave home and hearth to go to that last jungle, that last barrio, that last metroplex, that last valley, that last frozen wasteland and that last neighbor next door. Some of the men in our churches may well be called to take the gospel abroad and plant churches where none are currently found. Let's do our part to see to it that good men are trained and available for the Lord's call.

GATHERING MEN TO TRAIN

Gathering men precedes training them. That seems obvious but we must keep it in mind. And to rightly gather men we must do several things. First, we must pray. I said earlier that the Lord Jesus specifically tells His people in

Matthew 9:35–38 to pray earnestly to the Lord of the harvest to send out laborers into His harvest. God raises up men. We can work until we are blue in the face but without prayer it is not faithfulness, it is only fleshly activity. God can bring men out of nowhere and right from under your nose. Early in my ministry days I needed to learn two lessons. The first was hard prayer. The second was hard work. Both together comprise the Christian ministry. I spent months, from September through March, laboring from dawn till dusk. I labored to contact and meet with many young men. But while the prospects were many, I did not see where "my men" were. Then I began to pray in earnest. John 15:16 jumped off the page. "You did not choose me, but I chose you and appointed you that you should go and bear fruit and that your fruit should abide, so that whatever you ask the Father in my name, He may give it to you." What I saw so clearly then was that God's sovereign calling of men was intertwined with my prayer for my men. As I began to pray in earnest, that week God raised up the men who would become the backbone of my first ministry. Only God can give enduring fruit. Only the Lord of the harvest sovereignly chooses and calls men. And in answer to prayer, He enables His churches to recognize His called leaders-to-be.

Second, you must sow broadly. Jesus preached to the multitudes and invited those who knew themselves to be weary and burdened with their sins to come to Him (Matthew 11:28–30). And those effectually called did come. It is a mistake to sow narrowly and hope to see a mega-harvest from a small plot of land. The more you sow, the more men the Lord may raise up. Besides preaching on the Lord's

Day, take opportunities to preach to service clubs, baccalaureate services, jails, nursing homes, military bases and wherever else you have opportunity. Also have an occasional men's night out where you gather at the church or someone's home to watch a movie together and analyze its implications biblically.

You can also offer things that require a bit more commitment. For thirty years I also have led men's groups. Schedule them early in the morning on a work day (like 6:15–7:30 A.M.) or on a Saturday morning. Make them open to all men in the church. Make your invitations to come public and clear. Then pray and see who the Lord brings. Requiring that they go outside the normal church comfort zone of Sunday morning, Sunday evening and Wednesday evening shows whether spiritual growth and usefulness is important to them. I also privately exhort some men whom I believe to be underdeveloped to come also. They have heard the public invitation. Then I give them a private invitation. The Lord will winnow out those who will not be faithful in little things or who have no appetite to hunger and thirst for righteousness.

Third, identify clearly those with whom you are going to spend additional time training. You cannot be too careful here. Our Lord is recorded to have spent a whole night in prayer before choosing the twelve. If you have one chance to pour your life into men, which men are you going to choose? To choose poorly and wrongly is to waste your precious time. Make this mistake repeatedly and you risk wasting a lifetime. Have the biblical markers of faithfulness before you as you pray over your men. Who seems to be truly hungry and thirsty for righteousness? Who is regularly poor of spirit and seeking first the kingdom of God and His righteousness? Who is faithful in little things (Luke 16:10)? Who has a heart for God and a teachable attitude? Which men pursue holiness? Which men are jealous for Christ's glory? Which men are zealous for Christ in witnessing? Which men so walk with Christ that there is an overflow of their lives into their families first and then to others outside their families also?

Fourth, test them. Give them things to do that require faithfulness and humility. Ask them to do things that are detestable to the flesh. Fleshly egos want to do flashy and "important" things but will not do the everyday, faithful things. Those who do not show up for practice don't start on game day! Neither should men think that they can be unfaithful in little things and be called to do "big things." Also give men things to do that will test their metal. Take them witnessing. Take them with you when you are to speak somewhere and have them give a testimony. Have them publicly identify themselves with Christ and His cause. This will help a man burn some psychological bridges and help burn the gospel into his mind. See if they can teach by giving them a small group to lead and teach for a defined period of time. When the time is up, debrief and critique their work. If no one learns by listening to them, they probably do not have the gift of teaching. They are not lost to the kingdom, but you had better learn their strengths and weaknesses now.

Fifth, personally challenge them. Our Lord challenged men to follow Him with the promise that He would train them to become "fishers of men" (Matthew 4:19). We should do no less. Paul could challenge men and churches to follow him as he imitated Christ (1 Corinthians 4:6 and 11:1). In doing so we make clear the chain of command and the goal. It is Christ's kingdom and we are His undershepherds. We should never be authoritarian, but we should biblically wield authority, clearly asking men to follow us as we follow Christ. Be neither vague or nebulous but clear and forthright. "Here is where I am going. I believe God has worked in your heart to go down this road with me in ministering to others. I want you to follow me as I follow Christ. Will you come with me?" Give them a vision of where you want to go and pray that the Lord will work in their hearts.

Sixth and last, publicly identify them. In your local church context, explain publicly that Joe is being asked to teach Sunday School and that Bob is being asked to lead a small group study. All authority is delegated, coming down from the Father. Your people need to know that these men occupying new positions have delegated authority from the elders. People should not have to guess and wonder "who appointed him teacher over us." The answer should have come up front—you did!

Training the Men You Gather

Once God has given you men in whom to invest your life, you must be faithful to lead and train them. First, do so by example. The Lord Jesus Christ's incarnation is one great argument for the role of a godly example as the foundation of training men. Our Lord did not drop sermon outlines from heaven nor a manual on sacrificial love to God and to man. He became the proverbial picture that says more than ten thousand words. Our Lord consciously acted in such ways as to leave His disciples and us today examples to follow. John 13:1–5 is the great example of "greater love." Peter could never lose the memory of our Lord's example that night and other times and exhorted his readers to follow Christ's specific example of suffering in meekness (1 Peter 2:21–23) and serving others rather than lording it over them (1 Peter 5:1–5). The apostle Paul taught much about the place of being an example in his pedagogy. He used the word translated as "example" or "model" (think "template") to illustrate spiritual truth. He called Timothy, even though he was young, to be an "example" to the people, in speech, conduct, love, faith and purity (1 Timothy 4:12). He admonished the Corinthians to remember the kind of example he had been to them and challenged them to imitate his life's pattern of faithfulness (1 Corinthians 4:14–17 and 10:31–11:1). He lauded the church in Thessalonica for being an example to the other churches (1 Thessalonians 1:7) and later used himself as an example of the maxim that "if a man will not work for his food, he should not be helped by the church" (2 Thessalonians 3:9). He warned the Philippians to keep their gaze focused upon those who walk "according to the example you have in us" (3:17). He instructed young pastor Titus to be an example to the believers in Crete (2:7). He used an augmented form of the word *example* when he wrote Timothy to tell him that Jesus was the prototype or supreme example we are to follow (1 Timothy 1:16).

The power of an example cannot be over-stated. The old adage, "I cannot hear what you say because your actions speak too loudly" is still true today. If your life and conduct puts others off, if your life speaks a different message than your sermons, if you are not to some degree embodying what you profess and preach, you cannot train others—except in hypocrisy. That is what we call someone who does not practice what he preaches. The Bible does not teach or expect perfection this side of heaven but it does hold up faithfulness. Faithfulness is fulfillment of a stewardship as well as conformity with a code or standard. If I am a pastor who does not trust God, if I am known to be always under the pile, if I whine a lot about how hard life and the ministry are, if I am not leading and loving my family, then I am a bad example and must repent.

Martyn Lloyd-Jones was right when he said it was a sin for a minister to fail to express confidence in God. Men who obviously know God and are hopelessly in love with His Son and consciously dependent upon His Spirit and His Word are going to be attractive to others and impact others. Like begets like. If you are burdened for the lost and are witnessing as a way of life, so will your men. If you bring all of life before God's providence in Romans 8:28 fashion, so will your men. If you are a thorough repenter of your sins, so will your men be. You cannot take your men where you yourself have not gone. And if the Lord is teaching you, you ought to be passing on these lessons to your men.

Second, you train other men with sound doctrine. Teach your men the Bible. Christianity in the West is weak because it no longer has any skeletal structure. It is an "evangelly fish." It no longer teaches the great core doctrines of the Word of God. And before we cluck our tongues at others, we must be careful that we don't fall into the error of some of our forefathers who thought that holding on to a few fundamentals were enough. That great early twentieth-century champion of the Bible and the historic Protestant faith, J. Gresham Machen, once said something to the effect that he did not use the term "fundamentalist" to describe himself because "fundamentalism" was too small a ledge to stand upon as the great waves of unbelief smashed upon the shores of America. He was a full-blooded and hearty confessionalist. Introduce your men to the historic confessions of the Protestant churches.

Remember that you are teaching the truth to make them holy, not to make them smart. Nothing is more repugnant than a professed Calvinist whose life is consumed with looking for real or imagined "semi-Pelagians" in the bushes with whom to sword fight. The truth is given to make us like Christ, not to position us atop the Hill of Vain Glory to rain down scorn on brethren with less biblical theology. Paul warned the gifted and learned but unholy Corinthian congregation that knowledge puffs up but love builds up (1 Corinthians 8:1). If we keep clearly in mind that we are "teaching them to obey all that I have commanded you," then we will avoid the danger of "notional religion" and truly be "experiential Calvinists."

Don't neglect a key weapon in your arsenal—good books. Protestants have always championed literacy because of the primacy of the Word of God (a Berean spirit) and the priesthood of all believers. To have the Bible and the great legacy of Protestant theological and devotional writings and not use them is a sin! Have your men read the best books by the best teachers. After the Bible, your men should become lovers of the best books.

Start them on good authors who put the cookies down where everyone can reach them. Even men who are not great readers can become great readers when they are spiritually motivated and exposed to the good stuff. Begin with Peter Jeffrey, Jerry Bridges, Martyn Lloyd-Jones, James Boice, R. C. Sproul, Don Whitney, Richard Belcher, John Blanchard, Sinclair Ferguson, James Packer, John MacArthur and similar contemporary writers who make the truth come alive and are biblically and historically faithful. You won't agree with everything each author says but without being unduly critical tell your men where you disagree and why. It will help them learn discernment and know that no man, not even you, is perfect.

Give them back their great Protestant heritage by introducing them to the wealth of helpful literature that has been handed down to us. Encourage them to read the more accessible works of the Reformers (Martin Luther, John Calvin), the Puritans (Thomas Watson, Thomas Brooks, John Bunyan and Richard Sibbes), Jonathan Edwards, Charles Spurgeon, the writers of old Princeton (Alexander, the Hodges and Warfield) and the founders of the Southern Baptist Convention (Dagg, Boyce, Mell, Broadus, Manly, et al.). Encourage them to read church history and biographies (the writings of Iain Murray are particularly helpful here).

Third, train them by speaking the truth in love. What I mean by that is that you should become their encourager when they need it and their rebuker (both gently and more sternly) when they need it. Paul's admonition of "speaking the truth in love" (Ephesians 5:15) is literally "truthing in love." Our men need the hard edge of unbending truth and the tender sensitivity of love. And you too must be a man who takes rebuke and admonition well without reacting and becoming defensive. You must be a man who receives encouragement and not act like you always have it all together.

Fourth, train men by doing (with them) and delegating (to them). Earlier I said that you must test your men by giving them things to do. You should always be the example who is out doing it yourself. Take them with you to watch and learn. Never do anything by yourself if you can help it. Always take one of your men with you. Jesus did. Paul did.

When riding together in the car on the way to speak, pray about the upcoming engagement, explain how you make decisions on what to preach about or how you discern things and then debrief and rejoice (or grieve) on the way home. Think of how our Lord spoke to the multitudes or to a person along the way and then discussed the events with His men. Or when you have a spontaneous opportunity to counsel a person with a tricky problem, let your associate pretend he is a fly on the wall and be quiet and learn.

Jesus was not an ivory tower theologian. He was not the general who led from the rear of the army. Biblical shepherds led their sheep to green pastures and still waters by walking out ahead and they followed. So must we. We must take them where we want them to go. Don't send them witnessing, take them witnessing. Don't just delegate, take them with you. Don't just tell your men to pray, pray with them.

Fifth, train your men in various formats. Churches have many places to give men places to serve. Let them try several things, even if they fail briefly. Do not leave a failing man in a responsibility forever. Take him out, debrief as to why failure occurred. Give him other things to do. One man may have gifts that do not make him a public leader, he is more of a behind-the-scenes kind of guy. But if he ever has to lead a public meeting, he will appreciate the man who is gifted in that way. Similarly, the man with public gifts should learn to take a back seat and minister in quiet obscurity for a time. It will cause him to appreciate the brother whose gifts are not as public but are nevertheless necessary if the whole body is to function well.

Well, brother, I have gone on way too long and tried your patience. I could say other things but I have given you enough to chew on (and hopefully not choke on). May the Lord give you wisdom in giving your time to the best things and not just to good things. Look to your Lord and He will guide your steps.

Your brother, co-worker and fellow pilgrim
on the road to the Celestial City,
Steve Martin

PS—I have taken the liberty to suggest where you might get more help. These men have forgotten more than I will ever learn on the subject of training men.

1. *The Training of the Twelve* by A. B. Bruce (Grand Rapids, MI: Kregel, 1971).
2. *The Master Plan of Evangelism* by Robert Coleman (Grand Rapids, MI: Fleming H. Revell Co., 1994).

3. *Christ's Call to Discipleship* by James Montgomery Boice (reprint, Grand Rapids, MI: Kregel, 1998).
4. *Following the Master: A Biblical Theology of Discipleship* by Michael J. Wilkins (Grand Rapids, MI: Zondervan, 1992).
5. *The Lost Art of Disciple Making* by Leroy Eims (Grand Rapids, MI: Zondervan, 1978).

Chapter 18

Care for the Nations

Phil Newton

Dear Timothy,

Greetings to you in the wonderful name of the Lord Jesus Christ! I'm thankful for the new door of ministry that the Lord has granted you. Shepherding a congregation of believers will prove to be challenging and rewarding. The Lord has been preparing you for such a time and I know that you will be faithful to God's calling on your life to "shepherd the flock of God among you."

You are likely beginning to get the feel of what serving as a pastor demands on your time and energy level. I'm sure that you are finding surprises every day! As always, I want you to know that I stand ready to assist you any way that I am able.

You will be busy in many things as you get to know your congregation—ministering to them in times of need and crisis, preparing weekly sermons and Bible studies, organizing the ministries of the church, meeting with committees and leaders and occasionally putting out "brush fires." But as your pastor and friend, I want to remind you of an area that can easily be left out of the hectic pace of pastoral life—namely, *missions*. I know that you will diligently observe the emphases of our denomination on missions but that can almost be done unconsciously. Pastors tend to relegate missions to the denomination's mission agency or to para-church organizations, but you must see this as *your* work, leading your flock to have a passion for the world. The local church must be the launching pad for global missions. As pastor of a local church, you are the key to launching missions from your congregation.

No doubt, you are dealing with busy, preoccupied people. They hustle through a daily routine, fighting traffic, commuting to work, shuttling children from school to sports to music lessons and barely find time for church services! In the process they likely pay only scant attention to world events, unless they feel that the events have a direct bearing upon their daily lives. So while they are hectically running, the world about them languishes in the darkness of sin. Hundreds of Christians are butchered in Somalia and Nigeria. A church service is savagely attacked in Pakistan. Missionary work is suppressed on every continent. Many Islamic countries forbid any type of evangelism upon pain of imprisonment or even death. Earthquakes, floods, typhoons, famines and ravaging diseases decimate hundreds of thousands. All the while, members of your congregation rush about their daily routine oblivious to all but the weather, box scores and partisan politics. You bring up the challenge of global missions and voices pipe up, "Why do we need to go somewhere else? We have plenty of lost folks right in our city. Why spend all that time and money to go to people that aren't interested?" Others may cavil that missions belongs to the professionals and not to the untrained members of the church, so leave it alone.

Your confidence must be that of standing upon God's Word as you lead your people into the realm of global missions. Interestingly enough, the first century church may have had similar preoccupations. The first major missions work recorded in the book of Acts was not carefully planned but rather set in motion as a result of persecution. Once persecution struck the church after the stoning of Stephen, the church began to scatter and everywhere they went they preached the Word. The term that Luke uses for "preaching the word," comes from the same root word as "gospel." I like to think of it as "they were announcing the good news" or to create a word, "they were *gospelizing*" (Acts 8:4). Persecution brought about the spontaneous proclamation of the gospel outside the familiar trappings of Jerusalem. "The suffering of the church is used by God to reposition the missionary troops in places they might not have otherwise gone," as John Piper expressed it in *Let the Nations Be Glad!*[1] Our great Sovereign brought this about to move the church beyond its borders and into the world. Most importantly, it was *not* professional missionaries that were scattered into the world, but the church at large. They soon embraced the missionary challenge as their own.

To our own shame, Christians in the darkest areas of the world still seem to be the most buoyant in telling

---

[1] John Piper, *Let the Nations Be Glad! The Supremacy of God in Missions* (Grand Rapids, MI: Baker Books, 1993), 96.

others the good news. Persecution brings out the best while our freedom appears to breed complacency. Yet we must not let that discourage or dissuade us from pursuing global missions. Let us learn from our brothers and sisters that live in difficult lands!

The challenge that all of us face as pastors remains, "How do we help our churches develop a heart for the world?" It begins with *you!* Think of the missionaries that have passed through our church, whom you have heard speak about their work. Can you forget Dane's passionate vision for global missions, particularly among unreached people groups? Can you forget the night that Paul Ndungu answered your questions about his work with Maasai tribesmen in Kenya? Do you remember our dear friend Philippe's testimony of evangelizing post-modern students at a French university? Or how about the Sunday when we had national pastors from a dozen countries in our worship service and our homes for dinner? Can you forget their faces and stories? Can you forget the many who have suffered greatly for the gospel?

I'm almost brought to tears, and certainly to prayer, when I recall the conversation with David, the Liberian church planter that is attempting to reach the displaced nationals of warn-torn Liberia, Sierra Leone and Burkina Faso. I'm struck by my own complacency when I consider Pastors N.N. and Moses in Ghana and Raymond in Nigeria as they have carried the gospel into Muslim villages, risking their lives for the sake of precious souls living in darkness.

I remember your first short-term mission trip—you were only a teenager. I watched as you worked through a translator to communicate the existence of God with an atheistic university student. You endured his scorn and patiently answered his questions. Though he never acknowledged believing anything you said to him, you continued praying for him months after our return.

This fire must be communicated to your congregation. They must see in you a man with the world on his heart. Like John Wesley who said, "The world is my parish," you must feel the burden of the nations on your shoulders. While building your own congregation up in a most holy faith, you must likewise see the broader work of God's kingdom to the ends of the earth.

It begins with seeing that our God is a missionary God. His promise to Abraham, "And in you all the families of the earth will be blessed," demonstrates that the divine concern was not for a single family or nation, but for the world (Genesis 12:3). John Stott says that this expression more than any other shows that the living God of the Bible is a missionary God.[2] The balance of Scripture demonstrates what God has done through Christ to redeem men "from every tribe, tongue, people, and nation" (Revelation 5:9).

You can increase your congregation's heart for the nations through your faithful exposition of God's Word. As you work your way through one passage after another, you will squarely face the missionary mandate for the people of God. Expound it and apply it with passion. Work your way through Genesis 12, 17 and 22. Preach through the Psalms, especially the Messianic Psalms 2 and 110, as well as the kingly Psalms 93–99. Exegete Isaiah's multiplied

---

[2] Ralph Winter and Steven Hawthorne, eds., *Perspective on the World Christian Movement* 3rd edition (Pasadena, CA: William Carey Library, 1999), 9.

missionary texts in chapters 40–66. Study through the little missionary book of Jonah and then Habakkuk's promise of the earth being filled with the knowledge of God (2:14). The Gospels demonstrate Christ's passion for all people. Luke gives numerous examples of Jesus dealing with the Gentiles (or peoples). The prologues to John and Romans provide missionary motivation. Expound the book of Acts, and in doing so teach your congregation to think missiologically. The Epistles give clear examples of the gospel message being applied in missionary settings. Revelation is an extraordinary missionary book, especially chapters 4–5.

Let me give you some ideas that have helped me in addressing the Bible's missionary message. First, as you expound a text you will be showing the missionary mandate within a biblical context. That way you are never reduced to manipulation or gimmicks to motivate God's people for missions. In this manner, you are setting forth the eternal Word that becomes our highest motivation. Show the church that the ministry of missions is to call the nations to the worship of God so that His glory might be displayed throughout the earth. John Piper explains that worship "is the fuel and goal in missions. It's the goal of missions because in missions we simply aim to bring the nations into the white-hot enjoyment of God's glory. The goal of missions is the gladness of the peoples in the greatness of God."[3]

Second, prove from the Scriptures that missions are central to a true, New Testament church. John Calvin described a New Testament church as one that has the faithful exposition

---

[3] Piper, *Let the Nations Be Glad*, 11.

of Scripture, the right use of the sacraments and the discipline of its members. However, I think that we must add that a New Testament church has a missionary heart as well. That is part of the passion that bleeds through any reading of the book of Acts; missions show up from start to finish. More than any other, the book of Acts illustrates the dynamics of missions as a natural part of church ministry.

Third, exhort the congregation to total involvement in missions. Not everyone will be able to travel on a short-term mission or be involved in vocational missions. But everyone can pray, encourage and give. In William Carey's famous, *An Enquiry into the Obligations of Christians, to Use Means for the Conversion of the Heathen*, he points out what churches can do in the work of missions: "One of the first and most important of those duties which are incumbent upon us is fervent and united prayer." He explains, "We must not be contented however with praying without exerting ourselves in the use of the means for obtaining of those things we pray for."[4] In other words, prayer will lead to action. He then proposed that a society be formed to evaluate the character of those who would *go* in answer to the praying for the nations. Finally, he exhorted all churches to be involved in giving toward the work of missions as God enabled them. Carey wrote, "If congregations were to open subscriptions of one penny or more per week, according to their circumstances, and deposit it as a fund for the propagation of the gospel, much might be raised in this

---

[4] Quoted in Timothy George, *Faithful Witness: The Life and Mission of William Carey* (Birmingham, AL: New Hope Publishers, 1991), E.52, E.54.

way."[5] We've followed this pattern in our "Two-Per Offering," asking our congregation to give two dollars per person each week to fund short-term missions through our church in addition to regular giving. As you apply your missionary texts to the church, give them particular responsibilities in light of God's Word: praying, giving, encouraging others in the work, and going. Everyone will not find a niche in each area, but all can and must do something in the work of missions, for that is the New Testament church spirit.

Regular prayer for missionaries and the peoples of the world must be part of your personal and church discipline. I would encourage you to develop an extensive list of international contacts of both missionaries and national believers. Provide names, addresses and e-mail addresses for members of the congregation to establish contact and prayer (provide first names only for those in sensitive or closed countries). Pray for these missionaries and nationals in your worship services and prayer meetings. Read their letters to the congregation to help them get a sense of the battles they face and the victories that are being won through the gospel.

We've found it helpful to use Patrick Johnstone's *Operation World*[6] as a resource for writing a regular synopsis of mission work and global needs for our Sunday worship folder. In my pastoral prayer, I lead the church in praying for the country that has been identified on a given Sunday. Often I will know a missionary or national from the country, so that my praying takes on a more personal character. This allows your church to become familiar with peoples

---

[5] Ibid., E.56–57.
[6] Patrick Johnstone and Jason Mandryk, *Operation World*, 21st century edition (United Kingdom: Paternoster Lifestyle, 2001).

and countries (from Andorra to Zambia), to understand the religious complexities of nations and to grapple with the political, economic and spiritual problems they face. It will allow them to see that our God is a missionary God that has concern for the people of the world. In addition, various people groups are identified that will help to focus your praying and possibly your involvement. You might also lead your church to adopt a particular unreached, ethnolinguistic people group. You can find out more about them through the International Mission Board's (www.imb.org) or through the AD2000 (www.AD2000.org) websites.

As you know, I love to read missionary biographies. So often I've been encouraged and inspired while seeing how our Lord worked in their lives even in the most difficult settings. It has helped me to put things in better perspective! I've found that such biographies provide ample illustrative material, not only when addressing missionary concerns, but in other expositional contexts. This helps to familiarize the congregation with names like William Carey, Adoniram Judson, Hudson Taylor, Jim Elliot and Nate Saint. Recommend these books to your church. Perhaps you can even make some copies available for loan or purchase. You might even enlist the help of some to write book reviews of missionary biographies for your church newsletter.

In the past I have presumed that most church members know the names of Carey, Judson and Taylor, but I discovered when teaching an introductory missions course at the local college, that these missionary pioneers were strangers to many of the Christian students. I dare say that you will likely find the same impoverished understanding in your own congregation. I've made *Faithful Witness: The Life and Mission of William Carey* by Timothy George to be required reading for my students, and it might be a good idea to at least provide copies of this excellent work for your leadership. Of course you cannot make it required reading as I'm able to do in the classroom, but you can certainly exhort your leaders to grow in their understanding of the history of missions with this book. Maybe you could begin your deacons' meeting or missions committee meeting with a fifteen-minute discussion of *Faithful Witness* or *John Paton: An Autobiography*[7] or *Through Gates of Splendor*.[8] In this way you will help your leadership to think missiologically by using historical material to flesh out ideas for developing a mission-hearted church. As one of our elders expressed it, "Missions education leads to missions consciousness."

I want to challenge you to make missions a life-long area of study. In the past two hundred years, missionary borders have stretched into every corner of the globe. Since the early days of the "Baptist Missionary Society" and "The Society for the Propagation of Christian Knowledge," hundreds of mission organizations have arisen. Many of them will be good partners with you as you equip your congregation to mobilize on mission. But you must always remember that no organization can replace the local church as the launching pad for missions. Churches produce the personnel that eventually end up in a mission setting. You must cherish the role of equipping missionaries for the

---

[7] James Paton, ed., *John G. Paton Autobiography* (reprint, Edinburgh: The Banner of Truth Trust, 1994).
[8] Elisabeth Elliot, *Through Gates of Splendor* (reprint, Wheaton, IL: Tyndale House Publishers, Inc., 1981).

field. I will never forget one veteran mission leader telling our congregation that he valued the training by churches even more than seminaries for preparing his missionaries. Then he offered the plea that we train our people theologically and that we teach them to be "churchmen" that will understand how to develop biblically sound congregations. Seminaries were never designed to replace the local church in preparing men and women in ministry; they exist to supplement the church. If you are to be effective in training potential career and short-term missionaries in your congregation, then you must pursue a lifetime of missiological study.

You will begin this role by understanding the theological base for missionary work. That is what thrust William Carey, Andrew Fuller, John Sutcliff and John Ryland, Jr. into the forefront of the modern missionary movement: the first as "the missionary" and the other three as the support base. All of these eighteenth-century pastors were pastoral theologians that wrestled with their grasp of God's Word and its implications in congregational life. Their theological convictions enabled them to boldly confront the mission passivity among English Baptists. These same convictions from God's Word sustained them through dark days of the fledgling missionary society. Timothy George explains the theological basis for William Carey's *Enquiry* that became the primary outline for the modern missionary movement: "While his plan was a call for action based on genuine compassion for the lost, it was grounded in something deeper still; namely, the character of God Himself—eternal, holy, righteous, loving, giving."⁹ For Carey and his friends, theology motivated them toward missiological action.

While I advocate reading books that deal with missiological strategy, your foundation must always be in a clearly articulated theological basis for missions. Once the foundation is laid in Scripture, then you can sift through the many strategy issues confronting missionaries. You will be able to discern those strategies that are mere fluff and manipulation that will not leave lasting results.

In terms of studying missiological strategy, I am still amazed at how up-to-date Carey's *Enquiry* and the later *Serampore Compact of 1805* are for our own times. Carey laid out a clear vision for local church involvement in missions. The *Compact* outlines the "great principles" that directed Carey, Joshua Marshman and William Ward (The Serampore Trio) and others involved in their mission work. It addresses foremost their theological foundation in "the glorious doctrine of free and sovereign grace" as the motivation for "persuading men to be reconciled to God." They assess the value of a human soul, the importance of researching a given culture to understand how to communicate with them, abstaining from things that might culturally hinder gospel witness, living with the people rather than being isolated from them, maintaining the centrality of Christ crucified in their preaching and exercising patience with the nationals. Their section on working diligently with new converts stands in sharp contrast to the presumption so often characterizing modern missions. They sought to fos-

---

⁹ George, *Faithful Witness*, 58.

ter the leadership development of nationals, to focus upon translating the Scripture into various dialects and to educate nationals so that they might read the Word of God. The missionary's personal devotional life must be cultivated regularly. "Finally, let us give ourselves up unreservedly to this glorious cause," they concluded, with an earnestness to lay down their lives for the gospel in foreign lands.

I have found it helpful to insert mission strategies where appropriate in sermons. The church must learn to think missiologically if it is to have a burning passion for global missions. Strategies are really applications of your theological understanding of missions. So it is right that you help your church understand the practicality of biblical doctrine, even in the work of missions.

In addition to studying missiology, you must also keep abreast of news around the world. This will really help you in synthesizing your theological and missiological studies into real life situations. You must get to know the world. Keep a world map or globe in view so that you will become familiar with the far reaches of the world. Read about nations, people groups, civil conflicts, world religions, global political changes, economic issues, natural disasters, population trends and human suffering. In one sense, you must become a "theological-demographer"—studying people of the world, understanding their cultures, feeling the anguish of their cries, and yet all the while grappling with their need for the gospel. Pray often as you read. Once you begin investigating the world you will discover that Americans tend to have a myopic view toward the rest of the world. We're horrible geographers and we tend to know even less about people groups, cultures, worldwide suffering and spiritual needs. As you investigate the world you will need to intercede for particular nations and people groups. Include this type of praying in your pastoral prayers before the church so that the congregation will begin to think and pray beyond the walls of the church building.

You can start your investigation of the world by reading a good daily newspaper, focusing on world news. Add to this various journals, such as WORLD, *National Geographic, U.S. News & World Report, Commission;* and in addition, subscribe to *Compass Direct* for up-to-date information on the plight of Christians throughout the globe. Web searches will yield more information than you can possibly assimilate, so you should never run out of resources for studying the world from a Christian/missiological worldview.

Finally, there's nothing quite like visiting an international setting to help foment your understanding of missions and intensifying your missions passion. I recommend that you establish a visit with a missionary friend or national. Plan your trip well in advance. Research the country, people groups, religious background and current mission work in preparation. Find out how you can be of service to those you visit. Realize that you cannot replace them during your brief stay, but you can be a helper to them. You are coming alongside them, joining hands and hearts with them in their work. Once you arrive, take the time to listen to them and learn from them. Ask lots of questions, not only of your hosts but of other nationals you meet. Immerse yourself in their culture. Walk in their shoes, even if it is only for a week. Feel the burden they bear for the lost in their community. Get to know the people to whom the missionary or national Christian leader ministers. Understand the dynamics of exercising a gospel ministry in that particular cultural setting. Then carry all of this back home.

I remember an older couple in Sommiere, France that I've visited several times during my mission teaching trips in that region. The missionary asked me to go with another couple to visit them. We made our way through this old city that has no evangelical work, driving through the narrow streets until we came to a small house in a development. The smiles were wide as we walked through the door! Since they could not speak English nor could I speak French, we depended upon our translators to assist. The translations were in broken English but our hearts communicated. We asked questions about their health, talked about their family and grandchildren. They reciprocated with questions about our families and church. We talked about Christ, the gospel and the church of the Lord Jesus Christ. Then we sang together—in English and French. I opened the Scriptures and briefly expounded a Psalm and led the small group in prayer while my friend translated for the edification of the older couple. Our hostess brought out juice and brioches for us to enjoy. We parted with the traditional double-kiss and a satisfaction that we had entered into their lives—and they, into ours. I've returned to their home in succeeding trips since that time. It has become a highlight to carry young people from our church with me to visit with them. They are now part of the picture that comes to mind when I think of France.

Similar pictures surface when I think of Russia—and eating a very questionable chicken soup with three students as we talked about the importance of sound doctrine and fidelity in ministry; Albania—where I had stamped on my mind the blank stares of people who had suffered deprivation of every sort for forty years; Brazil—where I preached the gospel on an outdoor platform as thousands rushed by, with a few pausing to listen; and Italy—where a middle-aged man struggling with the gospel, listened to me expound the sufficiency of Christ and commented, "You spoke this for me."

Nothing has been more rewarding than carrying others with me on these short-term mission trips. Once members of the church see another culture firsthand and sense the impact of cross-cultural gospel communication, they have a completely different attitude toward global missions. I do not have to convince them that the church must exercise care for the nations. I need only equip and mobilize them to action. They understand the power of the gospel of Christ that breaks down every barrier to transform lives in every culture and unite them with the body of Christ.

Yes, Timothy, your challenge is enormous; but the Lord of the church is greater. Be faithful in the journey as a good steward of the gospel through the manifold grace of God.

Warmly,
Pastor Phil

PS—By the way, aside from Piper's *Let the Nations Be Glad! The Supremacy of God in Missions*, Johnstone's *Operation*

World, and George's *Faithful Witness: The Life and Mission of William Carey*, let me commend a few more titles that will be treasured resources:

1. In the early twentieth century, Anglican missionary Roland Allen wrote *Missionary Methods: St. Paul's or Ours?* (reprint, Grand Rapids, MI: William B. Eerdmans Publishing Co., 2002). He demonstrates that our missiological strategy must have a clear, biblical foundation.
2. *Perspectives on the World Christian Movement*, edited by Ralph Winter and Steve Hawthorne 3rd edition (Pasadena, CA: William Carey Library, 1999), contains 124 essays on the broad field of global missions. You will not agree with all the content but you will find helpful material to stimulate your thinking on missions.
3. Dr. and Mrs. Howard Taylor's *Hudson Taylor: God's Man in China* (Chicago, IL: Moody Press, 1965), Elisabeth Elliot's *Through Gates of Splendor* (reprint, Wheaton, IL: Tyndale House Publishers, Inc., 1981) and John Patton's *Autobiography* (reprint, Edinburgh: The Banner of Truth Trust, 1994) will influence your missiological thought and probably keep you spellbound by their fascinating stories.

Chapter 19

Don't Neglect Revival

Ray Ortlund, Jr.

Dear Timothy,

I thrill to follow your progress in the ministry. God has put His hand upon you, my friend. I hope that, by faith, you are enjoying a sense of His favor through the finished work of Christ on the cross. Let the smile of God encourage you, embolden you, energize you, for His service. Radiate that grace to others—they need it, too. We are all so weak and need strong encouragement.

Now as you walk through these formative years of your ministry, you are doubtless aware that there are basically two ways you can proceed in the pastorate. On the one hand, you can work for a monthly paycheck. You can settle for a predictable church routine, keeping the various factions within the church happy, charting a safe middle course on every controversy, carefully protecting your job and so forth. On the other hand, you can serve your glorious Lord. Following His Word, you can reach out by faith for *more*. You can be a man of conviction. You can shape your ministry by the Bible. You can labor for the eternal advantage of your people's souls and the bold expansion of the gospel into your mission field. Basically, there are these two ways to do pastoral ministry. I know you will continue to strive for a God-sized ministry, no matter what the cost.

If you were to stoop to being a mere man-pleaser, your ministry would be simpler. Your default setting at all times would be popularity, ease, control, peace-at-all-costs, following the path of least resistance. You would aspire after the lofty height of becoming a "really nice guy," as one recent author has put it.

But since you have determined to be a God-pleaser first and foremost, your path forward is more complex. Naturally, you want to win people's good will. You love people and enjoy people, as you should. You want them to love you, for Jesus' sake. Paul said, "I try to please everyone in everything I do" (1 Corinthians 10:33). What a sweeping declaration of his generous willingness to listen, adjust, flex and adapt! Paul tried hard not to turn people off. He wanted to win a hearing, for the Lord's sake. So he shaped his strategies in order to fly in under their radar, disarm their prejudices and *please* them. "I try to please everyone in everything I do." You do too, Timothy, and this is right. Never become a mean-spirited, grumpy, narrow man. Paul wasn't. His ministry was so sweet it melted in people's mouths because he lived out Christ-like servanthood for the gospel's sake.

It is also true that, if, with Paul, you aim high, your vision will challenge people. You will stretch them. You may make them feel uncomfortable. They may even feel threatened at times. You will inevitably (sometimes you won't even realize you are doing it) challenge aspects of your church that some people would rather leave undisturbed. So as you follow God, you will take risks. You will disregard self-interest for the sake of the progress of the gospel. And nowhere is this more true than in the area of revival.

I have mentioned to you before the lectures by J. I. Packer that I heard as a seminary student years ago. That one sentence of his just will not let me go: "Do not neglect the revival dimension in your ministry." You know, Timothy, some men do. They don't even think in terms of revival. It never occurs to them. They're aiming at next Sunday's sermon and next year's missions conference. Their thinking is limited to their church programs. It never dawns on them that the greatest moment for a church is when God comes down with an irruption of His manifest presence and power and holiness, canceling events on the church calendar and establishing *Himself* as the felt center of a church's reverent fascination. God is wonderfully able to visit His people.

I remember as a boy, Timothy, in the early 1960s (maybe I was eleven or twelve, I can't remember), sitting in church one Sunday morning as my dad was preaching. He was just proclaiming a biblical message in his typically winsome way. He was not trying to incite any unusual response in the people. He never does. As I recall, I was doodling with a pencil in the bulletin, not paying much attention, when something happened. I noticed that one of the men in the choir, Ed Fisher, got up from his seat in the choir loft behind the pulpit and quietly, without any self-display, went down to the communion table at the front and knelt reverently in prayer. Ed was a man of God, not an eccentric. He had credibility. But God was speaking to him in a powerful way through Dad's sermon, and he was compelled by the

Holy Spirit to respond in some way. Then Leta, his wife—faithful, earnest Leta!—also in the choir, got up from her seat to join Ed in prayer down front. Mind you, Timothy, we did not do this sort of thing as a church. We were a staid, upper-middle class church of architects, scientists, doctors and got-it-all-together types. This was the historic Lake Avenue Congregational Church of Pasadena. Boy, were we respectable! But God came down to us that day with a remarkable visitation of His saving presence. And to my amazement, from all over the church more and more people began going quietly forward to kneel at the front of the sanctuary in prayer, doing business with God. Dad wasn't asking them to. He was as surprised as anyone else. In fact, as he became aware that God was moving in a special way, he didn't know what to do at first. Initially, he just kept preaching. But when it became clear that God was taking over in the service, Dad stepped back from the pulpit and stood quietly in prayer himself. The organist had the presence of mind to begin to play in an appropriate, non-intrusive way. Everyone was quiet. But God came down among us, adding to the normal ministry such a demonstration of His power that we could not proceed in our usual way. And, in fact, Timothy, this happened again on later occasions, and it was never orchestrated by man. It makes me think of 1 Kings 8:10–11, when the priests could not continue in their ministries because "the glory of the Lord filled the house of the Lord."

That was the experience of just one church. And it was no silver bullet—it didn't solve all our problems. It didn't establish a new tradition of "altar calls." It didn't distract the church from the ordinary efforts of weekly preaching, counseling, teaching, encouraging and so forth. The leadership of the church kept steering the ship on a straight, non-eccentric, biblical course. But revival is biblical, too. And these experiences of God's reviving presence, through and according to His Word, marked us as a church. We knew that we had entered into an irreversible newness. We knew that there was more for us in Christ than we had yet apprehended, and our hearts opened to the "more" He wanted to give us. Those were years of great fruitfulness for Lake Avenue Church and to this day, I am moved when I think back on what God did. For the rest of my life, I can never be content with just "doing church." I want to see the Lord visit His people with nothing less than reviving mercies.

I know your heart longs for revival, too. Together we are praying for a great breakthrough for the gospel in our generation. We are not content with the present mediocrity of the evangelical church. We cannot endure existence without the name of Jesus being honored and esteemed and desired and obeyed more and more far and wide. We yearn for a spirit of repentance to subdue our glib, self-admiring churches, along with a spirit of faith to fill them full of the Holy Spirit. We pray for the privilege of re-living the book of Acts in our time—a massive outpouring of the Spirit, so that the Word runs like lightning through the church out into the world to change the face of our generation, according to the promises of God's prophetic Word.

But not everyone feels that way. Some Christians just don't feel that intense fire burning in their hearts. And when they encounter it in others, some don't understand it and they may even dislike it. You will be surprised, Timothy, at how good-hearted, sincere Christians can resist revival. You will hear their defensiveness: "What do you mean, we need revival? Pastor, are you saying we haven't been praying enough? Are you saying there's something wrong with us? Are you saying that God hasn't been blessing us all these years? Are you invalidating everything we have been and done? Are you implying that we have no heart for evangelism? What do you mean, we need revival? We were serving the Lord long before *you* ever showed up! And if you think you're going to *change* our church—well, we like it just the way it is, thank you very much."

Timothy, this is the church—the church as it is, in her pride and fear and backwardness. These are the needy people God loves and wants to awaken to a new awareness of Himself, a new desire for His glory, a new openness to His overruling will. And He wants to do this *through your influence*. You cannot make revival happen. Only God can. But He wants to use you for His awakening purpose. So how can you present yourself as useful to Him for a ministry He can own with His holy power?

Much could, and should, be said at this point. But I will content myself in the short span of this letter to propose three things you should keep clearly in mind.

First, lead your people *spiritually*. You are not there just to run church programs. Wisely deployed, such institutional devices have their uses. But some pastors don't seem to grasp that a church is not the religious equivalent to the local Y. Neither are you there just to stuff more and more Bible information into your people's heads. After a service some time ago, a wise but frustrated saint approached her pastor-teacher—and I emphasize *teacher*—with this plea: "Pastor, bring us to Jesus!" Now, Timothy, *that* is your great privilege and responsibility. Sunday by Sunday, take your people by the hand, as it were, bring them to their Lord and leave them there. Use the weekly services for head-and-heart engagement with the living God. Use your preaching to point people through the Word to the Lord revealed there. Use your praying to display how real God is, through Christ, to us sinners. It is not your job to protect people from the living God but to bring them to Him. Our constant tendency is to lapse into a hurried religious routine, running prayerlessly from one activity to the next without really thinking about what we are doing. Then, if the Lord does move, we ourselves may be caught so off-guard that we spoil the moment with a stupid joke. So I urge you, Timothy, to fight and pray, that you may remain spiritually awake yourself. Wherever you are, hide yourself in Christ and lead your people to live there too. Wonderful, surprising things can happen when our Bibles and our hearts are fully open before God.

Second, preach the gospel *expectantly*. Through Christ and for the sake of His name, you have been called to preach God's grace to sinners. What a joy! And He stands ready to pour out His Spirit upon you moment by moment in continual freshness for that saving purpose. What a resource! Martyn Lloyd-Jones concluded his lectures on preaching at Westminster Theological Seminary in 1969 by asking:

> What then are we to do about this? There is only one obvious conclusion. Seek him! Seek him! What can we do without him? Seek him! Seek him always. But go

beyond seeking him; expect him. Do you expect anything to happen when you get up to preach in a pulpit? Or do you just say to yourself, "Well, I have prepared my address, I am going to give them this address; some of them will appreciate it and some will not"? Are you expecting it to be the turning point in someone's life? Are you expecting anyone to have a climactic experience? That is what preaching is meant to do. That is what you find in the Bible and in the subsequent history of the church. Seek this power, expect this power, yearn for this power.[1]

The greatest battle in your ministry will be fought deep inside you, as you struggle to keep on *expecting* God's blessing in the face of your own sins and the sins of others. The only remedy against despair in the ministry is the gospel. Keep preaching the gospel to yourself first. Keep reminding yourself that God loves *sinners*, God works with *sinners*. Encourage yourself that the word of the Lord came to Jonah *a second time* (Jonah 3:1). And through Jonah—even Jonah!—that word transformed an evil city. Aren't you and I just as inadequate and problematic as Jonah? But the One who sent us is "a gracious God and merciful, slow to anger and abounding in steadfast love, and relenting from disaster" (Jonah 4:2). As someone put it pithily, "God does not call the qualified; He qualifies the called." So, Timothy, let the mystery of His grace sustain your expectancy in the face of plausible arguments for giving up on yourself and others.

---

[1] D. Martyn Lloyd-Jones, *Preaching and Preachers* (Grand Rapids, MI: Zondervan, 1972), 325.

Third, accept suffering *meekly*. Let's face it. Not many Christians are aflame with heroic spiritual aspirations. Too many of our fine, church-going people tend to be absorbed with next weekend's barbecue or next month's fishing trip or next year's retirement, pretty much like the world. As a result, my Great-heart, you might find yourself misunderstood, feared and rejected by some Christians. Precisely because you are living boldly for the Lord, you may be perceived as an enemy. After all, in one sense, you are. By setting yourself *for* the triumph of Christ alone, you are, more than you intend or even realize, setting yourself *against* the idols dominating the ethos of some churches.

Now, if you find yourself opposed, be as honest and impartial about it as you can be. Ask yourself if it is your fault. It may be, in part. You may need to repent of something yourself. So be open. Beware of the hardening power of your own self-righteousness.

But it might not be your fault at all. The conflict might have arisen because you are *obeying* God—as did the apostles and so many others who have been persecuted. Now, my brother, when you are reviled for righteousness' sake, ask the Lord to keep three things clearly before you. One, you have a great reward in heaven. In your own modest way, you have become identified with the noble army of martyrs and with your crucified Lord Himself. Savor the privilege. Stand tall. Be confident that God will take care of you. Two, the pastoral office in the church you serve deserves protection from being diminished by well-intentioned but uncomprehending people. Detach your self psychologically from the pastoral office you occupy and, for the sake of that church and her next pastor, try—as much as you can without complicating things further—to guard the authority and honor of the office as such. Three, your own person and reputation and feelings are expendable. My dear brother, your very life is expendable, for Jesus' sake. Of course, your elders ought to build a firewall around you. But whether they support you or fail you, do not hit back at your detractors for merely personal slights and attacks. Hard as it is, you must turn the other cheek. Frederick William Faber put it plainly in one of his hymns: "Learn to lose with God."

You know from the gospel that it is the cross that triumphs. It is death that conveys life. It is shame that brings honor. It is sacrifice that inherits abundance. In the ways of God—how strange, how counter-intuitive are His ways and experienced only as we trust Him more than we trust our own self-preserving but destructive instincts—you have a reason to accept adversity with meekness. Your humility has been ordained by God to pierce consciences and awaken slumbering hearts. In following the crucified Jesus, you will become an agent of revival for the resurrected Christ. He will make sure of it. So don't lose heart. When you are weak, you are strong.

Now, Timothy, keep your eyes firmly fixed on what only *God* can do. Shape your ministry by that exciting, biblical criterion. Isn't that the adventure, the mystery, the romance of the gospel ministry? And along the way, don't surrender your principles. When you have to stand alone, a clear conscience and strong principles make good companions. And, better still, there is a Friend who sticks closer than a brother.

May He preserve and enrich you in every grace, so that your life makes an eloquent statement to your generation of the reviving power of God, for His greater glory, your richer joy and the salvation of the nations.

Your brother in Christ,
Ray Ortlund, Jr.

PS—To study revival further, I suggest the following:

1. Begin with Edwards. No one thinks about revival as carefully and helpfully as he does. Read "Thoughts on the Revival" by Jonathan Edwards. You can find it in *The Works of Jonathan Edwards*, 2 vols. (reprint, Edinburgh: The Banner of Truth Trust, 1979).
2. After Edwards, why not try Martyn Lloyd-Jones' sermons on revival? Read the collection of his sermons entitled *Revival* (reprint, Westchester, IL: Crossway Books, 1987). If you haven't fallen in love with Lloyd-Jones yet, I hope you will. *Revival* is the Doctor at his prophetic best.
3. Finally, I hope you will forgive me for suggesting my own book, *When God Comes to Church* (Grand Rapids, MI: Baker Books, 2000). I dig into to the biblical text itself, to expound and defend true revival. But there are so many other wonderful books on this theme. Oh, I wish we could all take a year off just to read!

Chapter 20

Find a Place to Settle

Geoff Thomas

Dear Timothy,

Congratulations on your first charge! I trust you accepted the call to this pastorate with a sense of wonder that any church should have asked you to become its minister. I was more confident than most young men when I started in 1965 and the next decades were to be a voyage into weakness.

The full-time gospel ministry is still a protected oasis. We are relieved of so many of the tensions and temptations that the men to whom we minister are meeting each day. They work with their minds and bodies in this evil world and give their hard-earned money to us so generously that we may spend our days—think of it—in the quiet of our studies, in the Bible, in evangelism and in pastoring God's people. I hope you will never join with those ministers who sit around grumbling in their fraternals about all the alleged hardships of being preachers. What a marvelously privileged life we lead! I trust you earnestly believe that if it be God's will for you to spend the rest of your life caring for this particular congregation you will happily do so and thank the Lord at the end of each day for such blessings.

There is rich variety in the work of the minister. The seminary professor teaches one limited theological segment of the religious disciplines usually to one narrow age band of men between twenty-one and twenty-four. He has academic papers to write and publish to maintain his tenure. He has to work with colleagues who are of the same intellectual intensity as himself. There are papers to mark, exams to set, erring students to chase after, insouciant young men to face and high-flying colleagues to work alongside. Much of his labor is unknown and unprayed for by the churches. His parents never see him at work! What a one-string song he sings.

The preacher, on the other hand, often works from his home. There is his office with his wife moving through the nearby rooms and his children calling in to see him. Charles Hodge moved the doorknob on his study door lower so that his kids could come into the room and chat to him at any time. There is enormous freedom about the books of the Bible he chooses to study and preach on. There are his calls to the hospital and to the sick and elderly at home. There is evangelism of all kinds, counseling, desktop publishing, working with godly leaders of the congregation, pre-wedding talks and funerals with privileged conversations with widows and the children of the deceased. There are the godly old ladies to converse with. When the phone or doorbell rings, what might the caller want? There is no richness in any para-church work that can compare to the pastor's. I say you must thank the Lord every day for putting you in the ministry. Who, called of God to this work, could desire anything else?

There is a sea-change between your recent opportunities for itinerant preaching—visiting new congregations where not one face was familiar—and your present ministry, now settled behind one pulpit to address one people week by week. But those early experiences of encountering new assemblies should be repeated throughout one's life. There are few guaranteed tonics for a preacher's heart when discouraged with a hundred little worries, than going off and preaching to a distant congregation. It is like going to visit an unfamiliar city and surveying the square, the houses, churches and shops. All is pristine and fascinating, but in a congregation the people's eyes are on you too. The crowds walk the thoroughfares and there is a solemnity about that scene of which one may lose sight in one's own congregation. One sees that bustling community and thinks of Another's grief who once beheld another city, and then one recalls His words, "Broad is the road that leads to destruction, and many there be that find it." How earnestly we should be preaching the gospel.

But such visits should be occasional. Constant traveling to meet new people and consciously creating a good initial impression can warp our sense of humanity altogether. Many great preachers have been inseparably associated with the places where they labored and where, perhaps, they lived as pastors their entire lives. In many cases their place has passed into their names as if it were a true part of themselves. Chrysostom of Constantinople, Augustine of Hippo, Calvin of Geneva, Baxter of Kidderminster, Bunyan of Bedford, Rowland of Llangeitho, Jay of Bath, M'Cheyne of Dundee, Spurgeon of the Metropolitan Tabernacle, Lloyd-Jones of Westminster Chapel,

Chantry of Carlisle. In my Wales with our sparseness of surnames a multitude of such associations have become historic and compelled the Welsh to identify the man with the place and the place with the man.

In the New Testament there was both a dynamism and a stability about church leadership. The preachers were continually on the move going out to new areas with the gospel with little apparent control or financial support needed for their sowing and watering. Yet there were also the New Testament pastorates: John in Ephesus, James in Jerusalem and Titus in Crete. They established churches through preaching. The regular preaching ministry needs no defense. Its record is its best defense. Whoever would have heard of places in my own nation like Llangeitho, Trefecca, Talsarn, Bala and Clynog if it were not for the extraordinary changes wrought in those communities through the preachers who lived there? We must never lose confidence in the power of the preached Word of God and the office of the minister.

Through long pastorates preachers become rich in their knowledge of the ways of God with man and of human nature. Philips Brooks presented three rules to students, introducing them with due solemnity:

> I beg you to remember them and apply them with all the wisdom that God gives you. First. Have as few congregations as you can. Second. Know your congregation as thoroughly as you can. Third. Know your congregation so largely and deeply that in knowing it you shall know humanity.[1]

---

[1] Philips Brooks, *Lectures on Preaching* (given at Yale College in 1877; published by James Robinson in Manchester, 1899), 190.

Dr. James Stalker reminisced in this way:

It was my happiness, when I was ordained, to be settled next . . . to an aged and saintly minister. He was a man of competent scholarship, and had the reputation of having been in early life a powerful and popular preacher. But it was not to these gifts that he owed his unique influence. He moved through the town, with his white hair and somewhat staid and dignified demeanour, as a hallowing presence. His very passing in the street was a kind of benediction, and the people, as they looked after him, spoke of him to each other with affectionate veneration. Children were proud when he laid his hand on their heads, and they treasured the kindly words which he spoke to them. At funerals and other seasons of domestic solemnity his presence was sought by people of all denominations. We who labored along with him in the ministry felt that his mere existence in the community was an irresistible demonstration of Christianity and a tower of strength to every good cause. Yet he had not gained this position of influence by brilliant talents or great achievements or the pushing of ambition; for he was singularly modest, and would have been the last to credit himself with half the good he did. The whole mystery lay in this, that he had lived in the town for forty years a blameless life, and was known by everybody to be a godly and prayerful man. He was good enough to honour me with his friendship; and his example wrote deeply upon my mind these two convictions—that it may sometimes be of immense advantage to spend a whole life time in a single pastorate, and that the prime qualification for the ministry is godliness.[2]

The man to whom he was referring was a certain James Black of Dunnikier and little more than that paragraph of Stalker's is known of the man or even the place where he labored. Dunnikier is too small to appear in any British atlas. Black was one of that army of holy men who have served the Lord in obscure communities modestly and humbly for no reward other than the immense privilege of having so great a Master as our Christ.

The danger of the above portrait is its romanticism. Where are the wild beasts? The Lord Jesus sent His disciples forth as sheep amidst wolves. Paul preached the Word publicly but also from house to house. He spoke in an upper room but also in the open air. He was surrounded by weeping appreciative friends but also by mobs who stoned him. To live in a small community for many years liked by all men and then to die with the words, "He was a nice old boy," as one's epitaph would be a total betrayal of our calling. Such a life could not be blessed to anyone. "Blessed are you when people insult you, persecute you and falsely say all kinds of evil against you because of me. Rejoice and be glad, because great is your reward in heaven, for in the same way they persecuted the prophets who were before you" (Matthew 5:11–12).

We do not doubt that James Black not only comforted and exhorted but at times manifested the anger of rebuke.

---

[2] James Stalker, *The Preacher and his Models* (London: Hodder & Stoughton, 1891), 57–58.

He would have to live righteously if he were as faithful as his Lord who denounced the Pharisees and the king. As Stalker arrived in his first church near Dunnikier and observed Black he learned one great truth: Everything must preach in the preacher, not merely the tongue, but also gesture, manner, dress, walk and conversation. By the end of his life Black had, by the Spirit of Christ, developed a quite unselfconscious instinct and tact in following the Savior. There was a commentary that he furnished by his own personal walk with God that all of Dunnikier could read, and of which he was the last to be aware. Whether one's ministry in a certain community is going to be long or short it must be characterized by a Christian firmness of character, overcoming the timid fear of men and men-service and also popularity-hunting. The purer the pruned vine, the more fruit it brings forth. The people of the community as they get to know the minister are all too ready to use his faults as fig leaves for their own nakedness. The sins of the pastor are the greatest in the whole church because they do most to hinder the course of the Word of God. The longer the faults are placated before the community the more unattractive the Christian life will seem. But how powerful the sustained momentum of a holy walk.

In three ways should the preacher preach: with heart, with mouth and with life. The life must prove what the mouth speaks, and the mouth must speak what the heart feels. It was said of the Reformers that "The truth not merely sounded, it shone out of them." Richard Baxter warns men in his *The Reformed Pastor:*

One proud, surly, lordly word, one needless contention, one covetous action, may cut the throat of many a sermon . . . It is a palpable error for some ministers, who make such a disproportion between their preaching and their living; who study hard to preach exactly, and study little or not at all to live exactly. All the week long is little enough to study how to speak two hours; and yet one hour seems too much to study how to *live* all the week. . . . Oh, take heed, brethren, of every word you speak, and of every step you tread, for you bear the ark of the Lord—you are entrusted with his honour! . . . Take heed to yourselves, for the success of all your labors does very much depend on this.[3]

How ministers find a place to settle is an utter mystery to me. If ever God's sovereignty is evident it is in the manner and timing of a call to a church. I have seen holy men whom I consider to have the brightest gifts for pastoring and preaching, and they have waited while taking work as postmen, teachers and firemen for years before they were invited to become pastors. Some never became ministers and they spent their lives thinking their vocations had been second best. Yet other men, much less discerning, theological light-weights, have had the security of a pulpit held out to them before completing their seminary course. The leadings of providence are no safe confirmation that a man is called to gospel work. When runaway Jonah, in defiance of his Lord, arrived at Joppa he found a ship about to sail to Tarshish. There was a berth on board and Jonah had the

---

[3] Richard Baxter, *The Reformed Pastor* (reprint, Edinburgh: The Banner of Truth Trust, 1979), 63.

money for the fare. It was all for him a confirmation that his own thoughts of ministry in Tarshish were God-inspired, but in fact he was fleeing from the Lord. The testings of providence are not to be interpreted as divine guidance either crushing our desires or opening doors for us. Do we earnestly desire this work? Do we have a good biblical understanding of what it entails? Do we have the moral, intellectual, theological and affectionate gifts for this work? Do men whom we respect urge us to consider this as our own divine calling? Do we have any funny ideas? The ministry is no place for cranks, however orthodox they might be.

Then wait patiently on God. We have the same heavenly Father. He does not give gifts and then let them rust or atrophy by non-use. There is no reason why you should not preach for the rest of your life. You may not have a regular pulpit, a manse and a salary, but there is nothing to stop you preaching in all sorts of ways. Be involved in a local church. Sit under the best ministry you can find. Display an enviable contentment. Hew wood and draw water if that is God's will for you. Accept what opportunities the Lord through His church gives you. The grapevine is very efficient. The question preachers are asked more than any other is, "Can you recommend a minister for our church?"

I have remained in this small town of 15,000 people since 1965. I always felt that I began at the very top and could not consider a more perfect place to be a pastor-preacher. Aberystwyth is the cultural capital of Wales. As it is midway between the north and south of the country it was made the home of the National Library of Wales and the first Welsh university, which now has about 8,000 students. It is a bilingual community and we are a Welsh-speaking family. Situated on the Irish Sea it is a delightful place to live. God gave me a place in the sun. I wept when I heard the church had given me a call and I accepted their businesslike invitation that same week. Both our childhood homes (my wife's and mine) were a few hours away to the north and the south. One Saturday night after I had been here a couple of months I drove to speak on the North Wales coast at Bangor University Christian Union. The next morning I drove to Aberavon on the South Wales coast and preached in Sandfields where Dr. Lloyd-Jones had been a minister in the 1920s and 30s. I could speak anywhere in Wales and return home that same evening. I was not interested in another place but never had a serious call to a pastorate in all these years. If I had begun my ministry in a one-horse town I might not have stayed so long. I never played around with another church's affections in order to tell our congregation I was being appreciated somewhere else. When I was forty I felt restless, pinned into the local scene by a wife and three daughters and other family members who could never dream of living anywhere else. It was a brief mid-life crisis. The British churches needed men to preach the whole counsel of God in local congregations like ours, to show that assemblies could be reformed and hear with love the doctrines of grace and be happy united fellowships serving the Lord of all the earth. God, however, kept me here.

It is possible to keep fresh in a long ministry. The temptation having moved to a new church is to preach sermons earlier given in one's previous pulpit. That can rarely be done if one is confronting a beloved congregation for many years. I determined to preach through the whole Bible while I was here. I have, of course, failed. There are always challenges one sets—fascinating new books are published that one must read, classics remain yet unread. There are various series to preach on Sundays and different audiences to address—children, passers-by in the open air, a house group, a factory Christian union, an informal meal and message, a men's group, an early morning prayer meeting, students' meetings—the list is endless. One feels more relaxed in some than others.

The longer you stay in a church the more resolute you should be in attending ministers' conferences. As you grow in reputation you make a contribution just being with the men. No minister should go to conferences simply to address them. He should go to learn too. He should not be of the mindset, "I have something to teach you, but you have nothing to give to me." Conferences are important for meeting your brothers in the ministry. The messages are a bonus. They might stimulate and encourage you in your labors. Attendance at some of the range of conferences available to men in North America and the United Kingdom will provide a couple that prove to be consistently helpful to you.

There are challenges and dangers that are inherent to staying in a church for many years. The congregation you face constantly changes. Populations are dynamic. New faces appear and new problems arise in the lives of those who have long sat at your feet. The late Bernard J. Honeysett recently observed in his autobiography:

John Kemp was one of five pastors I knew personally who held pastorates for more than fifty years. In the case of Stanley Delves of Crowborough, his predecessor was also in the office for over fifty years, so that the two spanned over a century. It has been my observation that when men have continued so long, they can unwittingly become dictators. A generation grows up under their ministry and pastoral care, and their word can become law. I knew of one case where a church meeting was mentioned and the pastor said, "I will say when we are to have a church meeting." Sometimes such leaders make no provision for the future when they are taken, in some cases with very sad results.[4]

One is delivered from tyranny by self-restraint and integrity and also by the watchfulness and friendship of one's officers. There is enough consciousness of the priesthood of all believers in gospel churches to sound an alarm if a minister is becoming a one man band or throwing his weight around in the church. Good national Christian magazines bring other information and ideas into the congregation. One begins to invite suitable younger men to preach regularly in the pulpit especially before one is thinking of leaving.

The benefits of staying in a community for decades are legion. Many in the congregation are one's best friends. Some came to faith through your preaching. One has baptized some parents and then their children a generation later.

---

[4] Bernard J. Honeysett, *The Sound of His Name* (Edinburgh: The Banner of Truth Trust, 1995), 51.

One gets to know the town and how it operates. If one does not know significant men personally (because they are always changing), one knows the office of the editor of the local paper, the chief of police, the personalities of the local radio station, the headmasters of the schools, the political structures, the business leaders and their gatherings, the funeral directors, the clergy and their theologies. One knows how to contact these people, where they are heading, how they can be approached to serve the gospel of Jesus Christ. I can walk into our town center today and the vast majority of the people are strangers to me. I can stand in line in the post office and know few of the people waiting with me, but I do know the staff behind the counter. They know who I am. To some I have given invitations to our meetings and to one a copy of Bunyan's *The Pilgrim's Progress*. The same is true for check-out people, my mechanic, plumber, electrician and barber (with whom I have frequent noisy ecclesiastical debates. He is a young Roman Catholic, son of a Sicilian, and he always asks me loudly when I come into his shop "How is the Reverend today?"). We can hold open-air meetings during the winter fairs and on the promenade in summer and we are trusted by the police. Our own three children, having gone through the whole state school system in the Welsh language, had a wide circle of friends and through this contact we got to know scores of parents, greeting them in the town each week and now discussing grandchildren and their own cares. A month after I arrived in the town I was present at the opening of the new hospital here in November 1965. Since that time I have prayed in all the wards and practically by every bed, but there are few of the staff I know because they come and go.

I have learned what rare issues to write about in the columns of the local newspaper, far less these days than when I first came and was a bit of a hothead. Except for one widow we are the oldest folk on our street and we try to be good neighbors, but I am always going off in my car somewhere. If I walked (as my wife does) I would meet more people. So there are these obvious benefits of influence and presence from being in a community a long time. Some credibility is given to the historic Christian faith. When I arrived vague religion dominated the community. A university coming to a community has an enormous rationalistic influence on the pulpits. Every clergyman was thought to believe the same things and we were all considered to be supporters of the ecumenical movement. Now they have learned that there are a number of us who are unhappy with ecumenical religion and our position is grudgingly respected if not accepted by others.

When should a minister leave his pulpit to accept another position? Let him wait calmly for a call. If he is restless in his present church will he be happy somewhere else? Which sensible church would dream of calling the Rev. Rolling Stone—who has never spent longer than a few years in any place? Only the most immature congregation could shrug at that record and issue a call. When preachers move elsewhere they take themselves with them. So often the problem is not in the deacons or congregation; it is in the unresolved tensions located in our own hearts. Whenever a man moves he finds himself doing exactly the same work in the next church as he was doing in his old position, preaching the Scriptures and pastoring those who hear us. Someone else will have to do those labors in the old church.

If we are weary of that and want an external change, have we ever understood what the work of the pastorate is?

Wherever we go we will surely be exchanging one set of problems for another. A higher salary, a bigger reputation and an apparently easier position are not good reasons for quitting. Neither are larger numbers—it is enough to bear to the throne of judgment the number who hear you now and give account to God for them let alone a thousand people. Should we go because the wicked in a congregation are making life tough for us? That is questionable. Should we allow them to have all the church's assets and desert our friends and supporters, leaving them to the tender mercies of those who have been striving against the God of grace? There is also a doctrine of brushing the dust off one's feet and moving on. If the majority reject us we will accept their decision with sadness and dignity. Even Jonathan Edwards was rejected by his own congregation and, unlike our church, his people had known mighty times of refreshing from the presence of the Lord. It is amazing how any of us survive in this climate of hyped-up expectations that congregations have been given by church growth experts.

Maybe there will be too many deep tensions with a substantial group of people in the congregation to make a blessed ministry possible and another orthodox man might further what is proving hard for you to advance. Every preacher itching to leave argues with his own heart like that: "I can't take them any further." Why not? Aren't you a growing man yourself? They must grow with you. But every church passes through seasons, winter deadness and then the new life of spring, and our leaving is no guarantee of gospel advance. There will be no shortage of religious tosh to hand around as your reason for taking off. There is a fight everywhere. It is a good fight of faith. The future is as bright as God's promises. One thing we know most certainly is that God is going to work all things together for the good of them that love Him.

If a preacher does intend to accept a call, it must be evident to all that the new office is a more strategic sphere and that his gifts may be used for the greater benefit of Christ's church than where he now is. Paul did target the great cities for his ministries. Even if it is evident that the advantages of moving will further the gospel yet members of your present congregation may be stubborn and resentful of your desire to leave them, not thinking of the well-being of the greater testimony of Jesus Christ. Then the parting may not be so amicable. Of course one expects some mutual grief at any parting. But it would have been unthinkable for Spurgeon to have remained the country "Pastor of the Fens" at Waterbeach when New Park Street Church in London was calling him. The call of the church itself, accompanied by an enthusiastic vote and the encouragement of many of your respected friends, will carry heavy weight in your decision to go.

But, Timothy, you shouldn't be thinking of moving on since you have only just begun your first pastorate. Build up a happy church that loves the whole counsel of God. Don't aim for anything less than this. That is the New Testament goal.

With every blessing,
Geoff Thomas

PS—A book to recommend to you is the two-volume biography of Dr. Martyn Lloyd-Jones by Iain Murray, *D. Martyn-Lloyd Jones: The First Forty Years 1899–1939* (Edinburgh: The Banner of Truth Trust, 1982) and *D. Martyn Lloyd-Jones: The Fight of Faith 1939–1981* (Edinburgh: The Banner of Truth Trust, 1990). These two volumes provide a moving account of a thirty-year ministry at the heart of London by the greatest preacher of the twentieth century.

Recommended Reading

Armstrong, John, ed. *Reforming Pastoral Ministry*. Wheaton, IL: Crossway Books, 2001.

Baxter, Richard. *The Reformed Pastor,* 1862, reprint, Edinburgh: The Banner of Truth Trust, 1974.

Beardmore, Roger, ed. *Shepherding God's Flock*. Harrisonburg, VA: Sprinkle Publications, 1988.

Bebbington, David. *Patterns in History*. Downer's Grove, IL: Inter-Varsity Press, 1990.

Beeke, Joel. *The Quest for Full Assurance: The Legacy of Calvin and His Successors*. Edinburgh: Banner of Truth Trust, 1999.

Blue, Ken. *Healing Spiritual Abuse*. Downers Grove, IL: Intervarsity Press, 1993.

Boice, James Montgomery. *Christ's Call to Discipleship*. Reprint, Grand Rapids, MI: Kregel, 1998.

Bridges, Charles. *The Christian Ministry*. Reprint, Edinburgh: The Banner of Truth Trust, 1980.

Bridges, Jerry. *The Discipline of Grace*. Colorado Springs, CO: NavPress, 1994.

Brown, John, ed. *The Christian Pastor's Manual*. Reprint, Pittsburgh, PA: Soli Deo Gloria, 1991.

Bruce, A. B. *The Training of the Twelve*. Grand Rapids, MI: Kregel, 1971.

Bunyan, John. *The Pilgrim's Progress*. Reprint, Edinburgh: The Banner of Truth Trust, 1977.

Coleman, Robert. *The Master Plan of Evangelism*. Grand Rapids, MI: Fleming H. Revell Co., 1994.

Cunningham, William. *An Introduction to Theological Studies*. Reprint, Greenville, SC: Reformed Academic Press, 1994.

Edwards, Jonathan. *The Works of Jonathan Edwards*, 2 vols. Reprint, Edinburgh: The Banner of Truth Trust, 1979.

Eims, Leroy. *The Lost Art of Disciple Making*. Grand Rapids, MI: Zondervan, 1978.

Elliot, Elisabeth. *Through Gates of Splendor*. Reprint, Wheaton, IL: Tyndale House Publishers, Inc., 1981.

George, Timothy. *Faithful Witness: The Life and Mission of William Carey*. Birmingham, AL: New Hope Publishers, 1991.

Gregory, Joel. *Too Great a Temptation*. Irving, TX: Summit Publishing Group, 1994.

Grudem, Wayne. *Systematic Theology*. Grand Rapids, MI: Zondervan, 1995.

_____. *Bible Doctrine*. Grand Rapids, MI: Zondervan, 1999.

Hart, D. G. and John R. Muether. *With Reverence and Awe*. Phillipsburg, NJ: P&R Publishing, 2002.

Henry, Matthew. *A Method For Prayer*. 1716; reprint, Greenville, SC: Reformed Academic Press, 1994.

Hoekema, Anthony A. *Saved By Grace*. Grand Rapids, MI: William B. Eerdmans Publishing Company, 1989.

Hulse, Erroll. *Who are the Puritans?* Darlington, England: Evangelical Press, 2000.

Johnson, Terry. *Leading in Worship*. Oak Ridge, TN: Covenant Foundation, 1996.

_____. *Reformed Worship: Worship That is According to Scripture.* Greenville, SC: Reformed Academic Press, 2000.

_____. *The Pastor's Public Ministry.* Greenville, SC: Reformed Academic Press, 2001.

Johnstone, Patrick and Jason Mandryk. *Operation World,* 21st Century edition. United Kingdom: Paternoster Lifestyle, 2001.

Lewis, Peter. *The Genius of Puritanism.* Morgan, PA: Soli Deo Gloria, 1997.

Lloyd-Jones, Martyn. *Preaching and Preachers.* Grand Rapids, MI: Zondervan, 1971.

_____. *Revival.* Reprint, Westchester, IL: Crossway Books, 1987.

Logan, Samuel T., ed. *The Preacher and Preaching.* Phillipsburg, NJ: Presbyterian and Reformed Publishing Co., 1986.

Lundgaard, Kris. *The Enemy Within.* Phillipsburg, NJ: P&R Publishing, 1998.

Mack, Wayne. *Your Family, God's Way.* Philippsburg, NJ: Presbyterian & Reformed Publishing Co., 1991.

Martin, Robert P. *A Guide to the Puritans*. Edinburgh: Banner of Truth Trust, 1997.

Metzger, Will. *To Tell the Truth*. Downers Grove, IL: InterVarsity Press, 1981.

Miller, Samuel. *Thoughts on Public Prayer*. 1844, reprint, Harrisonburg, VA: Sprinkle Publications, 1985.

Morris, Leon. *The Atonement: It's Meaning and Significance*. Downer's Grove, IL: Inter-Varsity Press, 1983.

Muller, Richard. *The Study of Theology*. Grand Rapids, MI: Zondervan, 1991.

Murray, Iain. *D. Martyn Lloyd-Jones: The First Forty Years 1899–1939*. Edinburgh: The Banner of Truth, 1982.

_____. *D. Martyn Lloyd-Jones: The Fight of Faith 1939–1981*. Edinburgh: The Banner of Truth, 1990.

_____. *Jonathan Edwards: A New Biography*. Edinburgh: The Banner of Truth, 1987.

Oliphant Old, Hughes. *Leading in Prayer*. Grand Rapids, MI: Eerdmans, 1995.

_____. *Worship That Is Reformed According to Scriptures—Guides to the Reformed Tradition*. Atlanta, GA: John Knox Press, 1984.

Ortlund, Raymond C. *When God Comes to Church*. Grand Rapids, MI: Baker Books, 2000.

Owen, John. *The Works of John Owen*. Edited by William. H. Gould. Vol. 6, *Temptation and Sin*. 1853; Reprint, Edinburgh: The Banner of Truth Trust, 1967.

———. *The Works of John Owen*. Edited by William. H. Gould. Vol. 7, *Sin and Grace*. 1853; Reprint, Edinburgh: The Banner of Truth Trust, 1965.

Packer, James I. *A Quest for Godliness: The Puritan Vision of the Christian Life*. Wheaton, IL: Crossway Books, 1990.

———. *Evangelism and the Sovereignty of God*. Downers Grove, IL: InterVarsity Press, 1961.

———. *Knowing God*. Downers Grove, IL: InterVarsity Press, 1973.

Piper, John. *Brothers, We Are not Professionals*. Nashville, TN: Broadman & Holman Publishers, 2002.

———. *Let the Nations Be Glad! The Supremacy of God in Missions*. Grand Rapids, MI: Baker Books, 1993.

———. *The Supremacy of God in Preaching*. Grand Rapids, MI: Baker Book House, 1990.

Priolo, Lou. *The Complete Husband*. Amityville, NY: Calvary Press Publishing, 1999.

Rayburn, Robert. *O Come Let Us Worship*. Grand Rapids, MI: Baker Book House, 1980.

Ryken, Leland. *Worldly Saints: The Puritans As They Really Were*. Grand Rapids, MI: Zondervan, 1990.

Ryle, J. C. *Holiness*. Reprint, Darlington, England: Evangelical Press, 1979.

Sproul, R.C. *The Holiness of God*. Carol Stream, IL: Tyndale, 1998.

Spurgeon, Charles H. *Lectures to My Students*. Reprint, Grand Rapids, MI: Zondervan, 1954.

_____. *An All-Around Ministry*. Reprint, Edinburgh: The Banner of Truth Trust, 2000.

Stott, John R. *Between Two Worlds*. Grand Rapids, MI: William B. Eerdmans Publishing Co., 1982.

_____. *The Preacher's Portrait*. Grand Rapids, MI:. Eerdmans, 1961.

_____. *The Cross of Christ*. Downer's Grove, IL: Inter-Varsity Press, 1986.

Thomas, Derek. *Praying the Savior's Way*. Fearn, Ross-shire: Christian Focus Publications, 2001.

Tripp, Tedd. *Shepherding a Child's Heart*. Wapwallopen, PA: Shepherd Press, 1995.

Warfield, Benjamin B., *The Religious Life of Theological Students*. Reprint, Phillipsburg, NJ: P&R, 2001.

Watts, Isaac. *A Guide to Prayer*. 1715, reprint, Edinburgh: The Banner of Truth Trust, 2001.

Whitney, Donald. *Spiritual Disciplines for the Christian Life*. Colorado Springs, CO: NavPress, 1991.

Wilkins, Michael J. *Following the Master: A Biblical Theology of Discipleship*. Grand Rapids, MI: Zondervan, 1992.

Willard, Dallas. *The Spirit of the Disciplines*. San Francisco, CA: Harper & Row, 1988.

Winslow. Octavius. *The Precious Things of God*. Reprint, Pittsburgh, PA: Soli Deo Gloria, 1993.

Witsius, Herman. *On the Character of a True Theologian*. Reprint, Greenville, SC: Reformed Academic Press, 1994.